The Plain English

REAL ESTATE
DICTIONARY

FOURTH EDITION

ASHLEY
CROWN
SYSTEMS, INC.

This publication is designed to provide accurate and current information regarding the subject matter covered. The principles and conclusions presented are subject to local, state, and federal laws and regulations, court cases and revisions of same. If legal advice or other expert assistance is required, the reader is urged to consult a competent professional in the field.

Real Estate Publisher
Leigh Conway

Copy Editor
Emily Kazmierski

Academic Information Analyst
Laura King

Graphic Designer
Susan Mackessy Richmond

Senior Technical Writers
Judith Moyer
Nicole Thome

Technical Writer
Ben Hernandez

Writer
Sue Carlson

Contributors: Sherry Shindler Price and Roy Bottger

©2010 by Ashley Crown Systems, Inc.,
a division of Allied Business Schools, Inc.
Fourth Edition

Published by:
Ashley Crown Systems, Inc.
22952 Alcalde Drive
Laguna Hills, California 92653

Printed in the United States of America

ISBN: 978-0-934772-73-0

TABLE OF CONTENTS

A

abandonment – The act of voluntarily surrendering or relinquishing possession of real property, without transferring title to someone else. Non-use of the property does not prove abandonment.

abandonment of easement – The obvious and intentional surrender of the easement.

abandonment of homestead – A legal document that proves a homestead was abandoned. An owner must file an abandonment of homestead on the old property, in order to obtain a homestead on a new property.

abatement – A reduction or decrease in amount or worth; usually applies to rent or taxes.

abatement of nuisance – Legal process used to remove nuisances and code violations.

able – Financial ability, as in ready, willing, and able buyer.

above grade improvements – Improvements built above ground level.

abrogation – The revocation, rescission, or annulling of a contract by mutual consent of the parties to the contract, or for cause by either party to the contract.

absentee owner – A property owner who does not live on the property, and who may rely on a property manager to oversee it.

absolute net lease – Lease requiring the tenant to pay for all the expenses of operating and maintaining the property, including major repairs and any capital expenditures.

absorption analysis – A study of the number of units of residential or non-residential property that can be sold or leased over a given period of time in a defined location.

absorption bed – A shallow trench containing a pipe that carries effluent away from the septic tank into an open area, where it is absorbed into the soil.

absorption period – The estimated time period required to sell, lease, place in use, or trade the subject property in its marketing area at prevailing prices or rental rates.

absorption rate – The rate at which a type of property is either bought or leased, i.e., absorbed by the market. Usually, the rate is expressed in square feet per year or number of units per year.

abstract of judgment – A document summarizing a court decision and is used to execute a judgment lien.

abstract of title – A summary of the conveyances, transfers, and other facts appearing of record and relied upon as evidence of title to real property.

abstraction method – *See* extraction method.

abstractor – A person who searches historic records affecting the title to real property and summarizes the results in a report called an abstract of title.

abutter's rights – The reasonable right to light, air, and visibility that a property enjoys from another.

abutting property – Property that touches or is contiguous to another property, as opposed to being near to another property.

accelerated cost recovery system (ACRS) – For tax purposes, the system for calculating depreciation (cost recovery) on depreciable real property acquired and placed into service after January 1, 1981. This method of depreciation is based on recovery periods, instead of on the useful life of the property.

accelerated depreciation – A method of cost write-off in which depreciation allowances are greater in the first few years of ownership than in subsequent years. This permits an earlier recovery of capital and a faster tax write-off of an asset.

acceleration clause – A clause in a loan document describing certain events that cause the entire loan to be due. Possible events include sale of the property, failure to repay the debt, pay the property taxes, or provide adequate hazard insurance coverage.

acceptance – Unqualified agreement to the terms of an offer.

access right – The right of an owner to have ingress to and egress from owner's property over adjoining property.

accessibility – The ease of entrance and exit to a property. Accessibility is a factor in determining the most profitable use of a property.

accession – The acquisition of title to additional land or to improvements, as a result of natural increase or growth or by installation of improvements.

accessory buildings – Structures on a property that are secondary to the main building, such as sheds and garages.

access to property – A seller must provide reasonable access to the property to the buyer, inspectors representing the buyer, and representatives of lending institutions for appraisal purposes, or for any other purpose relating to the sale.

accommodation recording – The recordation of an instrument without consideration and without assumption of responsibility for correctness or validity.

accord and satisfaction – The discharge of an existing obligation by acceptance of a substitute agreement in which the creditor accepts less than the full amount owed as satisfaction of the debt.

accounting – The process of identifying, measuring, and communicating economic information to permit informed judgments and decisions by users of the information.

accounting method – A set of rules used to determine when and how income and expenses are reported.

Accredited Management Organization (AMO) – A property management designation offered by the Institute of Real Estate Management (IREM) to property management companies that meet prescribed high standards.

Accredited Residential Manager (ARM) – A property management designation offered by the Institute of Real Estate Management (IREM) to individuals. Requirements for designation include management experience, additional training, and adherence to a code of ethics.

accretion – A buildup of soil by natural causes on property bordering a river, lake, or ocean.

accrual method – An accounting method that reports revenue when earned and expenses when incurred.

accrue – To accumulate, grow, or mature over a period of time; as in accrued interest on a loan.

accrued depreciation – Depreciation that has already occurred, and is the difference between the cost of replacement or reproduction, and the current appraised value of a property.

acid rain – Precipitation containing harmful amounts of nitric and sulfuric acids formed primarily by sulfur dioxide and nitrogen oxides released into the atmosphere when fossil fuels are burned. Also called acid precipitation or acid deposition.

acknowledgment – A signed statement by a named person, made before a notary public, confirming that a document was signed voluntarily.

acoustical tile – Blocks of fiber, mineral or metal, with small holes or rough-textured surface to absorb sound, used as covering for interior walls and ceilings.

acquisition – (1) The act or process by which a person procures property. (2) A transaction in which a firm is absorbed by another firm, with the ownership vested in the acquiring firm.

acquisition appraisal – An appraisal that estimates the market value of a property facing condemnation under the government's powers of eminent domain. The appraisal is performed to determine the amount of just compensation due to the owner.

acquisition cost – The total cost of acquiring property. In addition to the purchase price, other costs include escrow fees, title insurance, lenders fees, etc.

acre – A measure of land equaling 43,560 square feet, or 4,840 square yards, or 160 square rods, or a tract about 208.71 feet square.

acre foot – A volume of material such as water, sand, coal, etc., equal to an area of one acre with a depth of one foot. If a liquid, equal to 325,850 gallons.

acreage – A large piece of property that is usually unimproved. Acreage may be used for agricultural, industrial, residential or commercial uses.

acreage zoning – Zoning that reduces residential density by requiring large building lots. This type of zoning is also called large-lot zoning or snob zoning.

action – A lawsuit brought to court.

action in *rem* – An action in which judgment is sought against property to determine its status.

active solar – As an energy source, energy from the sun collected and stored using mechanical pumps or fans to circulate heat-laden fluids or air between solar collectors and a building.

act of God – An act attributable to nature without human interference. Such acts include tidal wave, flood, hurricane, volcanic eruption, earthquake, and fire. The occurrence of an act of God may temporarily or permanently relieve parties from the responsibilities of their agreement.

actual age – The chronological, real age of a building. It is the opposite of its effective age, which is determined by the building's condition and utility.

actual authority – Authority expressly given by the principal or given by the law and not denied by the principal.

actual cash value – The monetary worth of an improvement. The cost of replacing the improvement, less any depreciation.

actual damages – Damages a court of law recognizes, as the result of a wrong.

actual depreciation – Depreciation occurring as a result of physical, functional, or economic forces, causing loss in value to a structure.

actual fraud – An act intended to deceive another, e.g., making a false statement, making a promise without intending to perform it, suppressing the truth.

actual notice – Notice in fact or in reality to or by a party directly and personally based on things actually seen, heard, read, or observed.

ADA – *See* American with Disabilities Act.

ADAM E. LEE – The mnemonic for the eight ways to terminate an easement: Abandonment, Destruction, Adverse possession, Merger, Express agreement, Lawsuit, Estoppel, and Excessive use.

addendum – An addition or change to a contract; a supplement. All addendums to an agreement should be dated and signed or initialed by all parties involved.

additional deposit – Additional earnest money given with a purchase agreement. This deposit is sometimes added to the offer, if the buyer can only make a small initial earnest money deposit when the offer to purchase is written, and the buyer agrees to add an additional deposit at a later date.

add-on interest – Interest charged to, and paid by, the borrower that is computed on the full principal amount of the loan for the entire loan term, regardless of how much principal is repaid. Also called block interest.

adjoining owners – Persons owning lands that share common boundaries and therefore have mutual rights, duties, and liabilities.

adjustable-rate loan – A type of loan whose interest rate is tied to a movable economic index. The amount and timing of interest rate adjustments are agreed upon in the note.

adjustable-rate mortgage (ARM) – The mortgage securing an adjustable-rate loan.

adjusted cost basis – The original purchase price of a property, plus any capital improvements and any costs of the sale, less depreciation. Also called adjusted book basis.

adjusted sales price – (1) The estimated sales price of a comparable property after adjustments have been made to compensate for differences between the subject property and the comparable. (2) The price the comparable property would sell for if it possessed all the characteristics of the subject property.

adjustment – In the sales comparison approach, a dollar or percentage amount added to or subtracted from the sale price of a comparable property, to account for a feature the property has or does not have, which differentiates it from the subject property.

adjustment grid – Lists important items affecting value, such as site area, location, design and appeal, quality, condition, gross building area, basement area, room count, view, age, amenities, etc. Also called a matrix.

adjustment guidelines – Appraisal guidelines established and regulated by the Federal National Mortgage Association, and applied when a comparable property ceases to be an appropriate comparable; i.e., one has to make too many adjustments to the comparable.

administration expense – The cost of direct management and services related to the management of property.

administrator – Personal representative of the estate of an intestate decedent.

adobe – A kind of natural clay that is sticky when wet, but dries hard. Adobe soil is expansive.

adobe bricks – Bricks made from a mixture of clay and straw, which were dried in the sun rather than in a kiln.

ad valorem – According to value.

advance fee – A fee paid in advance of any services rendered.

advances – Payments made by the lender to a delinquent borrower to cover such charges as taxes, insurance, and foreclosure costs.

adverse possession – A method of acquiring title to property by continued possession and payment of taxes, rather than by purchase or conveyance.

adverse use – The access and use of property without the owner's consent, such as a pathway across another's property.

advertising – An impersonal form of mass communication promoting a product or company that is paid for by the company.

advertising campaign – A plan with a common theme describing the mode and frequency through which someone communicates a marketing concept.

advertising media – The different channels available to convey a message to a target market.

Advisory Opinions – The Appraisal Standards Board (ASB) issues Advisory Opinions to illustrate the applicability of USPAP in specific situations and offers advice for the resolution of appraisal issues and problems.

aerator – A device installed on faucets to get air into a water stream.

aesthetic value – Relating to beauty, rather than to functional considerations.

aesthetic zoning – Regulates the appearance of buildings in the area.

affidavit – A written declaration under oath.

affidavit of service – Details the method and date of delivery of the eviction notice, is signed by the person who delivered it, and is notarized if required by statute.

affiliated business arrangement disclosure – An affiliated business arrangement disclosure is required whenever a settlement service refers a buyer to a firm with any kind of business connection to the service, such as common ownership.

affirmation – A declaration in writing under penalty of perjury.

affirmative easement – One that requires the owner of the servient estate to do something to benefit the dominant estate.

affordable housing – Housing for individuals or families considered low-income by HUD (U.S. Department of Housing and Urban Development).

afforestation – The establishment of a forest, stand, or tree crop on an area not previously forested, or on land from which forest cover has been absent for a long time.

afiant – A person who has made an affidavit.

A-frame style – The triangular-shaped roof going all the way to the ground on two sides of the house, giving this housing style its name. This style is ideal for cold, snowy regions.

after-acquired title – Title accepted by a grantor after his or her previous conveyance.

after-tax cash flow (ATCF) – The cash flow remaining from the net operating income after paying income taxes, debt service, and loan repayments.

after-the-fact-referral fee (ATF) – Fee requested after a real estate agent has established a relationship with a buyer or seller.

age – The chronological lifespan of a person or object. A consideration when determining legal capacity to enter into contracts, also a feature of anti-discrimination housing laws.

age-life depreciation – An appraisal method of computing accrued depreciation. It assumes a building depreciates at a fixed rate over the course of its life. The depreciation is calculated by dividing the total economic life by its current effective age. Also called the straight-line method.

age-life method – A method of computing accrued depreciation. The cost of a building is depreciated at a fixed annual percentage rate. This is the method most frequently used by residential appraisers. Also known as the straight-line method.

agency – A legal relationship of trust by which one person (agent) is authorized to conduct business, sign papers, or otherwise act on behalf of another person (principal) when dealing with third parties. This relationship may be created by express agreement, ratification, or estoppel.

agency by estoppel – An agency relationship between a broker and a principal created when a principal causes a third party to believe the agency exists by words or actions. If the third party then deals with the supposed agent, the principal is estopped, or prevented, from denying the agency relationship, because of his or her earlier words or deeds.

agency by ratification – An agency relationship created when the agent acts as if an agency relationship exists, before an official agreement or contract is expressed. The principal agrees to the relationship after the act is performed, thereby ratifying the act and the agency relationship.

agency coupled with an interest – An agent acquires an interest in the subject of the agency (the property).

agency relationship disclosure – A disclosure statement confirming the agency relationship exists in a particular transaction.

agent – A person who has the authority to act for and in the place of another, called a principal, for the purpose of affecting the principal's legal relationship with third persons.

agents of production – Land, labor, capital, and management. *See* principle of increasing and decreasing returns and principle of surplus productivity.

age-restricted housing – Housing that generally restricts residency and ownership to active seniors 55 years and over.

aggregate – (1) Sum of all individual variates. (2) A surfacing material or ballast for a roof system. Aggregate can be rock, stone, crushed stone or slag, water-worn gravel, crushed lava rock, or marble chips.

aggregate deductible – The deductible in some property insurance contracts assessed on an annual aggregate, or cumulative, basis rather than on a per claim basis. In this arrangement, the insured pays a fixed amount, and the insurance provider pays the rest, once the aggregate deductible amount is exceeded.

agrarian – Relating to land.

agreed boundary line – Adjoining owners of property with an uncertain boundary set a new boundary line.

agreement – A mutual exchange of promises (either written or oral). Often synonymous with a contract.

agreement of sale – An agreement entered into for the sale and purchase of property.

agricultural property – Property zoned for use in farming, including the raising of crops and livestock.

agricultural waste – Waste from farming and livestock operations, including animal manure and harvest residues. such wastes are sources of pollutions but also potential energy sources.

AIDA formula – In marketing, a formula for writing an ad designed to get maximum results: Mneumonic: **A**=Attention, **I**=Interest, **D**=Desire, **A**=Action.

air barrier – A layer of material resistant to airflow usually in the form of polyolefin. A material which is applied in conjunction with a building component (such as a wall, ceiling or sill plate) to prevent the movement of air through that component.

air changes per hour (ACH) – The number of times in one hour that the air in a building is completely replaced with outside air.

air cleaner – A device using filters or electrostatic precipitators to remove indoor-air pollutants such as tobacco smoke, dust, and pollen.

air collector – A medium-temperature collector used predominantly in space heating, utilizing pumped air as the heat-transfer medium.

air conditioner – A device that changes the humidity levels, temperature, or quality of air.

air conditioning – Cooling and dehumidifying the air in an enclosed space by use of a refrigeration unit powered by electricity or natural gas.

air flow volume –The amount of air circulated in a space, measured in cubic feet per minute (cfm).

air pollution – Contamination of the atmosphere by substances that are damaging to health and the environment.

air-pollution abatement equipment – Equipment used to reduce or eliminate airborne pollutants, including particulate matter (dust, smoke, fly, ash, dirt, etc.), sulfur oxides, nitrogen oxides (NO_x), carbon monoxide, hydrocarbons, odors, and other pollutants.

airport hotels – Serves as a destination point for business meetings and conferences.

airport mall – Has specialty retail, restaurants, and other services concentrated in airports.

airport zoning – Zoning regulations in and around airports, restricting building height and natural growth, in order to minimize potential hazards to aircraft.

air quality standards – Regulatory limits set by the U.S. Environmental Protection Agency for the maximum safe levels of pollutants or contaminants in the atmosphere.

air rights – The rights in real property to the reasonable use of the air space above the surface of the land.

airspace – (1) The interior space in an apartment, office, or condominium. (2) Airspace above buildings and land is included in the ownership of real property, up to a reasonable height.

AITD – *See* all-inclusive deed of trust.

alarm systems – Warning devices, installed or free-standing, including but not limited to: carbon monoxide detectors, flue gas and other spillage detectors, security equipment, ejector pumps, and smoke alarms.

alcove – A recessed part or addition to a room.

algae discoloration – (1) A type of roof discoloration caused by algae. (2) A fungus growth.

alien – A person not born in the United States, and who has not been naturalized and is not a citizen. In most states, aliens may acquire and hold an interest in land, with some limitations.

alienate – To voluntarily or involuntarily transfer, convey, or sell property to another.

alienation clause – A clause in a note or in a security instrument calling for automatic maturity in the event of sale or transfer of title by borrower.

alligatoring – (1) A term used to describe the cracking of surfacing bitumen on a built-up roof. These cracks result from the limited tolerance of asphalt to thermal expansion or contraction, and produce a pattern resembling an alligator's hide. (2) Cracking paint can also be described using the term alligatoring.

all-inclusive deed of trust (AITD) – A deed of trust securing payment of an obligation owing under a prior deed of trust.

allocate – To assign or set apart for a specific purpose.

allocation method – The allocation of the appraised total value between land and improvements. Allocation made by using a ratio comparing building value to the total price (or value).

allodial system – Our modern system of free and full land ownership by individuals, as opposed to the feudal system in which land ownership was vested in the king and represented only the right to use the land.

allowance for vacancy and collection losses – The percentage of potential gross income that will be lost due to vacant units, collection losses, or both.

all-suite hotels – Offers full suite accommodations for guests.

alluvial deposit – Soil built up as a result of accretion; the gradual build-up of soil. Also called alluvium.

ALTA title policy – American Land Title Association policy of extended title insurance expanding the coverage for risks normally insured against under a standard title policy, to include unrecorded mechanic's liens; unrecorded physical easements; facts a physical survey would not show; water and mineral rights; and rights of parties in possession, such as tenants and buyers under unrecorded instruments. The policy is designed to protect lenders and can be purchased by the lender or buyer.

alterations – Changes made to the interior or exterior of a building that do not change its exterior dimensions.

alternative dispute resolution – A procedure to settle a dispute using mediation or arbitration rather than litigation.

amenities – Features that add value to a property. The qualities of a property, both tangible and intangible, that bring the owner satisfaction and non-monetary benefits.

amenity value – That value, difficult to measure in monetary terms, that is attributable to a property because of pleasant surroundings, such as a pretty view, quiet area, or ideal climate.

American foursquare style – This practical housing style is a sub-style of the Prairie. They are simple, space-efficient, and box-shaped, with a wide porch across the entire front of the house.

American Institute of Real Estate Appraisers (AIREA) – A professional organization promoting professional practice and ethics in the real estate appraisal industry.

American Land Development Association (ALDA) – A national trade association of the real estate development industry. Membership includes professionals primarily involved with recreational and second homes.

American Land Title Association (ALTA) – An association of land title companies that promotes the safe and efficient transfer of ownership and interest in real property and provides information to consumers, while maintaining professional standards and ethics.

American Society of Appraisers (ASA) – The oldest professional organization of appraisers. It promotes professional excellence through education, accreditation, publication, and other services. Members include personal property appraisers, business appraisers, and machine and jewelry appraisers in addition to real property appraisers.

American Society of Home Inspectors (ASHI) – A professional organization of home inspectors building public awareness of home inspection, and promoting excellence and exemplary practice.

Americans with Disabilities Act (ADA) – A federal law passed in 1990 designed to eliminate discrimination against individuals with disabilities, by mandating equal access to jobs, public accommodations, government services, public transportation, and telecommunications.

Americans with Disabilities Act Accessibility Guidelines (ADAAG) – A document providing standards to be observed in the design, construction, and alteration of buildings falling under the jurisdiction of the ADA.

amortization – The payment of principal and interest at stated periods for a stated time until debt is extinguished.

amortization schedule – A schedule for payment of a loan showing the amount of each payment, the payment number, interest payment, principal payment, total payment, and unpaid principal balance.

amperage – The measurement of the quantity of electricity in an electrical circuit available to do a given job.

ampere – (1) A measure of electrical current. (2) The steady current produced by one volt applied across a resistance of one ohm.

analysis of alternatives – Analysis to determine whether a property needs a change in operations or a physical change that will justify a rent increase or elevate the occupancy levels.

anchor bolt – Attaches mud still to foundation; embedded in concrete foundation.

anchor tenant – A major department or chain store located in a shopping center. The anchor tenant draws large numbers of consumers, generating maximum sales volume for the entire shopping center.

ancillary – An addition to.

angle – The measurement in degrees between two intersecting lines.

annex – To add or attach.

annexation – Addition to property or to territory.

annual – Once per year.

annual budget – Annual report that proposes planned income and expenses. It is an important tool used for planning growth and for anticipating borrowing needs.

annual debt service – The total amount of all mortgage payments required in one year on a loan.

annual net income – The amount of income left from an income-producing property after all expenses have been deducted. Also called net operating income.

annual percentage rate (APR) – The relationship of the total finance charge to the total amount to be financed, as required under the Truth-in-Lending Act.

annualized fuel utilization efficiency (AFUE) – The ratio of the total useful heat a gas furnace delivers to a building to the heat value of the fuel it consumes.

annuity – A yearly payment of money for life or for a term of years.

annuity capitalization – An income capitalization method, providing for annuity recapture of invested capital. Discounts the future income to an estimate of present value. Also referred to as yield capitalization.

annuity method – A method of capitalization that treats income from real property as a fixed, regular return on an investment. The annuity method can be applied, if the lessee is reliable and the lease is long-term.

answer – In law, a written pleading filed by a defendant to respond to a complaint in a lawsuit filed and served upon that defendant.

anthracite – The highest rank of coal; used primarily for residential and commercial space heating. It is a hard, brittle, and black lustrous coal, often referred to as hard coal, containing a high percentage of fixed carbon and a low percentage of volatile matter.

antitrust laws – The laws created to protect and preserve business competition.

"A" paper loan – A loan given to a borrower with excellent credit, who receives the benefit of the lowest interest rate and lowest cost loan, with the best terms available to finance a home purchase or refinance a home loan. Also known as a prime loan.

appeal – The act of requesting a higher court of law to reconsider a decision made by a lower court, especially in order to reduce or prevent a punishment. Also, the request itself.

appearance – Presence of a party litigant before the court.

appliance – Non-industrial equipment such as dishwasher, electric range, air-conditioning, etc.

appointment of a receiver – Lease clause that outlines what is to take place if one of the parties involved in the agreement files for bankruptcy.

appointments – Equipment or furnishings used in the interior of a building, especially a home, which tend to increase comfort, appeal or utility.

appraisal – An appraiser's unbiased estimate or opinion of the value of a property, reached in a competent, objective, and impartial manner.

appraisal approaches to value – Any of the following three methods used to estimate the value of real estate: sales comparison approach, cost approach, and income capitalization approach.

appraisal consulting – The act or process of developing an analysis, recommendation, or opinion to solve a problem, where an opinion of value is a component of the analysis leading to the assignment results.

a priori – From the past. From what goes before. Used in legal writing to indicate a cause and effect relationship.

appraisal process – An orderly systematic method to arrive at an estimate of value.

appraisal report – A written statement, in which an appraiser gives his or her opinion of the property value, as of the date of appraisal.

appraisal review – The review of an appraiser's analysis, research, and conclusions by another appraiser.

Appraisal Standards Board (ASB) – An organization created by The Appraisal Foundation. The ASB establishes the rules for developing an appraisal and reporting its results. It is also responsible for the enforcement of USPAP (Uniform Standards of Professional Appraisal Practice).

appraised value – An appraiser's estimate of the amount of a particular value, such as assessed value, insurable value, or market value, based on the particular assignment.

appraiser – A person qualified by education, training, and experience who is hired to estimate the value of real and personal property based on experience, judgment, facts, and use of formal appraisal processes.

Appraiser Qualifications Board (AQB) – An organization created by The Appraisal Foundation. The AQB establishes licensing and certifying Standards and examination requirements for appraisers.

appraiser trainee license – In some states, this is the lowest level of appraisal license. The education, experience, and exam requirements to obtain a trainee license vary widely by state.

appreciation – The increase in market value of real estate.

appropriative water rights – The right to take riparian surface water for a beneficial use on non-adjacent property.

appurtenance – All rights, privileges, and improvements that belong to and pass with the transfer of the property, but that are not necessarily a part of the actual property.

appurtenant – Belonging, appended, or annexed to.

APR – *See* annual percentage rate.

aquastat – A device that senses and controls water temperature in a boiler. In hydronic heating, the aquastat controls boiler water temperature and the thermostat controls room air temperature.

aquifer – A subsurface layer or layers of rock or other geological strata of sufficient porosity and permeability to allow either a significant flow of groundwater or the abstraction of significant quantities of groundwater.

arbitration – A method of dispute resolution in which the claims are submitted to an objective third party. Arbitration is frequently used to settle real estate disputes and avoid court costs.

arbitrator – A neutral person hired to listen to both sides of a dispute. The arbitrator may award a binding decision on the parties to the dispute.

arch – A concave, curved span over a doorway, entire room, or building, such as an arched ceiling or roof.

arch rib roof – A roof usually used in industrial buildings, having the shape of an arch or crescent. It is supported by a bowstring truss that spreads the roof load evenly.

architectural style – Generally the appearance and character of a building's design and construction.

area – The space or size of a surface defined by a set of boundaries.

arid – Regions where precipitation is insufficient in quantity for most crops and where agriculture is impractical without irrigation.

armored cable – Two or more insulated wires enclosed in a metal sheathing.

arm's-length transaction – A transaction, such as a sale of property, in which all parties involved are acting in their own self-interest and are under no undue influence or pressure from other parties.

arranger of credit – A person who is not party to the real estate transaction, but is compensated for arranging the credit, negotiating the credit terms, completing the credit documents, and facilitating the transaction.

arrears – (1) A payment made at the end of a time period. (2) A delinquent payment of a debt.

art deco style – A housing style popular in the early 1900s, in which glass blocks, metals, and plastics are used extensively. Angular and boxy housing style, with a flat roof and simple, clean lines.

artesian well – A well in which the water rises under hydrostatic pressure above the level of the aquifer in which it has been confined by overlying impervious strata.

articles of incorporation – An instrument setting forth the purposes, power and basic rules under which a private corporation is formed.

artificial intelligence – The intelligence of machines and the branch of computer science, which aims to create it.

art moderne style – A simple housing style with a horizontal, cube-like shape and a flat roof and rounded corners. The exterior walls are smooth stucco with rounded corners.

ASB – *See* Appraisal Standards Board.

asbestos – Naturally occurring mineral fibers formerly used for insulation and home products, but that were found to cause lung and stomach cancer and are no longer used.

asbestos abatement – Procedures to control fiber release from asbestos-containing materials in a building or to remove them entirely, including removal, encapsulation, repair, enclosure, encasement, and operations and maintenance programs.

asbestos containing material (ACM) – Asbestos combined with other materials. The resulting substance can be more dangerous than asbestos alone, since it can easily flake or crumble and be ingested or inhaled.

Asbestos Hazard Emergency Response Act (AHERA) – A law passed by Congress in 1986 amending the Toxic Substances Control Act (TSCA) requiring all public schools to be inspected for the presence of asbestos and to remedy problems considered hazardous to people's health.

aseptic system – The clean water system.

ash – Impurities consisting of silica, iron, alumina, and other noncombustible matter that are contained in coal.

ASHI – *See* American Society of Home Inspectors.

"as is" – Words in a contract signifying the property is being sold in its current state, and stating that the seller will not be responsible for the cost of repairing any defect. The seller must still disclose all known defects of the property to the buyer.

asking price – The price at which a piece of real estate is offered to the public.

asphalt – Smooth, hard, tar-like, brittle black or brownish-black resinous mineral made of a variety of bitumen.

assemblage – The process of putting several smaller less valuable lots together under one ownership to increase total value.

assess – The act of determining a property's value for tax purposes.

assessed value – Value placed on land and buildings by a public tax assessor as a basis for use in levying annual real estate taxes.

assessment base – The total value of all the assessed properties in a tax district or assessment district.

assessment ratio – The assessed value of a property in comparison to its market value, expressed as a fraction.

assessment roll – A list of all taxable property showing the assessed value of each parcel; it establishes the tax base. Also called a tax roll.

assessor – The official who determines value of property for taxation purposes.

asset – Real or personal property that is owned and has value.

asset manager – In property management, an executive who works either for a large corporation or a professional property management firm, who oversees the company's real estate assets, and sets goals and strategies on behalf of the owners. Also called a portfolio manager.

assign – To transfer all of an interest in personal property.

assignee – One to whom property is assigned.

assignment – The transfer of an entire leasehold estate or a property's right, title, and interest to a new person.

assignment conditions – In appraisal, the conditions that the assignment results are based upon such as extraordinary assumptions, hypothetical conditions, limiting conditions, jurisdictional exceptions, and supplemental standards.

assignment elements – Crucial sub-steps in appraisal problem identification.

assignment of rents – A lender's right to take possession and collect rents in the event of loan default.

assignor – The person transferring a claim, benefit or right in property to another.

assisted living facility – Offers medical and limited nursing care.

associate licensee – Another term used for a licensed real estate salesperson employed by a licensed real estate broker.

association – A group of people who come together for business purposes. The group may be treated and taxed as a corporation by the IRS.

assumable mortgage – A mortgage that may be transferred to a third party without first obtaining approval from the lender.

assume – A term used in real estate transactions where the buyer may take over, or assume, responsibility for a pre-existing mortgage.

assumption clause – A clause in a document allowing a buyer to take over the existing loan and agree to be liable for the repayment of the loan.

assumption fee – The charge made by a lender when a buyer assumes seller's existing loan.

assumption of mortgage – The taking of a title to property by a grantee wherein grantee assumes liability for payment of an existing note secured by a mortgage or deed of trust against the property, becoming a co-guarantor for the payment of a mortgage or deed of trust note.

atmosphere – The layer of gases surrounding the Earth and composed of considerable amounts of nitrogen, hydrogen, and oxygen.

attachment – The seizure of a defendant's property by court order in a lawsuit, where the property is held as security for satisfaction of a judgment.

attic – The open area above the ceiling and under the roof deck of a steep-sloped roof.

attorney-in-fact – A competent and disinterested person, authorized by another person, through a power of attorney, to act in his or her place in legal matters.

attornment – A tenant's acceptance of a new owner or landlord on the same property.

attractive nuisance – Any inherently dangerous object or condition that is likely to attract and harm children. A property owner is liable for injuries to a child due to such a hazard. For example, an unfenced swimming pool is an attractive nuisance.

auction – Usually, a public sale of goods or property, where people make successively higher offers of money for each item, until it is sold to the person who will pay the highest price.

authorization to sell – A contract signed by a seller of property, authorizing an agent to obtain a potential buyer for the property. However, it does not authorize the agent to enter into a binding sales contract.

automated valuation models – In appraisal, computer software programs that analyze data using automated systems.

automatic damper – A device that cuts off the flow of hot or cold air to or from a room as controlled by a thermostat.

average deviation – In statistics, the measure of how far the average variate differs from the mean of all variates.

avigation easement – An easement affecting land near airports. It allows aircraft to fly at low elevations over private property and prevents property owners from making improvements or allowing trees to grow above a certain height. The extent of restriction depends on the glide angle required for safe landing and take-off.

avulsion – The sudden washing or tearing away of land by the action of water.

awning window – A window that is hinged at the top and opens out.

B

baby-boomers – The name given to the large number of people who were born in the years following World War II, from 1946 to 1964.

back-end ratio – The ratio of all fixed debt, including housing expenses, to gross income.

backfill – Material, usually earth, used to refill an excavated area or to fill in holes or support a foundation.

back surfacing – Fine mineral matter applied to the back side of shingles to keep them from sticking.

back-to-back escrow – An escrow agreement established by one party who is simultaneously selling a property and purchasing another.

back-to-back lease – An agreement by a lessor to take over a prospective lessee's existing lease in another property, in return for the lessee's commitment to lease space in the lessor's commercial property.

backup generator – A generator that is used in the event of an emergency, such as a shortage of power needed to meet customer load requirements.

backup offer – A secondary offer. An offer to buy a property, submitted with the knowledge that a prior offer has been submitted and accepted. The seller often accepts the backup offer, if the first offer fails.

balance sheet – A financial statement that reflects detailed information about the company's assets, liabilities, and owner's equity or net worth at a given point in time.

balcony – An open air platform extending outward from a building and enclosed by a railing.

balloon frame construction – A type of wood framing in which the studs run from the floor of the first level to the ceiling of the second story uninterrupted.

balloon payment – Final installment payment of a promissory note larger than any single preceding installment payment.

Baltimore method – An early appraisal method used to determine the value of a corner lot. *See* corner influence.

bamboo – Bamboo is a fast growing grass—up to 24 inches in a day. Along with other construction uses, bamboo may be cut and laminated into sheets and planks for flooring.

band of investment approach – Method of estimating interest and capitalization rates, based on a weighted average of the mortgage interest rate (or other cost of borrowed funds) and the rate of return on equity required.

banker's rule – A calendar standard by which prorations are calculated. When closing a real estate transaction, most escrow agents use a 360-day year (30 days in each month) to calculate prorations.

bankruptcy – A proceeding in U.S. Bankruptcy Court wherein assets of a debtor (unable or unwilling to pay debts) are applied by an officer of the court in satisfaction of creditor claims.

bare title – Title conveyed using a deed of trust, in which the trustee holds title to property without the usual rights of ownership.

bargain sale – Property sold for less than its fair market value.

baseboard – A finishing board affixed to the bottom of interior walls at the point where the base of the wall meets the floor.

baseboard heating – A heating system in which the baseboards of a house are replaced by the heating units.

base lashing – The upturned edges of a watertight membrane on a roof.

baseline – In the Public Land Survey System, the imaginary east-west lines that intersect meridians to form a starting point for measurement of land.

basement – A building's lowest story or the floor of a building that is partially or entirely below ground.

base rent – The minimum rent due in a percentage lease agreement. *See* minimum rent.

basic industry – In economic base analysis, an industry that attracts income from outside the community.

basis – The value the Internal Revenue Service assigns an asset. This value is used as a point of reference to determine subsequent depreciation or appreciation of the asset.

basis point – Increments used to measure the change in interest rates. There are 100 basis points in one percent.

batten – Narrow strips of board, wood, or metal used to hide or cover joints between panels on the interior or exterior of a building. Also used for decorative effect. In roofing, strips of wood used as the base for slate, clay tiles, or wood shingles.

bay window – A window that protrudes from the exterior of a building, leaving a recess within.

beam – A long thick piece of wood, metal or concrete, used to support weight in a building or other structure.

bearing wall – A wall supporting a floor or the roof of a building as well as its own weight. In condominiums, all bearing walls are common walls shared by two or more units.

bedrock – Solid rock usually found a few feet beneath the topsoil. Bedrock is a good foundation support for structures.

before-and-after method – An appraisal technique used to determine the amount of compensation due to the owners of land that has been partially taken through condemnation. The value of the land before and after condemnation is calculated. The value of the remaining property is the difference between before and after condemnation.

before-tax cash flow (BTCF) – The portion of net operating income after debt service is paid, but before income tax is deducted. Also called equity dividend or pre-tax cash flow.

belly-up – A slang term used to describe a failed business or real estate project, as in the sentence, "The clothing store went belly-up."

below grade improvements – Improvements below ground level.

benchmark – A survey reference mark made on a monument indicating a known location and elevation, used in a metes and bounds survey.

beneficiary – The individual who benefits from a will, insurance policy, trust or other contract. Also, the lender under a note and deed of trust.

beneficiary statement – Statement of a beneficiary under a deed of trust as to principal balance due on a promissory note and other information concerning the loan.

benefit – The good or helpful effect of an improvement made to a previously private property, which was acquired under eminent domain.

bequeath – To convey real or personal property by will.

bequest – A gift of personal property by will. *See* legacy.

betterment – An improvement made to property increasing its value.

bid – An offer to purchase property for a certain amount, or the act of submitting an offer to purchase something.

big-box retailer – Large stand-alone store that specializes in a single line of products.

bilateral contract – An agreement or contract in which each person or party promises to perform an act in exchange for another person's promise to perform.

bilateral instructions – One set of escrow instructions signed by both the seller and buyer.

billboard – Large outdoor sign (15 square feet or larger) used for advertising purposes.

bill of sale – A written agreement used to transfer ownership in personal property.

binder – Written agreement to issue, within a specified time, a policy of title insurance. Contract to insure.

biodegradable – The ability of a substance to be broken down over time by sun, wind, water and microorganisms.

biodiversity – The variety of animals, plants, fungi and micro-organisms that inhabit a place is its biodiversity.

biofuel – Liquid fuels and blending components produced from biomass feedstocks, used primarily for transportation.

biomass – Organic nonfossil material of biological origin constituting a renewable energy source.

biomass energy – Energy produced by combusting renewable biomass materials such as wood.

biomass waste – Organic non-fossil material of biological origin that is a byproduct or a discarded product., such as municipal solid waste from biogenic sources, landfill gas, sludge waste, agricultural crop byproducts, straw, and energy crops grown specifically for energy production.

bioremediation – The use of living organisms such as bacteria to remove pollutants from water or land.

bird dogging – Obtaining the initial lead regarding property, buyers, investors, potential home improvement customers, etc. The lead is then handed over to, and followed up by someone else, whose goal is to close the deal.

bird stop – In addition to preventing birds from nesting in the hollows of the roof tiles, this length of formed metal or foam elevates the starter course/layer of roof title so it is positioned at the same angle as subsequent courses/layers.

bitumen – Mineral pitch or any material obtained as a type of asphalt residue in the distillation of coal tar, wood tar, petroleum, etc., or occurring as natural asphalt.

bituminous coal – A dense coal, usually black, sometimes dark brown, often with well-defined bands of bright and dull material, used primarily as fuel in steam-electric power generation, with substantial quantities also used for heat and power applications in manufacturing and to make coke. Bituminous coal is the most abundant coal in active U.S. mining regions.

bi-weekly payment loan – A loan that requires payment every two weeks. This results in an earlier loan repayment, and lower interest costs.

blackletter law – Well-established legal principles. The term derives from the practice of printing law books in a bold, black Gothic type.

black liquor – A byproduct of the paper production process, alkaline spent liquor, that can be used as a source of energy.

blacktop – Asphalt paving used in streets and driveways.

blackwater – Water from toilets, kitchen sink, or other dirty sources (e.g. washing machines used for diapers), which may be contaminated with microorganisms or harmful bacteria.

blanket insurance – Insurance covering multiple pieces of personal property at one location, or multiple pieces of personal property at more than one location.

blanket mortgage – A mortgage or deed of trust on more than one lot or parcel.

blended rate – The interest rate of a newly refinanced loan. The interest rate is greater than the rate on the old loan, but is still less than the current market rate.

blighted area – A section of a city, generally the inner city, where a majority of the buildings are run-down, and the property values are extremely low.

blind advertising – Advertising that fails to disclose that the party is a licensee acting as an agent.

blind pool – A type of syndication where money is raised for unspecified properties meeting specific investment criteria.

blisters – Bubbles that appear on the surface of asphalt roofing after installation.

blockbusting – The illegal practice of causing panic selling by telling people property values in a neighborhood will decline because of a specific event, such as the purchase of homes by minorities.

blower door – A variable speed fan, mounted in a doorframe, used to pressurize and depressurize a house to measure air leakage.

blue-sky law – A law (generally of a state) protecting the public from investing in fraudulent companies. Usually requires full disclosure of risks associated with investment before the investment entity puts investor's monies at risk.

board foot – A unit of measurement for lumber: one foot wide (12 inches) by one foot long (12 inches) by one inch thick (1 inch), or144 cubic inches.

board of directors – Central governing body of an association elected into office by the association members.

Board of Governors (BOG) – Created by the Federal Reserve Board, the BOG regulates the banking system and supervises certain types of financial institutions, overseeing a network of 12 Federal Reserve Banks (FRBs) and 25 branches that make up the Federal Reserve System.

boiler – A sealed tank in which water is turned into steam for heating or power.

bona fide – A Latin term meaning, in good faith.

bona fide purchaser – A purchaser in good faith, for fair value and without notice of any adverse claim or right of third parties.

bona fide sale – The sale of property in a competitive market, at the current market price, where good faith between the buyer and seller is present in the transaction.

bond – A written undertaking to pay a certain sum of money.

bond rating – An assessment by financial reporting organizations of the relative financial risk of a bond issue.

book depreciation – An accounting concept which refers to an allowance taken to provide for recovery of invested capital.

book value – The current value (for accounting purposes) of a property, calculated as the original cost, plus capital improvements, minus accumulated or accrued depreciation.

boot – Money or other property used to equalize the trade in a 1031 tax deferred exchange transaction, if the value of one property is greater than the other.

borrower – A debtor or one who borrows money in the form of a loan, and who is obligated to repay the debt in full, with interest.

boundary – Artificial or natural perimeter of a parcel of land, separating it from adjacent parcels of land.

bounds – A directional reference, as in metes-and-bounds. Metes measure the length, and bounds limit the lengths to a certain area designated by monuments or landmarks.

boycotting – The deliberate exclusion of a particular business or group from the benefits of competition and inclusion.

BPI Building Analyst – Contractor and home energy rater or auditor certified by the Building Performance Institute (BPI).

bracing – Diagonal board or framing lumber nailed across wall framing in order to prevent sway and provide rigidity.

bracketing – When using the sales comparison approach in an appraisal, the idea that the sales prices of the comparables chosen for the appraisal will not all be higher than the value of the subject property, nor will they be lower. The market data is selected so that the subject property is contained within the mid-range of comparable properties, with one or two sales that are higher and one or two sales that are lower.

brand – A distinctive name, logo, image, service, or style.

branding – Making yourself known to a specific area, group of people, or segment of the market.

breach of contract – Failure by one party to comply with all of the terms and conditions of contract.

breakdown method – A method of calculating accrued depreciation by analyzing and measuring each cause of depreciation separately. The different types of depreciation are then added together to find the total depreciation. Also known as observed condition method.

breakeven point – Point at which income is equal to costs.

breezeway – A canopy that extends from the house over the driveway, and serves as protection from the weather for an automobile and for people going between the house and the automobile. Used in a house with no garage. Also, a covering over a porch or patio, connecting two sections of a house or a house and a garage. It is open on two sides, allowing air circulation.

bricks and clicks office – An office that is a combination of a bricks and mortar business and virtual office.

bricks and mortar office – An office with a physical presence. Also called a traditional office.

bridge loan – A short-term loan (usually interest only with a balloon payment) made to bridge the gap between the end of one mortgage and the beginning of another, such as when a borrower purchases a new home, before receiving cash proceeds from the sale of a prior home. When the home sells, the loan is paid off with the profits. Also known as a swing loan.

bridging – The addition of small pieces of wood or metal, which are nailed in a diagonal position between floor joists, at mid-span, to prevent the joists from twisting.

British Thermal Unit (BTU) – A measurement of heat. One BTU is equal to the amount of heat required to raise the temperature of 1 pound of water 1 degree Fahrenheit at approximately 39.2° F. BTUs measure the capacity of heating and air-conditioning equipment.

broker – Individual licensed by the state to arrange the sale or transfer of interests in real property for compensation.

brokerage – An activity involving the sale of something through an intermediary who negotiates the transaction for compensation.

broker associate – A licensed broker who acts as an agent under the sponsorship of a broker-owner.

broker owner – The broker on record with the state as the owner of a real estate brokerage firm who creates and establishes all policies for the firm.

brownfield – An abandoned commercial or industrial site or under-utilized neighborhood, where redevelopment is complicated by actual or perceived contamination.

brownstone – Type of row house, with little street frontage, constructed with reddish-brown sandstone. Commonly built in the 19th century and located in cities such as New York.

BTU – *See* British Thermal Unit.

budget – A balance sheet that identifies estimated or future receipts and expenditures.

budget loan – A type of standard loan in which the monthly payments are applied to property taxes and insurance, as well as principal and interest. As a result, the borrower begins to build equity with the first monthly payment.

buffer zone – Section of land separating one land use area from another, especially when the two zones may be incompatible, such as industrial and residential areas.

building capitalization rate – The sum of the discount and capital recapture rates for a building.

building code – Municipal ordinance regulating type and quality of building materials and permitted methods of construction. Minimum standards are designed to protect the public health and safety.

building ecology – Physical environment and systems found inside the building.

building employment density – Refers to the ratio of employees to floor space.

building engineer – Inspects the structural parts of a building. He or she also inspects the permanent systems.

building envelope – An area or barrier that separates conditioned space from unconditioned space or the outdooors.

building insurance – Covers buildings or structures and any completed additions listed on the declarations page of a policy.

building line – A line, as established by law, beyond which there can be no construction. For safety and aesthetic reasons, the line prevents buildings from being constructed too close to the street. Also called a setback line.

building manager – A person employed by a property manager or directly by an owner, and usually manages a single large building or office complex.

building moratorium – Temporary suspension of new building construction in order to control growth.

building paper – Waterproof paper used between sheathing and roof covering.

Building Performance Institute (BPI) – National standards and contractor credentialing organization for residential energy efficiency and weatherization retrofit work.

building permit – Written permission to construct a new building or other improvement, or to demolish or repair an existing structure. Building permits generally must be obtained before any work may be started.

building-related illness (BRI) – Clinically verifiable diseases that are attributed to a specific source or pollutant within a building and are more serious than sick building syndrome (SBS) condition. The symptoms of the disease persist after the occupant leaves the building, unlike SBS in which the occupant experiences relief shortly after leaving the building.

building residual technique – An appraisal method used to determine the total property value. The income from the land is subtracted from the net operating income. The remainder is divided by the building capitalization rate and the result is the building value. The building value is then added to the land value to arrive at the total property value.

building restrictions – Limits put on the size or type of improvements allowed by zoning laws or private restrictions. They appear in building codes or title documents.

build-out allowance (BO) – Tenant improvement allowance that gives credit or reimbursement to a tenant in order to cover the cost of improvements that the tenant makes to a property.

build-to-suit – A type of lease arrangement in which the lessor builds or modifies the property to meet the tenant's specifications. The cost of the construction is figured into the rental amount, which is usually for a long term.

built-ins – Fixtures, such as stoves, ovens, dishwashers, and other appliances, that are built into the walls and not movable.

built-up rate – A method of calculating a capitalization rate. It takes into consideration the yield amount each investor requires. Also called weighted rate.

built-up roof – An outer covering of a comparatively flat roof, consisting of several layers of saturated felt. As laid, each layer is mopped with hot tar or asphalt. The top layer is finished with a mineral or rock covering and a special coating.

bulk transfers – A transfer in bulk of a major part of the materials, inventory, or supplies of a business. The uniform commercial code regulates bulk sales transfers. Refer to Article 6 of the Uniform Commercial Code (UCC).

bulk zoning – Controls density and prevents overcrowding. Bulk zoning regulates setbacks, building height, and percentage of open area.

bullet loan – A short-term, interest-only loan without periodic payments, with the entire loan due upon maturity. Generally, prepayment is not allowed, or not without large penalties.

bundle of rights – An ownership concept describing all the legal rights attached to the ownership of real property. The bundle of rights includes the right to use, possess, transfer, encumber, and enjoy property.

bungalow style – A house style found in older neighborhoods, characterized by simplicity, with an emphasis on horizontal rather than vertical lines.

bus bar – A heavy, rigid conductor which serves as a common connection between the electrical power source and the load circuits inside a service panel.

business appraisal – The appraisal of business entities, including the intangible assets of a business, like goodwill, a logo, or copyright.

business cycle – The constant fluctuation of levels of income, employment, and the amount of goods and services produced in one year. Stages of the cycle include prosperity, recession, depression, and recovery.

business insurance – The insurance purchased to protect a business by minimizing financial risks associated with unexpected events, such as a death of a partner, an injured employee, a lawsuit, or a natural disaster.

business opportunity – Any type of business for lease or sale.

business park development – A cluster of commercial properties. The properties may include warehouse space, research and development facilities, or production space.

business plan – A written statement of business goals, objectives, and plans for reaching a company's goals.

business property insurance – An insurance policy that covers loss or damage to the building that houses your business, as well as everything related to the loss or damage of company property.

business risk – The uncertainty of future income of a business. In real estate, business risk includes variability in rents, vacancies, and operating expenses.

business risk management – The process of analyzing exposure to risk (harm or loss) and determining how to minimize the physical and/or financial impact.

business taxes – Includes sales tax, use tax, and miscellaneous local taxes, which include environmental fees, excise taxes, and fuel taxes. Sometimes a business must pay business property tax.

business valuation – The estimated worth of complete or partial ownership rights in a business.

buttress – A support for a wall. If the buttress projects from the wall and supports it by lateral pressure, it is called a flying buttress.

buydown – A loan with an initially discounted interest rate, gradually increasing to an agreed-upon fixed rate, usually within one to three years. An initial lump sum is paid to the lender for the buydown of the rate. This allows a buyer to qualify for more property with the same income.

buyer representation agreement – Employment contract between a buyer and a broker.

buyer's agent – A broker or agent of a broker who represents only the buyer and has a fiduciary duty to find the best house for the least money at the terms most favorable to his or her principal (the buyer).

buyer's market – A market containing more supply than demand. A ready, willing, and able buyer is in the majority and is in control of the market.

buyer's profile – A document indicating the buyer's motivation and how much he or she can afford to spend on a home.

buyer's statement – A record of costs and credits incurred for the purchase of the property.

buying signs – Certain clues indicating when a buyer is seriously considering buying a property.

bylaws – Rules adopted for the internal government of a corporation or unincorporated association.

C

calendar year – Starts on January 1 and continues through December 31 of the same year.

call – In a metes and bounds description, the angle and distance of a given line or arc. Each call is preceded by the word then or thence. For example, N 22Ú E 100' (1st call), thence N 80Ú E 100' (2nd call).

call option – A provision contained in loan documents giving the lender the right to call in, or make due immediately, the balance of the loan. The call can be exercised due to a breach of specific terms or conditions, or at the discretion of the lender.

campanile – A freestanding bell tower.

CAN SPAM laws – Federal and state law regulating commercial e-mail messages.

cancellation clause – Instructions in an escrow document about what to do if both buyer and seller agree to cancel the transaction, how monies are returned, who pays fees or charges incurred, and holds the broker harmless.

cantilever – Any structural part of a building projecting beyond its support and overhang. Describes the beam fixed at one end to a vertical support used to hold the structure, such as a bridge, balcony, or an arch in position.

cap – A limit on changes in the interest rate of a loan. A limit placed on the amount the interest rate may vary during rate adjustments on variable-rate loans. The limits may be yearly or for the life of the loan.

capacity – One of the legal essentials of a valid contract. Legitimate legal status to enter into a contract (mentally competent and of legal age).

Cape Cod style – A house that is usually rectangular and has one to one-and-one-half stories, with a steeply pitched gable roof and small overhang.

cap flashing – A sheet metal strip which covers the top edge of base flashing to prevent water from entering. Also known as counter-flashing.

capital – Money and/or property owned or used by a person or business to acquire goods or services.

capital assets – Assets of a permanent nature used in the production of an income, such as land, buildings, machinery, and equipment. In accounting, cash or property that is easily converted to cash.

capital expenditure – The expense of investing in a capital asset, such as purchases of land, buildings, or machinery, as opposed to expenses of daily operations.

capital gain – At resale of a capital item, the amount by which the net sale proceeds exceed the adjusted cost basis (book value). Used for income tax computations. Gains are called short-term or long-term, based upon length of holding period after acquisition. Usually taxed at lower rates than ordinary income.

capital improvement – Any permanent improvement made to real estate for the purpose of increasing the useful life of the property or increasing the property's value.

capital loss – The decrease in value between the time an asset is bought and when it is sold.

capital recapture – The return of an investment.

capitalism – An economic system in which most of the economy's resources are privately owned.

capitalization – The process of calculating a property's present worth on the basis of its capacity to continue producing an income stream. This process converts the future income stream into the property's present worth.

capitalization loss – A financial loss as a result of the sale of a capital asset.

capitalization rate – The rate of interest which is considered a reasonable return on the investment, and used in the process of determining value, based upon net income. It may also be described as the yield rate that is necessary to attract the money of the average investor to a particular kind of investment. Also called a cap rate.

capitalized income approach – *See* income approach.

capture rate – The estimated percentage of a total real estate market currently saturated by existing construction or is projected to be saturated by planned construction.

caravan – The inspection of newly listed properties by a group of real estate brokers or licensees. Caravans usually occur on a regular basis, giving real estate licensees a convenient opportunity for a personal preview of each new listing.

carbon cycle – Cycle by which carbon compounds are exchanged among earth, atmosphere, oceans, plants, and animals.

carbon dioxide (CO_2) – A colorless, odorless, non-poisonous gas that does not support combustion. It is formed in animal respiration and in the decay or combustion of animal and vegetable matter and is considered an atmospheric greenhouse gas.

carbon footprint – The total amount of greenhouse gases produced to directly and indirectly support human activities, usually expressed in equivalent tons of carbon dioxide (CO_2).

carbon monoxide (CO) – A colorless, odorless, poisonous gas, produced by incomplete burning of carbon-based fuels, including gasoline, oil, and wood.

carbon sequestration – A fixation of atmospheric carbon dioxide in a carbon sink through biological or physical processes.

carbon sink – A reservoir that absorbs or takes up released carbon from another part of the carbon cycle. The four sinks, which are regions of the Earth within which carbon behaves in a systematic manner, are the atmosphere, terrestrial biosphere, oceans, and sediments (including fossil fuels).

carport – A structure, covered by a roof, but open on the sides, which shelters cars.

carryback financing – Financing by a seller, who takes back a note for part of the purchase price.

carrying capacity – (1) The population a segment of land can support without consuming its natural resources. (2) Refers to the number of animal units or tonnage of crops per acre the land can support.

carrying charges – The various costs involved in property ownership including taxes, insurance costs, and maintenance expenses.

casement window – A window hinged at its sides and opened with cranks, allowing it to swing open horizontally.

cash dividend – Cash payment to a corporation's stockholders, usually based on profitability.

cash equivalency – The price for which real estate would sell if paid for in cash, without financing.

cash equivalency technique – Method of adjusting a sales price downward to reflect the increase in price due to assumption or procurement by buyers of a loan at an interest rate lower than the prevailing market rate.

cash equivalent sale – A sale where the financing does not affect the price; a sale with typical financing.

cash flow – The net income of an investment, after operating and other expenses are deducted from the gross income. A negative cash flow exists when the expenses are greater than income.

cash flow statement – A summary of the sources and the uses of cash.

cash method – An accounting method that reports income when received and expenses when paid.

casing – The decorative wood finish trim surrounding doors and windows.

casualty insurance – Insurance coverage primarily for the liability exposure of an individual, business, or organization.

category killer – Large national chain store specializing in one line of products, such as home improvements or office supplies.

catwalk – A narrow, elevated walkway along a wall, or over a stage or other area, where a person may need to go to operate or repair equipment.

caulk – To fill a joint with mastic or asphalt cement to prevent leaks.

caveat emptor – Let the buyer beware (Latin).

cavity wall – A wall constructed of brick or stone which is actually two separate walls, joined only at the top and the ends, making it hollow. Also called a hallow wall.

CC&Rs (covenants, conditions, and restrictions) – Detailed limitations applying to the use or enjoyment of real property.

C-corporation – Standard corporation.

cellulose insulation – Cellulose insulation is made from wastepaper, such as used newspaper and boxes. It is shredded into small particles, and chemicals providing resistance to fire and insects are added.

central business district (CBD) – The downtown area of a city, containing primary business, retail, recreational, and governmental activities of the community.

central heating system – A heating system consisting of four different elements: heat producer, exchanger, distributor, and controls. The system is designed to supply heat adequately for an entire structure.

central tendency – The numeric value that is suggested as a typical value in a statistical sample.

certificate of deposit – Financial instrument representing a time deposit with a bank or other lending institution.

certificate of eligibility – A document certifying a veteran is eligible for a loan guaranteed by the Department of Veteran's Affairs.

certificate of occupancy – A certificate issued by a local building department to a builder, certifying the building is in compliance with its permitted use, all required approvals have been obtained from the appropriate agencies, all fees have been paid by the builder, and the building is ready for occupancy.

certificate of reasonable value (CRV) – A document indicating the appraised value of a property being financed with a VA loan. The loan amount may not exceed the CRV.

certificate of sale – Evidence of a purchaser's acquisition of legal title at a judicial sale, subject to redemption rights, if any.

certificate of title – A written opinion by an attorney as to land ownership based upon examination of record title.

Certified Apartment Maintenance Technician (CAMT) – A designation offered by the National Apartment Association (NAA).

Certified Apartment Manager (CAM) – A designation offered by the National Apartment Association (NAA).

Certified Apartment Property Supervisor (CAPS) – A designation offered by the National Apartment Association (NAA).

certified check – A check bearing the issuing bank's guarantee that sufficient money is on deposit to cover the check.

certified financial statement – Statement of the financial condition of a company that has been certified by an independent certified public accountant after the financial records of the company are reviewed, found to be accurate, and prepared in accordance with generally accepted accounting principles.

Certified General Appraiser – An individual who has met specific education, experience, and examination requirements. May appraise any property. *See* appraiser.

Certified International Property Specialist (CIPS) – A property management designation offered by FIABCI-USA (French acronym for International Federation of Property Managers and Real Estate Consultants).

Certified Leasing Specialist (CLS) – A designation offered by the International Council of Shopping Centers (ICSC).

Certified Manager of Community Associations (CMCA) – A designation offered by the Community Associations Institute (CAI).

Certified Marketing Director (CMD) – A designation offered by the International Council of Shopping Centers (ICSC).

Certified Property Manager (CPM) – The most advanced property management designation offered by the Institute of Real Estate Management (IREM).

Certified Residential Appraiser – An individual who has met specific education, experience, and examination requirements. May appraise any 1-4 unit residential properties.

Certified Shopping Center Manager (CSM) – A designation offered by the International Council of Shopping Centers (ICSC).

certiorari – A writ from a higher court to a lower court directing the forwarding of a certified record of a proceeding up for review.

cesspool – An excavation in the earth which receives and retains drainage and sewage from a building.

chain – A unit of measurement used by surveyors. One chain is equal to four rods, or 66 feet. Ten square chains of land equal one acre.

chain of title – A chronological history of all documents affecting and transferring title of a property, beginning with the original transfer and ending with the latest document transferring title. Additional documents recorded in the chain include conveyances, liens, and encumbrances.

chalet – A style of housing design originating in the Swiss Alps. The design features an A-frame with large, overhanging eaves protecting against heavy snowfall.

change of venue – The removal of a cause for trial from one county to another.

characteristics – In appraisal, distinguishing features of a property.

chargebacks – The expenses for services provided by the brokerage that are deducted from the agent's share of the commission split.

charter city – Generally, a city organized under a charter.

chattel – An item or article of personal property.

chattel mortgage – Obsolete name for mortgage of personal property. These mortgages have now been replaced by security agreements.

chattel real – An item of personal property which is connected to real estate; for example, a lease.

check – A printed form, used instead of money, to make disbursements from a bank account.

chemical energy – The energy stored in the bonds of atoms and molecules.

chimney – Vertical masonry shaft of reinforced concrete or other non-combustible heat-resistant material that carries smoke and ash through the roof, away from the furnace or fireplace.

chimney pot – Round or octagonal pot on top of each flue in a Queen Anne style home.

chlorofluorocarbons (CFCs) – Any of various compounds consisting of carbon, hydrogen, chlorine, and fluorine used as refrigerants. CFCs are now thought to be harmful to the Earth's atmosphere.

chord – A component of a truss which acts as a rafter (upper chord) or joist (lower chord).

chose in action – A personal right not reduced to possession but recoverable by an action at law.

churning – The excessive sale and purchase of properties for financial gain.

CID – *See* common interest development.

cinder block – A building block made of ashes and cement. Cinder blocks do not have the weight or the strength of cement blocks.

circuit – A conductor or a system of conductors through which electric current flows.

circuit breaker – An electrical device which automatically interrupts an electric circuit when an overload occurs; may be used instead of a fuse to protect each circuit and can be reset.

civil law – Body of law imposed by the state or government for its citizens.

cladding – The external protective skin of the exterior surfaces of a home (surface coatings, siding, doors, windows, trim, shutters, entryways, and flashings).

clapboard – Narrow boards used as siding for frame houses, and having one edge thicker than the other. The boards run horizontally with the thicker edge overlapping the thinner edge.

Class A building – Excellent location and access, building is in excellent physical condition, meeting or exceeding building codes, and rents are competitive with new construction.

Class B building – Good location, building is in good condition and meets building codes, but suffers some functional obsolescence or physical deterioration, and rents are below new construction.

Class C building – Building is 15-25 years old and may not meet building codes, it suffers physical deterioration and functional obsolescence, has reasonable occupancy rates at lower rents.

Class D building – Have sub-optimal space and are located in less-desirable areas. Generally, the property is over 30 years old, with fewer or no amenities, and needs rehabilitation. Rental rates and occupancy rates are low.

classified ad – A small advertisement designed to give basic information. Reasonably priced ads placed in newspapers and magazines, using only text.

clay – Soil made of finely ground minerals and rocks other than quartz.

Clean Air Act – Passed in 1970, requires the EPA to establish national standards for clean air.

clean air delivery rate (CADR) – The measure of an air purifier's ability to reduce smoke, pollen, and dust particles in the 0.1 to 11 micron size range.

Clean Water Act – A law passed by Congress in 1972 prohibiting the discharge of pollutants into natural waters.

clear cutting – The felling of large forest tracts for agriculture or development, a practice that destroys habitat, kills flora and fauna and can lead to erosion, flooding, and sedimentation of streams and lakes.

clear span – An interior area of a building or house not using columns or posts to support the roof. This creates a large, open area with maximum visibility and use of floor space.

clear title – Title to property free from any liens, clouds, or defects.

client – The person who employs an agent to perform a service for a fee.

client segmentation – Identification of those people most likely to buy the service and targeting those groups.

climate – The prevailing or average weather conditions of a geographic region. Weather conditions include temperature, rainfall, sunshine, wind, humidity, and cloudiness.

climate change – Term used to refer to all forms of climatic inconsistency, but especially to significant change from one prevailing climatic condition to another.

closed bid – A real estate transaction not open for usual negotiations. The bids from potential buyers are sealed until a specified time when they are opened and the seller picks the best offer. The seller benefits from this method, because bidders often overbid to ensure their bid is chosen. Closed bidding is not a common practice.

closed cut valley – A roof valley where the shingles from one slope overlap the valley, and the shingles from the opposite slope are trimmed back from the valley centerline. The valley flashing is not exposed.

closed-end credit transaction – The term closed-end credit transaction is defined by exclusion. That is, it includes any credit arrangement (a consumer loan or credit sale) that does not fall within the definition of an open-end credit transaction. Open-end credit includes credit arrangements, such as revolving credit cards, where the borrower (the credit card holder) is not required to pay off the principal amount by any particular point in time.

closed-end mortgage – A mortgage that cannot be used as security for additional loans.

closed listing – A contract between a principal and an agent, giving the agent the exclusive right to market the principal's property for a fixed period of time. Also called an exclusive listing.

closed-loop recycling – A recycling system in which a product made from one type of material is recycled into a different type of product (e.g. used newspapers into toilet paper).

closed mortgage – A mortgage that cannot be prepaid until a certain time or until maturity.

closed period – Regarding a mortgage, the period of time during which the loan cannot be prepaid.

closed sheathing – (1) Foundation for exterior siding. (2) Boards nailed to studs.

closing – Process by which all the parties to a real estate transaction conclude the details of a sale of real property. The process includes the signing and recording documents and distribution of funds.

closing costs – The miscellaneous expenses buyers and sellers normally incur in the transfer of ownership of real property over and above the cost of the property.

closing statement – An accounting of debits and credits prepared by a closing agent for the lender, borrower, seller, and buyer showing the details of the transaction.

cloud on title – Any condition affecting the clear title of real property or minor defect in the chain of title which needs to be removed.

cluster development – An area of housing development in which the parcels are smaller than typical sites, and larger common areas are incorporated into the development.

CMA – *See* comparative market analysis.

coal – A readily combustible black or brownish-black rock whose composition, including inherent moisture, consists of more than 50 percent by weight and more than 70 percent by volume of carbonaceous material. It is formed from plant remains that have been compacted, hardened, chemically altered, and metamorphosed by heat and pressure over geologic time.

code – A collection of laws.

code of ethics – A set of rules and principles expressing a standard of accepted conduct for a professional group and governing the relationship of members to each other and to the organization.

codicil – A testamentary disposition subsequent to a will altering, explaining, adding to, subtracting from, or confirming it, but not revoking it.

codify – Compile, arrange, systemize, and write the laws of a given region into a code.

coefficient of performance (COP) – The ratio of energy input to heating capacity. This is the instantaneous measurement of the heating performance of a heat pump. It is comparable to knowing how many miles per gallon of gasoline a car gets when it is going full speed.

coinsurance – Insurance issued by two or more insurers.

coinsurance penalty – Paid by the insured to the insurance company at the time of loss if the building being covered is not insured to value.

cold calling – The practice of making unsolicited calls to people you do not know in order to get new business.

collar – Pre-formed flange placed over a vent pipe to seal the roof around the vent pipe opening. Also known as a vent sleeve.

collar beam – A horizontal beam connecting the pairs of opposite roof rafters above the attic floor.

collateral – Something of value given as security for a debt.

collateral assignment – Transfer of an interest in personal property for security purposes.

collateralized mortgage – A mortgage secured by something of value in addition to real estate.

collection loss – A loss incurred if tenants do not pay their agreed-upon rents.

collusion – An agreement between two or more people to do something unlawful. Generally, an agreement between people who represent different interests and sell out these interests for personal gain.

colonial architecture – Architecture following the style of New England colonial houses with two stories and windows divided into small panes, usually with shutters. The main façade is detailed and symmetrical, generally with a center entrance.

colonial revival style – Large houses, with two or more stories, featuring dark green or black shutters and wood exteriors with tall wood columns, typically painted bright white.

colonnade – A structure composed of a roof or series of arches supported by columns.

color of title – The false appearance of clear title, free of any clouds.

color rendition (CRI) – The CRI rates the ability of the bulb to render an object's true color when compared to sunlight. Look for lamps with a CRI of 80 or higher.

column – A slender upright structure consisting of a base, a round or square shaft, and a capital. Columns integrated into exterior walls are known as pilasters.

combination trust – A type of real estate trust combining real estate investment trusts and real estate mortgage trusts. Combination trusts are sometimes called balanced trusts.

combustion – The reaction of a material with oxygen gas or other oxidant, producing heat and flame.

combustion efficiency – A measure of useful heat extracted from a fuel source by an operating heating appliance. For example, a furnace with a combustion efficiency of 70% converts 70% of the fuels energy content into useful heat. The rest is lost as exhaust gases.

Comments – Extensions of USPAP DEFINTIONS, Rules, and Standards Rules that provide interpretation, and establish context and conditions for application.

commercial acre – The area remaining from an acre of newly subdivided land after deducting the area devoted to streets, sidewalks, alleys, curbs, etc. Also known as a buildable acre.

commercial bank – A financial institution designed to act as a safe depository and lender for many commercial activities.

commercial e-mail message – Any electronic mail message whose primary purpose is the commercial advertisement or promotion of a commercial product or service.

commercial leasehold insurance – Leasehold insurance for commercial and industrial properties provided by the Commercial Leasehold Insurance Corporation (CLIC). The policy guarantees the insurance company will pay the insured, if the tenants to do not pay their rent.

Commercial Leasehold Insurance Corporation (CLIC) – A corporation, owned by MGIC (Mortgage Guaranty Insurance Corporation), which provides leasehold insurance for commercial and industrial properties not having prime-rate tenants.

commercial or industrial CID – Consists of either condos or separate buildings situated in a commercial park or industrial complex.

commercial paper – Short-term loans issued by banks and savings institutions for business enterprises. They are usually issued to companies with high credit ratings, thus the investment is usually relatively low risk.

commercial property – A property where commerce is conducted, such as an office building or retail shopping center.

commingling – The illegal practice of depositing client's funds in a broker's personal or general business account.

commission – A fee for services rendered, usually based on a certain percentage of the sales price of a property. The amount is agreed upon before the transaction takes place.

commissioner – A member of a state real estate commission.

commission split – The agreed upon division of money between a broker and his or her associate licensees when the brokerage has been paid a commission from a sale made by the associate licensee.

commitment – A pledge, promise, or firm agreement; also, a title insurer's contractual obligation to insure title to real property.

commitment fee – A charge imposed by a lender for holding credit available for a borrower to use at a future date.

common area – An area of land or improved area in a common interest development that is shared by owners or tenants, such as hallways, staircases, playgrounds, landscaped areas, or parking areas.

common area maintenance (CAM) – Fee that covers the cost for taking care of the elevators, lobby, restrooms, and other common areas in the building. It is the expense of operations and common area maintenance of the property that is shared by the landlord and the tenants.

common elements – The facilities and features that owners and tenants share in a common interest development, such as common walls, roofs, pools, clubhouses, restrooms, and elevators.

common interest – An owner's undivided ownership interest in shared common areas and elements in a common interest development.

common interest development (CID) – A development of residential or commercial property that combines the individual ownership of dwellings or buildings with a shared undivided ownership of common areas and elements of the entire project. A homeowners' association usually governs the common areas.

common law – Body of law based on custom and judicial precedent rather than on codified statutes.

common law dedication – When a property owner implies through his or her conduct the intent that the public may use the land.

common wall – A wall shared by two or more buildings or by two or more units in the same building.

community apartment project – One type of common interest development (CID) in which the owner has an undivided interest in the land with the exclusive right to occupy a particular unit.

community association – Organization composed of people who own condominium units, the right of exclusive occupancy in a community apartment, or ownership interest in a stock cooperative or planned development.

community association manager – Administers the daily affairs and oversees the maintenance of property and facilities jointly owned and used by the homeowners through the association.

community center – A retail center anchored by a small department store and supported by up to 50 smaller stores. Typically, at least 5,000 households are necessary to support a community center.

community property – Form of concurrent property ownership that exists only between spouses. Property acquired by a husband and wife, or either, during marriage, when not acquired as the separate property of either prior to marriage.

community property with the right of survivorship – A type of vesting used in some states by spouses to hold title in property. This type of title combines the benefits of community property and joint tenancy. Upon the death of a spouse, community property with right of survivorship gives the surviving spouse title to the property and excludes the property from probate proceedings.

Community Reinvestment Act (CRA) – Legislation enacted by Congress in 1977 requiring banks and other lenders to make capital available to low and moderate-income urban neighborhoods.

compact fluorescent lamps (CFCs) – A fluorescent light bulb that is compacted to fit into an Edison light socket.

compaction – Extra soil matted down or compressed, added to a lot to fill in the low areas and raise the level of the parcel, or used where the soil is unstable.

company dollar – The income remaining from gross commission income (GCI) after paying the cost of sales.

comparable sales (comps) – Sales having similar characteristics as the subject property and used for analysis in the appraisal process. They are recently sold properties situated in a similar market. Commonly called comps.

comparative market analysis (CMA) – A comparison analysis of recent sales used, by real estate brokers when working with a seller, to determine an appropriate listing price for the seller's house.

comparative property analysis – In property management, an analysis that looks at the specific attributes of a particular property compared against the competition.

comparative-unit method – An appraisal method used to determine the value of a building by multiplying the cost per square foot of a recently built comparable building by the number of square feet in the subject building. *See* square-foot method.

comparison – An appraisal method of determining the capitalization rate of a property by looking at the operational capitalization rate of similar properties in the area.

comparison approach – A real estate appraisal method comparing a given property with similar or comparable surrounding properties. Also called sales comparison approach or market comparison approach.

compensating balance – When a borrower deposits funds with the bank in order to induce the lender into making a loan.

compensation plan – The written statement describing how associates are paid and listing any charges and expenses that are the associates' responsibility.

compensatory damages – Damages designed to compensate the injured party for the injury that was sustained.

COMPETENCY RULE – Per USPAP, the COMPETENCY RULE "identifies requirements for experience and knowledge, when completing an appraisal and prior to accepting an appraisal assignment."

competent party – A person entering into a contract who is legally capable to enter into a binding contract. Criteria for competency include age of majority and mental capacity.

competitive advantage – Something that places the company above the competition.

competitive area – The geographic area in which competition for a subject property occurs and may affect its revenues, expenses, and value.

complaint – The first document (pleading) that starts a civil action summarizing the plaintiff's case against the defendant including a demand for relief.

completion bond – A guarantee by an insurance company that a builder will complete a construction project.

compliance clause – A clause in a lease agreement designating the laws with which each party must comply.

component – (1) A part of a system. (2) Completed sections of housing parts delivered to a construction site and assembled into one housing unit.

composite rate – A capitalization rate composed of interest and recapture in separately determined amounts.

compost – A mixture of decaying organic matter, such as plants, leaves, and food scraps that is used for fertilizer.

composting – The controlled biological decomposition of organic material in the presence of air to form a humus-like material.

composting toilet – A self-contained toilet using little or no water that uses the process of aerobic decomposition (composting) to break down the waste composts into humus and odorless gasses.

compound interest – Interest paid on original principal and also on the accrued and unpaid interest which has accumulated as the debt matures.

Comprehensive Environmental Response, Compensation and Liability Act (CERCLA) – A law passed by Congress in 1980 establishing two trust funds to help finance the cleanup of properties impacted by the release of hazardous wastes and substances; commonly known as superfund.

compressor – The pump that moves the refrigerant from the indoor evaporator to the outdoor condenser and back to the evaporator again.

comps – *See* comparable sales.

computerized maintenance management system (CMMS) – In property management, a computer software solution that assists the user in developing and storing the information for a maintenance program.

concentric zone model – A theory of land development stating that cities grow by adding rings around existing rings of activity. At the center of the rings is the Central Business District. The next ring contains manufacturing, warehousing, and low-end commercial activities. The next ring contains low-income housing. As the rings continue outward, the level of housing increases.

concessions – Discounts or enticements given by a landlord or seller to attract prospective tenants or buyers into signing a lease or purchasing property.

conclusion – An appraiser's final estimate of value, realized from facts, data, experience, and judgment, set out in an appraisal.

concrete – A mixture of cement, sand, aggregate, and water used as a structural material.

concurrent ownership – Ownership of a piece of property by two or more persons at the same time. Examples of concurrent ownership include joint tenants, tenants by entirety, tenants in common, and community property owners. Also known as co-ownership.

concurrent recording – When the closing of an escrow is contingent upon the simultaneous closing of another escrow.

condemnation – The process by which the government acquires private property for public use, under its right of eminent domain.

condemnation guarantee – An evidence of title issued to a governmental agency naming persons to be made defendants in an action in eminent domain.

condensation – The cooling of a gas or vapors into a liquid state. It appears as a film or water droplets.

condenser – A device that transfers unwanted heat out of a refrigeration system to a medium (either air, water, or a combination of air and water) that absorbs the heat and transfers it to a disposal point. There are three types of condensers: air-cooled condensers, water-cooled condensers, and evaporative condensers. Most residential systems have an air-cooled condenser.

condition – A limiting restriction in the ownership of real property. The penalty for breaking a condition may result in the return of the property to the grantor or modification of the estate.

condition of sale – A comparison factor used in the direct sales comparison approach of appraisal. It refers to the motivations of the buyer and seller in the sales transaction. Examples are the relationship between buyer and seller, financial needs, and lack of market exposure.

condition precedent – A condition A condition that must be fulfilled before a right accrues or an estate vests.

condition subsequent – A condition which, if it occurs at some point in the future, can defeat a previously accrued right or vested estate.

conditional sales contract – A contract of sale in which title remains in seller until all conditions of the contract have been fulfilled.

conditional use – A use that does not meet the current use requirements, but may be allowed by obtaining a special permit.

conditional use permit – Allows a land use that may be incompatible with other uses existing in the zone. Also called special use permit.

conditions of sale – In appraisal, circumstances of the sale, such as exposure time, marketing process, and buyer motivation. Unusual conditions may affect the final purchase price of a comparable sale and cause the sales price to reflect the market improperly.

conditions, covenants, and restrictions – *See* CC&Rs.

condominium – An undivided interest in common in a portion of real property coupled with a separate interest in space called a unit.

Conduct – The Conduct section of the USPAP ETHICS RULE that identifies issues regarding appraisers' conduct.

conduction – The transfer of heat through a solid material.

conductor – Metal wires, cables, and bus-bar used for carrying electric current. Conductors may be solid or stranded, that is, built up by an assembly of smaller solid conductors.

conduit – Plastic or metal tubing housing electrical wiring.

Confidentiality – Per USPAP, the Confidentiality section of the ETHICS RULE states, "the appraiser must protect the confidential nature of the appraiser-client relationship and is obligated to obey all confidentiality and privacy laws."

conforming loans – Loans which conform to Fannie Mae guidelines, which sets loan limits to a certain amount.

conformity – When land uses are compatible and homes are similar in design and size, the maximum value is realized.

congruous – Suitable or appropriate. In appraisal, describes a property suitable to the area.

connector – Device used to join an electrical wire to a piece of equipment or another wire.

consequential damages – Payment made to compensate for a breach of contract. Also, damage to a parcel of land done by a public body or adjacent owner, impairing its value.

conservation – The preservation and renewal of natural resources through good management for use by future generations.

consideration – Something of value—such as money, a promise, property or personal services; one of the essentials of a valid contract.

consistent use – An appraisal concept stating that land and improvements must be valued on the same basis. Improvements must contribute to the land value in order to have any value themselves. *See* principle of consistent use.

constant – A percentage of the original loan paid in equal annual payments over the life of the loan. For example, a $1 million loan with a 10.8 percent constant requires a $108,000 annual payment.

constant payment mortgage – A mortgage with fixed payments of principal and interest for the life of the loan.

constructed wetland – Any of a variety of designed systems that approximate natural wetlands, use aquatic plants, and can be used to treat wastewater or runoff.

construction classification – A system that rates the basic frame, walls, and roof of a structure, as to their relative fire resistance (e.g., Class A, B, C, or D construction. Class A is the most fireproof).

construction cost – The cost of building a structure, including labor, materials, contractor's overhead and profit, taxes, and construction loan interest. Construction cost is different from original costs (the price the owner paid). The original costs may be more or less than the construction cost.

construction loan – A short-term interim loan made to finance the actual construction or improvement on land. Funds usually disbursed in increments as the construction progresses.

constructive eviction – Conduct by a landlord that impairs tenant's possession of the premises, making occupancy impossible.

constructive fraud – A breach of duty legally declared fraudulent, because it deceives others, despite the fact that there is no dishonesty or deceptive intent.

constructive notice – Knowledge, which the law presumes a person has, as in the case of documents which have been recorded as a matter of public record.

consumer confidence – Measure of the level of optimism consumers have about the performance of the economy.

Consumer Credit Protection Act – A federal law that includes the Truth-in-Lending Law.

consumer goods – Goods sold or purchased primarily for personal, family, or household purposes.

Consumer Price Indexes (CPI) – Program produces monthly data on changes in the prices paid by urban consumers for a representative basket of goods and services.

contact list – A record of everyone you know—family members, friends, teachers, former and current business associates, and members of associations to which you belong.

contaminant – Any physical, chemical, biological, or radiological substance or matter that has an adverse effect on air, water, or soil.

contamination – Introduction into water, air and soil of microorganisms, chemicals, toxic substances, wastes, or wastewater in a concentration that makes the medium unfit for its next intended use. Also applies to surfaces or objects and buildings, and various household and agricultural use products.

contemporary style – An asymmetrical housing style that is characterized by attractive, simple, clean lines and the combination of stone, glass, masonry, and wood in the exterior.

contiguous – Touching, connecting, adjoining, or in close proximity.

contingency – A provision in a contract requiring the completion of a certain act or the occurrence of a particular event, before the contract is binding.

contingent – Dependent upon an uncertain future event.

contingent beneficiary – A person who may share in an estate or trust depending upon the happening of an event.

contingent interest – An interest which may vest depending upon the happening of an event.

contingent liability – Responsibility extending beyond personal actions or deeds.

contingent valuation – A method used to identify how a particular feature affects the value of a property by asking those who are knowledgeable about that market, i.e. other appraisers and agents; used when there is no sales data available.

contingent valuation method – An appraisal method used to identify how a particular feature affects the value of a property by asking those who are knowledgeable about that market (other appraisers and agents) when no sales data is available.

contour – The surface configuration of land. Shown on maps as a line through points of equal elevation.

contract – A legally enforceable agreement made by competent parties, to perform or not perform a certain act.

contract date – The date the contract is created. The contract is created when the final acceptance is communicated back to the offeror.

contract documents – In real estate, the documents explaining and serving as proof of the agreement entered into by the buyer and seller.

contraction phase – Phase in the real estate cycle in which supply grows faster than demand and activity in the real estate market falls.

contract of sale – A contract for the sale of real property, where the seller gives up possession, but retains title until the total of the purchase price is paid off. Also called an installment sales contract, a contract for deed, an agreement of sale, a conditional sales contract, or a land sales contract.

contractor – A person or company supplying materials or work, for a set price, in the construction industry. Since the individual or company is not a regular employee, they receive no benefits.

contract rate – The agreed-upon interest rate of a loan, adjusted for inflation. Also called the nominal rate.

contract rent – The rent established by agreement or contract.

contractual intent – Intent to enter into a contract or an action understood by another party to imply intent to enter into a contract. A clear understanding of intent prevents jokes and jests from becoming valid contracts.

contra proferentem – Ambiguous terms in a contract should be interpreted against the party drafting the document.

contribution – What an element of real property adds to the overall property value.

contributory value – Value given by appraisers to site improvements after identifying them.

convection – (1) Gravity-caused heat transmission by the movement of air, due to the density differences between air currents of differing temperatures. (2) The transfer of heat in water, air, or another fluid, as the substance descends when it is cooler, and rises when it is warmer.

convenience center – (10,000 – 30,000 SF) has half-a-dozen to a dozen small stores designed in a straight line.

convention hotels – Large hotel designed to accommodate thousands of convention attendees.

conventional loan – Any loan made by lenders without any governmental guarantees (FHA insured or VA guaranteed). The loan typically requires a substantial down payment and is usually available only to those with good credit.

conversion – (1) Change from one character or use to another, as converting an apartment building to condominium use. (2) The appropriation of property or funds belonging to another.

conversion ratio – In property management, the number of prospects who visit a rental property compared to the number who actually sign a lease.

convertible loan – An adjustable-rate loan allowing the borrower to change to a fixed rate at any time during the life of the loan.

convey – To transfer ownership or title to property from one person to another.

conveyance – The written instrument transferring title to or an interest in land.

cooling capacity –A measure of the ability of a unit to remove heat from an enclosed space.

cooling-off period – A period of time after entering into a contract in which either party may legally back out of the contract.

cooperating broker – A real estate broker who assists another broker by finding a buyer for a property.

cooperative – Form of common interest development in which a corporation holds title to all of the real property and owners purchase shares of stock in that corporation. Each resident possesses a proprietary lease.

cork oak – The cork oak is native to the Mediterranean basin. Once the trees are about 25 years old, the outer layer of bark is harvested to make cork products, such as bottle stoppers, bulletin boards, and cork flooring. The tree is not harmed and the layer renews for harvesting every nine years. The trees live for about 200 years.

corner influence – The affect on property value a corner lot location produces. The value may be greater or less than inside lots, depending on the perceived benefits of being located on a corner.

corner lot – A lot found at the intersection of two streets. It may be desirable because of its accessibility, but may also be noisy and expensive to maintain because of the increased frontage.

corporate rental – Fully furnished apartment with all the comforts of home. The maximum stay is generally one month.

corporation – A legal entity or organization whose rights in business are similar to that of an individual. It exists indefinitely and has centralized management in a board of directors.

corrective maintenance – Involves fixing items that require repairs.

correlation – A step in the appraisal process involving the interpretation of data derived from the three approaches in value (cost, market, and income) leading to a single determination of value. Also called reconciliation.

correlative water right – A law exercised in some states restricting riparian owners who share a common water source to taking a reasonable amount of the total water supply.

corrosion – The gradual wearing away of a metal by rusting or chemical usage.

co-signer – A joint signer of a contract or note. The individual becomes obligated to the agreement along with the principal party.

cosmetic maintenance – Refers to maintenance that focuses on retaining or improving the physical attributes of the property to increase its value.

cost – The amount paid (in labor, material, or sacrifices) for goods or services.

cost approach – An appraisal method whereby a value estimate of a property is derived by estimating the replacement cost of the improvements, deducting the estimated accrued depreciation, then adding the market value of the land.

cost basis – Original price paid for a property (real or personal).

cost-benefit ratio – The ratio of the benefits of an improvement to the cost of that improvement. In order for the improvement to be considered desirable, the ratio must exceed 1.00.

cost index – Figure representing construction cost at a particular time in relation to construction cost at an earlier time, prepared by a cost reporting or indexing service.

cost-index trending – Converting known historical costs into current cost estimates.

cost multiplier – Regional or local factor used in adjusting published construction cost figures to estimate local costs.

cost-of-living index – A government indicator of the fluctuating cost of living for an average person on a monthly basis.

cost-per-unit fee – Determined by dividing total direct and indirect costs by the number of units within a building or buildings on the property.

cost recovery – The deduction of value from an income-producing property over a period of time. Similar to depreciation. However, cost recovery is not limited by the useful life of the property. The entire cost of the property may be deducted over a certain period of time.

cost services – Companies who collect and provide information regarding cost trends.

cost-to-cure – The dollar amount necessary to restore a deteriorated item to new or reasonably new condition.

cost-to-cure method of depreciation – Method of estimating accrued depreciation based on the cost-to-cure or repair observed building defects.

cotenancy – Ownership by two or more persons.

cottage – Originally, a house with no surrounding land belonging to it. In modern times, cottage refers to a small house, perhaps used as a seasonal home.

counterflashing – Flashing used on chimneys at roof-line to cover shingle flashing and prevent moisture entry.

counteroffer – The rejection of an original purchase offer and the submission of a new and different offer.

court – (1) A short road or open area, partially or wholly enclosed by buildings. (2) A judicial body that hears legal cases.

court confirmation – The approval by a court of the sale of property by an executor, administrator, guardian, conservator, or commissioner in a foreclosure sale.

covenant – (1) A promise to do or not do certain things. (2) An agreement written into deeds and other instruments promising performance or nonperformance of certain acts or stipulating certain uses or non-uses of property.

covenant of seisen – A clause in a general warranty deed that guarantees at the time of conveyance, the grantor owns and possesses the property and has the authority to sell it or hold it as collateral.

covenants, conditions, and restrictions (CC&Rs) – *See* CC&Rs.

CRA – *See* Community Reinvestment Act.

cradle-to-grave analysis – Analysis of the impact of a product from the beginning of its source gathering processes, through the end of its useful life, to disposal of all waste products. Cradle-to-cradle is a related term signifying the recycling or reuse of materials at the end of their first useful life.

craftsman style – Craftsman homes are generally one and one-half stories, with long, sloping rooflines and wide, pillared porches. The pillars typically widen at the base. Other features include tile or stone fireplaces, dark, heavy woodwork, beamed ceilings, rows of high, small ribbon windows, and full-width porches framed by tapered columns.

crawlspace – The space between the first floor and the ground surface, often found in houses with no basement or space between the ceiling of the top floor and the roof, taking the place of an attic. The opening must meet building code requirements.

creative financing – Financing techniques that are atypical. Creative financing may have different principal amounts, interest rates, or payment terms.

credit – A bookkeeping entry on the right side of an account, recording the reduction or elimination of an asset, an increase in income, the addition of a liability, or increase in equity.

credit bureau – An agency that collects the credit records of consumers and summarizes the findings in a factual credit report.

credit loan – A mortgage that is granted based upon the financial strength of a borrower, not taking into consideration equity or collateral.

credit rating – An estimate of the creditworthiness and responsibility of a consumer.

credit report – A document listing the credit history of an individual. Lenders use it as an indicator of the strength of an individual's credit.

credit scoring – Objective, statistical method that assesses the tenant's credit risk.

credit union – A cooperative, non-profit organization established for banking purposes. Credit unions are owned and operated by their members.

crime or fidelity insurance – Used to cover losses caused by employee dishonesty.

criminal law – Wrongs against persons or society.

cripple – Stud above or below a window opening or above a doorway.

cross-collateralization – When collateral for one loan also serves as collateral for one more additional loans.

cross-connection – A condition which permits connection between a potable water supply system and a drain or wastewater system. There may be a flow from one system to the other, and the direction of flow depends on the pressure differential between the two systems.

cross-defaulting clause – A clause, usually included in a secondary loan contract, stipulating that a default in the primary loan will also cause a default in the junior loan.

crown molding – A type of large molding with a curved face and beveled edges, used on a cornice or to cover the angle where the wall meets the ceiling around a room.

crude oil – A mixture of hydrocarbons that exists in liquid phase in natural underground reservoirs and remains liquid at atmospheric pressure after passing through surface separating facilities.

CRV – *See* certificate of reasonable value.

cubic-foot method – Similar to the square-foot method, except it takes height as well as area into consideration.

cul-de-sac – A street or alley, open at one end only, with a large, rounded, closed end to facilitate a U-turn.

cumulative zoning – Zoning laws allowing so-called higher uses (residential) to exist in lower use zones (industrial), but not vice versa.

curable depreciation – Items of physical deterioration and functional obsolescence which are customarily repaired or replaced by a prudent property owner.

curb appeal – The good or bad impression of a property one gains from an initial viewing, usually while driving by or standing on the curb.

current (electric) – A flow of electrons in an electrical conductor. The strength or rate of movement of the electricity is measured in amperes.

curtesy – The common law interest of a husband in estate of deceased wife.

curtilage – The grounds and additional buildings surrounding a house, commonly used in connection with the everyday use of the house. This area is usually fenced.

customer – A prospective buyer of real estate; not to be confused with a property seller, who is the listing broker's client.

cycle – The ups and downs that occur in a period of time.

D

dam – A physical barrier constructed across a river or waterway to control the flow of or raise the level of water.

damage – A deterioration in the quality of the environment not directly attributable to depletion or pollution.

damage or destruction clause – A clause in a lease detailing how the partial or total destruction of the property would be handled between the parties to the lease.

damages – Compensation a plaintiff may be paid as a result of injuries to himself or his property, through an act or default of another. Complex laws determine the amount of damages awarded.

damper – A movable plate or valve used to control airflow. In a fireplace or wood stove, a damper is used to control the amount and direction of air going to the fire. When the fireplace is not in use, the damper should be closed to prevent air from being drawn up through the flue.

data – Information pertinent to a specific appraisal assignment. Data may be general (relating to the economic background and the region), local (relating to the city and the neighborhood), or specific (relating to the subject property and comparable properties in the market).

data mining – Data processing using sophisticated data search capabilities and statistical algorithms to discover patterns and correlations in large pre-existing databases.

data services – The numerous companies engaged in the business of selling data to real estate appraisers.

data sources – Any of a variety of sources used by appraisers when collecting general, local, and specific information.

date – The exact date a legal document or contract is signed. Certain documents may have several dates indicating when different aspects of the agreement will take place or take effect.

date of acceptance – The date the seller accepts the offer or the buyer accepts the counteroffer.

date of appraisal – The date on which the opinion of value applies. The date of appraisal is not necessarily the same as the date the report is written. Also called the valuation date or date of value.

date of closing – The date the title of a recently sold property is transferred to the buyer.

date of value – *See* date of appraisal.

daylight factor (DF) – The ratio of daylight illumination at a given point on a given plane, from an obstructed sky of assumed or known illuminance distribution, to the light received on a horizontal plane from an unobstructed hemisphere of this sky, expressed as a percentage.

daylighting – The use of controlled natural lighting methods indoors through skylights, windows, and reflected light.

dead mall – Mall with a high vacancy rate, low consumer traffic level, or is dated or deteriorating in some manner.

debenture – A bond backed only by the credit of the borrower, and not secured by a mortgage or lien on property. The debt is recorded by an indenture agreement.

debit – The opposite of a credit. A bookkeeping entry on the left side of an account, recording the increase to or addition of an asset, disbursements from income, or reduction of an outstanding liability.

debt financing – Borrowed funds.

debtor – A person who is in debt; the one owing money to another.

debt ratio – The ratio of an individual's debt payments to his or her monthly income.

debt service – The periodic payment specified in the loan contract necessary to repay the total amount of debt.

debt-to-equity ratio – The ratio of the total debt to the total amount of equity possessed by the owner.

debt-to-income ratios – Guidelines used by lenders to determine a consumer's maximum mortgage amount.

decedent – A person who has died.

Deceptive Trade Practices and Consumer Protection Act (DTPA) – Serves as a valuable protection for consumers engaging in real estate transactions, which include the services rendered by property management.

decibel (dB) – Unit of sound level or sound-pressure level. It is ten times the logarithm of the square of the sound pressure divided by the square of reference pressure, 20 micropascals.

deciduous – Plants and trees that lose their leaves seasonally in the fall.

declaration – A legal document that must be filed by condominium developers in most states. The declaration describes the land to be developed, and the resulting condominiums, the type of lease, and other legal requirements.

declaration of homestead – The recorded notice to protect the equity in a home from forced sale by unsecured creditors.

declining annuity – Evenly spaced, periodic payments that are decreasing in amount. Also called decreasing annuity.

dedication – The giving of land by its owner to a public use, and the acceptance for such use by authorized officials on behalf of the public.

deductible – The amount the insured must pay when any insurance claim is filed.

deed – A written document used to convey an ownership interest in real property.

deed in lieu of foreclosure – A deed conveying mortgaged property that is in default. The owner deeds the defaulting mortgage to a lender to avoid foreclosure action. It is also called a voluntary deed or voluntary conveyance.

deed of reconveyance – A document used to transfer legal title from the trustee back to the borrower (trustor) after a debt secured by a deed of trust has been paid to the lender (beneficiary). Also called a release deed.

deed of sale – Evidence of a purchaser's acquisition of legal title at a judicial sale, subject to redemption rights, if any.

deed of trust – A three party security instrument conveying title to land as security for the performance of an obligation. Also called trust deed.

deed restrictions – Limitations in the deed to a property dictating certain uses that may or may not be made of the property.

de facto – In fact.

default – Omission or failure to fulfill a duty, observe a promise, discharge an obligation, or perform an agreement.

default clause – A clause in a lease specifying the lessor's rights, and the possible penalties facing the lessee, in the event of a default.

default interest rate – A higher interest rate charged on a loan if certain terms or conditions are not fulfilled by the borrower, such as a loan default.

default judgment – A judgment entered in favor of the plaintiff when the defendant defaults, or fails to appear in court.

defeasance clause – The provision of a mortgage giving the mortgagor the right to redeem the property upon satisfaction of the obligation it secures.

defeasible – Capable of being defeated, annulled, or revoked.

defendant – Person who sued in a civil proceeding or accused in a criminal proceeding.

deferred maintenance – Negligent, postponed care or maintenance of a building. A type of physical deterioration, resulting in physical depreciation and a loss of value.

deficiency – A feature of a property considered faulty or insufficient.

deficiency judgment – A personal judgment against a borrower for the unpaid balance of a debt owed when the security for the loan is not sufficient to repay the debt.

define the problem – Part of the appraisal process, includes identifying the client and other intended users, the intended use of the appraiser's opinions and conclusions, the type and definition of the value sought, and the effective date of the appraiser's opinions and conclusions.

defined channel – Any natural watercourse, even if it is dry during a good portion of the year.

definite and certain – Precise acts to be performed are to be clearly stated.

deflation – A state of the economy when price levels decrease and purchasing power increases.

deforestation – The loss of forest resulting in the loss of habitat for countless animal and plant species and soil erosion.

defunct – Deceased, dead.

degrees of freedom – Mathematical way of manipulating data to obtain credible results from a data set that is less than statistically significant.

dehumidifier – A device that removes humidity or moisture from the air.

delinquency – The failure of a borrower to make payments on time, as specified under a loan agreement.

delinquency report – List of all occupied units for which rent has not been received by a certain date. The delinquency report shows the tenants who are behind in rent payments and the number of payments missed.

delivery – The unconditional, irrevocable intent of a grantor immediately to divest (give up) an interest in real estate by a deed or other instrument.

demand – (1) The desire to buy or obtain a commodity. (2) The rate at which electricity is delivered to or by a system, part of a system, or piece of equipment expressed in kilowatts, kilovoltamperes, or other suitable unit, at a given instant or averaged over a specified period of time.

demise – To rent an estate for years, for life, or at will.

demographic profile – The statistical study of human populations, from a variety of sources used to create a broad profile of any community. A profile of a specific area that contains general information, such as employment, education, average age, average salary ranges, gender, occupation, number of children, etc.

demographics – The statistical characteristics of human population studies.

demolition cost – The expense required to demolish a building. It may be used in an appraiser's highest and best use analysis.

demurrer – A written response to a complaint, which pleads for dismissal on the point that even if the facts alleged in the complaint were true, there is no legal basis for a lawsuit. Also called notice to dismiss.

densitometer – A photometer for measuring the optical density (the opposite of transmittance) of materials.

density zoning – A type of zoning ordinance restricting the average number of houses per acre (gross density) that may be built within a specific subdivision.

Department of Energy – Government department whose missions are to advance energy technology and promote related innovation.

Department of Housing and Urban Development (HUD) – U.S. Department of Housing and Urban Development. HUD, created in 1965, administers the federal program dealing with better housing and urban renewal.

Department of Veteran's Affairs (DVA) – Established in 1944, the DVA guarantees a portion of an eligible veteran's loan.

depleted uranium – A radioactive waste comprised primarily of U-238.

depletion – A reduction in the value of an asset, due to the removal or exhaustion of a resource or material.

deponent – A witness; an affiant.

deposit – Money given to show intent to follow through with a purchase agreement. It is given along with an offer to purchase. *See* earnest money.

Deposit Insurance Fund (DIF) – A fund created by merging the Bank Insurance Fund (BIF) and the Savings Association Insurance Fund (SAIF), effective March 31, 2006.

deposition – Live, oral testimony under oath that is reduced to writing.

depository institution – A financial institution accepting deposits in the form of checking and savings accounts, and making loans using their depositors' monies.

depreciable rate – The rate at which an asset loses a limited resource or material.

depreciable real property – Property that is used as a business or produces income, and is subject to wear and tear.

depreciated cost method – Method for adjusting comparable sales where adjustments are calculated from an analysis of the depreciated replacement cost for each differentiating feature.

depreciation – (1) Loss in value from any cause, such as age, physical deterioration, functional, or economic obsolescence. (2) A tax advantage of owning income property.

depreciation rate – The degree of lessening in value of an object or property, usually applied on an annual scale.

depreciation reserve – An account into which the estimated replacement cost of equipment is accumulated each year over the life of the asset, so it can be replaced when it becomes obsolete and totally depreciated. Commonly used in the accounting of public utilities.

depression – A stage in the business cycle following a recession characterized by extremely high unemployment and very little purchasing power.

depressurization – A condition that occurs when the air pressure inside a structure is lower that the air pressure outdoors.

depth – Distance from the frontage of a lot to the rear lot line.

depth table – A statistical table used to estimate the value of the added depth of a lot.

deregulation – A process by which financial institutions, formerly restrained in their lending activities by the law, are allowed to compete freely for profits in the marketplace.

descent – Manner of succession to title to property of an intestate decedent.

description – A section of a conveyance document that legally defines the property to be transferred. The property is generally described in two ways; first, by general location, such as a street address, and then, more specifically, by the use of public or plat maps or other recorded information.

desk cost – Profitability measure calculated by dividing the fixed expenses of the firm by the number of associate licensees. It shows how much each associate licensee must earn to cover expenses.

deterministic model – Input determines the output or result.

development – The process of planning and building on an area of land. During development, property values may be established and/or may increase.

development method – Method of vacant land valuation in which development costs and developer's profits are subtracted from estimated gross sales, resulting in a raw land value estimate. Also called the land development method.

development rights – The right to build on or improve a property. The rights may be sold separately from the land.

devise – A gift of real property by will.

devisee – A person who receives land or real property in the last will and testament of the donor.

dew point – The temperature at which dew starts to form, or vapor to condense and deposit as a liquid.

diminished utility – A loss in the usefulness of a property resulting in a loss in property value. *See* accrued depreciation.

diminution – The act or process of decreasing, lessening, or taking away.

diminution in value – The difference between the before and after values of properties that have been damaged.

direct capitalization method – Income capitalization technique where value is estimated by dividing net operating income by the overall capitalization rate.

direct costs – All of the costs directly involved with the construction of a structure, including labor, materials, equipment, design and engineering, and subcontractors' fees.

direct endorsement program – An FHA special program allowing eligible lenders to consider mortgage applications without first submitting paperwork to HUD for approval. This makes it easier and quicker for low- and moderate-income families to buy homes.

direct lender – A lending institution dealing directly with its customers. There are no intermediaries between the borrower and the lender.

direct marketing – An activity sending promotional materials to individuals or businesses using mail, telemarketing, or via email.

direct sunlight – That portion of daylight arriving at a specified location directly from the sun, without diffusion. Also called beam sunlight.

directional growth – The location or direction toward which the residential sections of a city are destined or determined to grow.

discharge of contract – The cancellation or termination of a contract.

discharge of the loan – Cancellation or termination of a loan contract.

disclaimer – A statement denying legal responsibility for the product sold. It is also a denial or renunciation of one's legal right to property.

disclosure – The act of showing, or making something known. In real estate, it is an important risk reduction tool used by brokers.

disclosure statement – (1) A required statement listing all the information relevant to a piece of property, such as the presence of radon or lead paint. (2) A written statement of a borrower's rights, under the Truth-in-Lending Law, or a statement of all financing charges in a transaction, which must be disclosed by a lender.

discount – To sell a promissory note before maturity at a price less than the outstanding principal balance of the note at the time of sale.

discount point – The amount of money the borrower or seller pays the lender to get a mortgage at a stated interest rate. This amount is equal to the difference between the principal balance on the note and the discounted amount a purchaser of the note pays the original lender, under current market conditions. A point equals one percent of the loan.

discount rate – The interest rate charged by the Federal Reserve Bank to its member banks for loans.

discounted cash flow – Estimated future investment returns, mathematically discounted to their present value.

discounting a note – Selling a note for less than the face amount or the current balance.

discretionary income – The portion of an individual's income available for investment or spending after the necessities (rent or mortgage, food, clothing, etc.) have been paid.

discrimination – The practice of making a selection or choice, such as treating a person fairly or unfairly. *See* Fair Housing Act.

disintermediation – The process of depositors removing funds from savings.

display ad – A large, expensive ad that uses text, graphics, and pictures to sell a product or property.

disposable personal income – An individual's total income for spending or investment, after deductions for taxes.

distressed property – (1) Property in poor financial or physical condition. (2) Foreclosed real estate or property included in a bankruptcy.

distributed sales force – Sales associates working primarily in the field or working out of their homes and coming into the office for meetings with management or customers.

divest – To sell; to release one's interest in a property.

dividend – Payment to shareholders of a share of the profits from the company in which they hold stock.

division fence – Fence lying exactly on the boundary line separating two properties.

Do Not Call – Federal and state law regulating unsolicited telephone calls. The National Do Not Call law resulted from the passage of the Telephone Consumer Protection Act in 1991. The Act was written to protect the privacy of residential telephone customers.

doctrine of correlative use – A law exercised in some states, restricting riparian owners who share a common water source to taking a reasonable amount of the total water supply.

document – Legal instrument, such as mortgages, contracts, deeds, options, wills, bills of sale, etc.

domain name – Unique name that identifies one or more IP addresses on the Internet.

domicile – Fixed and permanent home.

dominant tenement – The property that benefits from an easement.

door jamb – The framework surrounding a door or door opening.

dormer – A projection from the roof of a building, usually a house, which contains a window. The projection is built at an upright angle from the slope of the roof. Dormers are usually used in second story bedrooms or bathrooms.

double dumbbell shape – Cross-shaped shopping center with anchor stores at the end of each cross.

double escrow – Two escrows on the same property, at the same time, having the same party as the buyer and seller of the property. The process is illegal in many states, unless full disclosure is made.

double-glazed window – *See* dual-glazed window.

double-hung window – A window opening vertically from the top and bottom, containing two separate sashes with a locking device at the center, where the top of the lower sash meets the bottom of the upper sash.

double net lease – A lease arrangement in which the tenant pays the rent, utilities, property taxes, special assessments, and insurance premiums.

down payment – The portion of the purchase price that is not financed.

downspout – The vertical pipe or duct of the gutter system used to carry rainwater from a gutter to the ground.

downtown hotels – Located near the center of a city's busiest economic activity.

downzoning – A change in a zoning standard, reducing the usage allowed for the property. An example of downzoning is reducing a property's zoning from residential use to a conservation site use.

drain – A channel or pipe for drawing off water or sewage in a building drainage system.

drain field – The area into which the liquid from the septic tank drains.

drainage – The removal of excess surface water or groundwater from land by means of ditches or drains.

draws – Monetary advances made to a borrower.

drip irrigation – Above-ground, low-pressure watering system with flexible tubing that releases small, steady amounts of water through emitters placed near individual plants.

dropped ceilings – A ceiling built below the actual ceiling, made of acoustic tiles and a T-bar suspension. The T-bar suspension is a framework of steel or metal channel suspended by wires, with pre-cut acoustic tiles placed into the framework.

dry rot – Wood decay due to fungi caused when wood is subjected to a constant source of moisture. Dry rot appears as brown, crumbling wood.

drywall – An interior wallboard made of any number of materials other than plaster, such as gypsum board, plywood, or wood paneling, used in place of wet plaster to finish the inside of buildings.

dual agency – An agency relationship in which a real estate broker represents both buyer and seller in a transaction. Some states require written consent before a broker may act as dual agent, and some states prohibit dual agency.

dual agent – A broker acting as agent for both the seller and the buyer in the same transaction.

dual-glazed window – A type of window having two layers (panes or glazing) of glass separated by an air space. Each layer of glass and surrounding air space reradiates and traps some of the heat that passes through thereby increasing the window's resistance to heat loss.

duct – Thin sheet metal, shaped either round, square, or rectangular, and used to convey air at low pressure.

duct blower – A variable speed fan that is attached to a duct system to measure duct air leakage.

ductwork – A network of metal, fiberboard, or flexible material flowing throughout a space, which delivers air from an HVAC unit to the respective zones of a home or office.

due diligence – The reasonable effort to secure accurate and complete information about a property.

due on sale clause – An acceleration clause in a mortgage or deed of trust granting the lender the right to demand full payment of the mortgage loan, upon sale of the property.

duplex – A residential building containing exactly two units. The units are side by side sharing a common wall and roof or stacked one above the other.

duress – The use of force to get agreement in accepting a contract.

DUST – The mnemonic for the four elements of value: **D**emand, **U**tility, **S**carcity, and **T**ransferability.

Dutch colonial revival style – Houses that are one to two-and-one-half stories with shed-like dormers and a distinctive gambrel roof.

Dutch door – A door divided horizontally into halves. The halves may open and close independent of the other, or they may be latched together to act as one door.

DVA – *See* Department of Veteran's Affairs.

dwelling – Any structure used for a residence or domicile.

E

early occupancy – A situation in which the buyer is allowed to take possession of a property before the close of escrow. This arrangement has a high risk for problems and is not recommended.

early termination clause – A clause that allows tenants to cancel their lease before it expires.

earnest money – Cash, a personal check, cashier's check, promissory note, money order, or other form of consideration given by the buyer at the time an offer is written on property.

earning potential – One's ability to earn income.

earth-sheltered construction – Constructing buildings below ground level, in-hill, or with berming using earth against external building walls for external thermal mass to reduce heat loss. An earth-sheltered structure provides a steady interior climate.

earth-sheltered home – A dwelling that is partially or totally underground or that has earth berms around some or all of its exterior walls.

earthquake insurance policy – Insurance that covers damage to the structure during an earthquake, but can vary greatly in terms of exclusions and deductibles.

easement – A non-possessory right to enter or use someone else's land for a specified purpose.

easement appurtenant – An easement connected to a particular property that transfers with the property when conveyed.

easement by prescription – Easement created by open, adverse, continuous, and uninterrupted use by a single party, for a number of years, as specified by law.

easement in gross – An easement that benefits a person, not a particular piece of land.

eave – The lower section of the roof that forms an overhang composed of a fascia, soffit, and soffit molding.

eco-efficiency – Combination of environmental and economic performance to create more value with less impact.

ecological economics – The idea that one must use the healthy and natural systems, services, and goods available from nature to be economically successful.

ecological footprint –A measure of the land area required to support a certain population or human activity. A city with an ecological footprint that is larger than its land area consumes more than its share of resources. The opposite of carrying capacity.

ecology – The relationship of living things to one another and their environment, or the study of such relationships.

economic age – Estimated age of a building based on its condition and usefulness.

economic base – The companies providing jobs for a community or defined geographic area.

economic base analysis – The study of economic forces affecting a certain community. The analysis is used to predict population, income, and other variables that may affect real estate or land use.

economic forces – In appraisal theory, one of several types of forces that affect property values.

economically feasible – Financially possible, reasonable, or likely. One of the four criteria for determining highest and best use.

economic life – The estimated period over which a building may be profitably used. Also known as useful life.

economic obsolescence – A type of depreciation occurring because of forces outside the property. Examples include changes in the social or economic make-up of the neighborhood, zoning changes, recession, or legislative restrictions. Also called external obsolescence.

economic rent – What a leased property would be expected to rent for, under current market conditions, if the property were vacant and available for rent.

economics – As related to real estate, a study of the factors that cause people to prosper and create a viable demand for real property.

economic-trend – Pattern of related changes in some aspect of the economy.

ecosystem – The interacting system of a biological community and its non-living environmental surroundings.

edible landscaping – Landscaping containing vegetation, such as fruit trees or grape arbors; cultivated for its ability to be eaten by humans.

effective age – The age of a building based on its physical condition and usefulness; not necessarily the same as its chronological age.

effective date – The specific day the conclusion of value applies to, whether it is a present, past, or future date.

effective demand – The demand or desire coupled with purchasing power.

effective gross income – The amount of income that remains after vacancy and credit losses are deducted from gross income.

effective interest rate – The percentage of interest that is actually being paid by the borrower for the use of the money, distinct from nominal interest.

effective rate – The interest rate a borrower actually pays on a loan, as opposed to the nominal rate stated in the loan contract.

effective rent – Average lease rate over the lease term after deducting all rent concessions.

efficacy – In lighting design, a measure of the luminous efficiency of a specified light source, expressed in lumens per watt. For daylighting, this is the quotient of visible light incident on a surface to the total light energy on that surface. For electric sources, this is the quotient of the total luminous flux emitted by the total lamp power input.

efflorescence – The white powdery substance that forms on the surface of masonry, by water leaching out certain chemicals.

effluent – Anything that flows out of a pipe, smokestack (which is emissions from stacks or chimneys), storage tank, channel, sewer, or septic system.

egress – The right to exit from a property using an easement.

EIR – *See* environmental impact report.

ejectment – Legal action for return of right to possession of land and for damages.

electric baseboard – An individual space heater with electric resistance coils mounted behind shallow panels along baseboards. Electric baseboards rely on passive convection to distribute heated air to the space.

electrical energy – The ability of an electric current to produce work, heat, light, or other forms of energy.

electricity – A form of energy characterized by the presence and motion of elementary charged particles generated by friction, induction, or chemical change.

electricity distribution system – That portion of an electricity supply system used to deliver electricity from points on the transmission system to consumers.

electric power – The rate at which electric energy is transferred. Electric power is measured by capacity and is commonly expressed in megawatts (MW).

electric power grid – A system of synchronized power providers and consumers connected by transmission and distribution lines and operated by one or more control centers. In the continental United States, the electric power grid consists of the Eastern Interconnect, the Western Interconnect, and the Texas Interconnect systems.

electric power plant – A station containing prime movers, electric generators, and auxiliary equipment for converting mechanical, chemical, and/or fission energy into electric energy.

electromagnetic spectrum – A continuum of electric and magnetic radiation encompassing all wavelengths from electricity, radio, and microwaves at the low-frequency end of the spectrum, to infrared, visible light, and ultraviolet light in the midrange, to x-rays and gamma rays at the high-frequency end.

electronic underwriting systems – The mortgage industry uses these systems to predict multiple-risk factors in a loan application. Users receive an analysis of the borrower's credit, estimate of the property's value, and an opinion of the risk involved.

element of comparison – Any aspect of a real estate transaction or any characteristic of the property that affects the property's sales price.

elements of value – Four prerequisites that must be present for an object to have value: demand, utility, scarcity, and transferability.

elevation sheet – A labeled diagram or cutaway of a home detailing its interior features and building components, as well as front and side exterior views of a building as it will be when finished.

Elizabethan style – This asymmetrical housing style has a very steep cross-gabled roof, a prominent chimney, half-timbered exteriors, rounded doorways, and multi-paned casement windows.

emancipated minor – Someone who is under age, yet legally set free from parental control/supervision. Emancipation may be achieved by marriage or by court order.

emblements – Growing crops that are cultivated annually for sale; considered personal property.

embodied energy – The total energy sequestered from a stock within the earth in order to produce a specific good or service including extraction, manufacture, and transportation to market.

emergency plan – The part of a disaster plan dealing with the first and immediate response to the disaster.

eminent domain – The right of a local, state, or federal government to acquire private property for public use. The government must pay the owner just compensation for taking the property.

emission standards – Regulatory limits set by governments on the pollutants that can be released into the atmosphere from sources like motor vehicles or manufacturing plants.

employment agreement – In real estate, this agreement is required by state law and must state the important aspects of the employment relationship, including supervision of licensed activities, licensee's duties, and the compensation arrangement.

employment hubs – Sources of employment.

encroachment – The unauthorized placement of permanent improvements that intrude on adjacent property owned by another.

encumbrance – Right or interest in land decreasing its value but not hindering its sale or transfer. Encumbrances that affect the title are financial encumbrances and those that affect the property's use are non-financial encumbrances.

Endangered Species Act – Federal legislation passed in 1973 that provides for the identification and protection of species (plants and animals) currently in danger of extinction or threatened by extinction within the foreseeable future.

endorsement – (1) The act of signing a name on the back of a check or promissory note to evidence its transfer. (2) A written document attached to an insurance policy expanding or limiting coverage.

energy – The capacity for doing work as measured by the capability of doing work (potential energy) or the conversion of this capability to motion (kinetic energy).

energy audit – A survey in which an auditor inspects a home and suggests ways energy can be saved.

energy conservation – Efficiency of energy use, transmission, or distribution that yields a decrease in energy consumption while providing the same, or higher, levels of service.

energy crop – A crop grown specifically for its fuel value. Energy crops include food crops, such as corn and sugarcane, and nonfood crops such as poplar trees and switchgrass.

energy efficiency – Using less energy or water to perform the same tasks.

energy efficiency retrofit – Improvement made to an existing structure that provides an increase in the overall energy efficiency of the building, or home.

energy efficient mortgage – A home mortgage for which the borrower's qualifying debt-to-income and housing expense-to-income ratios have been increased by 2% because the home meets or exceeds the minimum standards of the Council of American Building Officials 1992 version of the Model Energy Code.

energy efficient ratio (EER) – A measurement of the efficiency of energy; used to determine the effectiveness of appliances.

energy factor (EF) – The energy factor measures the efficiency of storage water heaters, which is based on an average hot water consumption of 64 gallons/day. The higher the EF, the more efficient the water heater.

EnergyGuide label – Label on all major home appliances indicating the appliance meets the Appliance Standards Program set by the U.S. Department of Energy (DOE). The label estimates how much energy the appliance uses, compares energy use of similar products, and lists approximate annual operating costs.

Energy Information Administration – An independent agency within the U.S. Department of Energy that develops surveys, collects energy data, and analyzes and models energy issues.

energy payback time – The time required for any energy producing system or device to produce as much energy as was required in its manufacture.

energy recovery – Recovery of useful material or energy from hazardous or municipal waste.

ENERGY STAR® – A program initiated in 1992 by the EPA establishing a standard set of guidelines to recognize the energy efficiency of various products.

engineered lumber – Recycled or reconstituted wood materials.

English cottage style – This asymmetrical housing style is patterned after the rustic cottages in southwestern England. They have an uneven sloping roof of slate or cedar that mimics the look of thatch.

English Tudor style – This traditional housing style is large, two-stories, with masonry or stucco, and has steep-gabled roofs with a medieval feel. This style is characterized by patterned brick or stone walls, rounded doorways, and multi-paned casement windows.

entertainment complex – Shopping center that features theaters, restaurants, amusements, and related retail stores.

entitlement – Eligibility; the degree to which a veteran deserves to receive a DVA loan.

entrepreneur – A person who attempts to make a profit by starting his or her own company or by operating alone in the business world, and thereby assumes a substantial portion of the risks, profits, and losses.

entrepreneurial profit – A market-derived figure representing the compensation the owner or developer expects to gain from developing the property.

entry-level home – A type of home for first-time buyers.

environment – The sum of all external conditions affecting the life, development, and survival of an organism in a broader context.

environment surroundings – All the external conditions and influences affecting the life and development of an organism, for example, human behavior, society.

environmental degradation – Deterioration of the environment due to depletion of resosurces, such as air, water, and soil.

environmental impact – Any change to the environment, whether adverse or beneficial, wholly or partially resulting from an organization's activities, products, or services. An environmental impact addresses an environmental problem.

environmental impact report (EIR) – Detailed report required by California Environmental Quality Act regarding projects potentially having significant environmental impacts.

environmental impact statement (EIS) – Detailed evaluation required by National Environmental Policy Act regarding the environmental impact of a proposed development.

Environmental Protection Agency (EPA) – A federal agency established in 1970 responsible for enforcing federal environmental regulations such as the National Environmental Policy Act, Clean Air Act and Clean Water Act.

Equal Credit Opportunity Act (ECOA) – Legislation passed that makes lender discrimination against a person, based on age, gender, national origin, marital status, religion, and race illegal.

equilibrium – (1) A status achieved when opposing characteristics of land in a specific market balance each other out. (2) When supply and demand in a market balance each other and prices stabilize.

equitable rights – The rights of an individual to occupy, lease, or sell a property.

equitable title – The right to obtain absolute ownership to property when legal title is held in another's name.

equity – (1) The difference between the appraised value and the loan. (2) Natural right or justice based upon ethics and morals.

equity buildup – The gradual increase of the borrower's equity in a property caused by amortization of loan principal.

equity capital – The amount an owner puts into an investment.

equity capitalization rate – Factor used to estimate the value of the equity in the band of investment method of capitalization and other mortgage and equity techniques.

equity dividend – The portion of net operating income after debt service is paid, but before income tax is deducted. Also called before-tax cash flow or pre-tax cash flow.

equity investors – Investors using venture capital to take an unsecured and thus relatively risky part in an investment.

equity loan – A loan made using the equity in the borrower's home as security. The equity is based on a percentage of the appraised value of the home.

equity of redemption – The right to redeem property after a judicial sale.

equity ratio – The percentage of a property unencumbered by debt. Calculated by dividing the equity interest of a property by its total value.

equity trust – An investment trust that deals in owning real estate, rather than in financing. One example of an equity trust is the Real Estate Investment Trust (REIT).

erosion – The gradual wearing away of land by natural processes.

errors and omission insurance (E&O) – A form of professional liability insurance, which protects business owners and professionals against liability claims or lawsuits for damage caused by errors, mistakes, and negligence.

escalation clause – A clause in a contract providing for the upward or downward adjustment of certain items to cover specified contingencies, usually tied to some index or event.

escheat – A legal process where property reverts to the state, because the deceased left no will (intestate) and has no legal heirs.

escrow – A small and short-lived trust arrangement used to close real estate transactions.

escrow agent – The neutral third party holding funds or something of value in trust for another or others.

escrow holder – A company that acts as a neutral agent of both buyer and seller.

estate – The ownership right or legal interest in property, and the degree, quantity, nature, and extent to which a person has that right or interest.

estate at sufferance – A tenancy created when one is in wrongful possession of real estate, even though the original possession may have been legal.

estate at will – The tenancy that may be ended by the unilateral decision of either party. There is no agreed upon termination date, and either party must give 30-days notice before ending the tenancy.

estate for life – A possessory, freehold estate in land held by a person only for the duration of his or her life or the life or lives of another.

estate for years – A tenancy agreement for a definite period. It can be for any period of days, weeks, months, or years. If the tenancy lasts for more than one year, the agreement must be in writing.

estate from period to period – A leasehold estate that is automatically renewed for the same term; a conveyance for an indefinite period of time; does not need to be renegotiated upon each renewal; commonly a month-to-month rental.

estate in remainder – An estate that has been conveyed to take effect and be enjoyed after the termination of a prior estate. Also known as remainder estate. *See* future interest.

estate in reversion – An estate that comes back to the original holder, as when an owner conveys a life estate to someone else, with the estate to return to the original owner on termination of the life estate. *See* future interest.

estate of inheritance – An estate which may descend to heirs. Also known as perpetual estate.

estate tax – A federal or state tax charged on the transfer of an individual's assets inherited by heirs.

estimate – (1) A preliminary opinion of value. (2) To appraise or determine value.

estimated remaining life – The number of years it takes for improvements to become valueless.

estoppel – A legal doctrine which prevents a person from denying something to be true or a fact, if the denial is contrary to previous statements or actions made by that same person.

estuary – Area at the mouth of a river where sea water and fresh water mix together creating brackish water.

et al – And others.

et con – And husband.

ethanol – Renewable colorless alcohol fuel made from the sugars found in plants, such as corn, sorghum, and barley.

ethics – A set of principles or values by which an individual guides his or her own behavior and judges that of others.

ETHICS RULE – Per USPAP, the ETHICS RULE "identifies the requirements for integrity, impartiality, objectivity, independent judgment, and ethical conduct."

et seq. – And following.

et ux – And wife.

eucalyptus – A fast-growing hardwood tree native to Australia that was introduced to many parts of the word. The tree can be harvested within 14-16 years due to the longer growing season of the climates where eucalyptus grows.

eutrophication – The increasing concentration of plant nutrients and fertilizers in lakes and estuaries, partly by natural drainage and partly by pollution. It leads to excessive growth of algae and aquatic plants, with oxygen depletion of the deep water, causing various undesirable effects.

evaluation – An analysis of a property and/or its attributes in which a value estimate is not required.

evaporation – The conversion of a liquid to a vapor (gas), usually by means of heat.

evaporative cooler – Cooling device used in low-humidity areas. Outside air passes over water-saturated pads, causing the water to evaporate into them. The cooler air is directed into the home and pushes warmer air out through windows. Also known as a swamp cooler.

event – In statistics, one or more outcomes of an experiment.

eviction – The legal process of removing a tenant from the premises for some breach or violation of the lease.

eviction notice – Written notice from the landlord to the tenant requesting that he or she move out of the property within the time specified by local or state law, or meet the landlord's requirements.

evidence of title – Proof of property ownership.

exception – The exclusion of some part of the property to be sold. Also, the liens and encumbrances not included in the coverage of a title insurance policy.

excess land – Surplus land beyond the land needed to support the property's highest and best use.

excess rent – The amount by which the total contract rent exceeds market rent.

exclusionary zoning – A type of illegal zoning which intentionally or unintentionally excludes racial minorities and low-income residents from an area.

exclusive agency – An employment agreement between a broker and a principal. The principal gives the broker the exclusive right to market and sell the principal's property for a fixed period of time. The principal may still sell his or her own property under this agreement, without any commission being due to the broker.

exclusive right to sell – An exclusive contract, in which the seller must pay the listing broker a commission if the property is sold within the time limit by the listing broker, any other broker, or even by the owner.

exclusivity clause – Lease clause giving a tenant the exclusive right to sell his or her product (cookies, shoes, cell phone accessories) or service (dry cleaners, travel agency) on the property.

exculpatory clause – A clause in designed to absolve a party from liability.

execute – To sign, perform, or complete.

executed contract – A contract in which the obligations have been performed on both sides of the contract, and nothing is left to be completed.

execution sale – The forced sale of a property to satisfy a money judgment.

executive suite – A shared office with services provided by a management firm.

executor/executrix – A person named in a will to handle the affairs of a deceased person.

executory contract – A contract in which obligation to perform exists on one or both sides.

exfilitration – The intentional or unintentional leakage of air out of a building.

exit strategy – The method planned by a business owner to sell or close the business.

expansion phase – Phase in the business or real estate cycle marked by speculation and expansion of credit, which stimulates the local, regional, and even national economy.

expansive soil – A type of soil that increases in volume when wet and decreases when dry.

expense stop clause – A clause that limits the lessor's responsibility for the costs of operating the premises.

expenses – The costs incurred in an enterprise. In appraisal, expenses are estimated on an annual basis regardless of the period in which they are incurred or paid.

experiment – In statistics, a situation involving chance or probability that leads to results called outcomes.

expert testimony – Testimony given in a court trial by a person qualified by the court as an expert on a particular subject, for example, as an expert witness on real estate values.

expert witness – One qualified to give expert testimony in a court of law on a particular subject, such as medicine, engineering, or real estate appraising.

expired listing – A property listing that did not sell during the specified period with the listing broker.

exposure – (1) The compass direction the front of a structure faces. (2) In marketing, the amount of visibility a property has in the market.

express agreement – A written agreement, usually in the form of a listing contract, authorizing the broker to represent the seller in finding a ready, willing, and able buyer. A contract created when the parties declare the terms and put their intentions in words, either oral or written.

expropriation – The seizure of private land for public use or purpose, under the government's right of eminent domain. The property is condemned, and fair market compensation is paid to the owner.

extended coverage policy – An extended title insurance policy that costs more than the standard title policy and broadens the scope of coverage to include off-the-record title related matters, for example, taxes or assessments or other claims, such as easements, encroachments, etc. not shown in public record. An extended coverage policy is required by secondary market lenders.

extension agreement – Agreement granting additional time for performance.

externalities – Outside influences that have a positive or negative effect on property value.

external obsolescence – Any influence negatively affecting a property's value that falls outside of the specific property site (i.e., a property located under an airport flight pattern). Examples of external obsolescence include zoning changes, proximity to nuisances, and changes in land use or population. *See* economic obsolescence and locational obsolescence.

extraction method – A method of determining the land value of a comparable property by deducting the depreciated costs of the improvements on that property from the property's known sale price. The remaining value represents value attributable to the land. This method is a variation on the allocation method and based on the same principles. Also known as abstraction method.

extraordinary assumption – Per USPAP, "an assumption, directly related to a specific assignment, which, if found to be false, could alter the appraiser's opinions or conclusions."

extrapolation – The process of predicting future trends based on current and past patterns and relationships. It assumes that the same economic factors that influenced past trends will affect future trends similarly.

eye appeal – Aesthetic appeal. A property's amenities and features such as landscaping or a pleasant view.

F

façade – The outer or front face of a structure. Often used to describe an exterior featuring a unique design.

face value – The stated amount of a bond or security, as opposed to its market or real value.

Facilities Management Administrator (FMA) – A property management designation offered by the Building Owners and Managers Institute (BOMI) with emphasis on the management of a commercial facility.

facility manager – Commercial property specialist who manages properties owned by the government and the military (public), colleges and universities (non-profit), or for-profit corporations (private entities).

factory-built housing – Housing built in a factory instead of on site. Includes manufactured, modular, panelized, and precut homes.

Fahrenheit – A temperature scale in which water freezes at 32 degrees and boils at 212 degrees at normal atmospheric pressure.

Fair Housing Act – The Fair Housing Act, including its amendments, provides protection against discriminatory housing practices against people, based on race, sex, religion, color, handicap, national origin, or familial status. Familial status refers to a family with at least one child under the age of 18 or pregnant women.

fair market value – The price the property would bring if freely offered on the open market with both a willing buyer and a willing seller. Also known as market value and objective value. *See* market value.

false promise – A false statement of fact.

familial status – Having at least one member of the family who is less than 18 years of age, or the presence of a pregnant woman.

Fannie Mae – *See* Federal National Mortgage Association.

farm – A specific geographic location that a real estate agent delivers or mails advertising pieces to once or twice a month, in order to obtain listings.

Farm Credit System – A separate national banking system that finances the needs of farmers, ranchers, rural homeowners, agricultural cooperatives, rural utility systems, and agribusinesses. Unlike other banks, Farm Credit System banks and associations do not take deposits. Instead, loanable funds are raised through the sale of System-wide bonds and notes in the nation's capital markets.

Farmers Home Administration (FmHA) – A relief agency that disburses emergency farm financing. It complements the activities of the Farm Credit System by creating and insuring loans to farmers who are unable to obtain financial assistance from other sources.

farming – One of the most effective prospecting tools used to identify and cultivate new leads, with the ultimate goal of gaining new business.

fascia – Horizontal, flat trim pieces used around the outer end of roof rafters at eave and wall junctures, sometimes used to support gutters.

fashion mall – Shopping center featuring stores that offer stylish clothing, upscale merchandise, and quality consumer goods.

fault creep – Movement along an earthquake fault caused by stress and/or earthquake shaking.

FDIC – *See* Federal Deposit Insurance Corporation.

feasibility study – An analysis performed on a proposed property to determine potential income and expenses, and most effective use and design.

Federal Deposit Insurance Corporation (FDIC) – An independent agency of the federal government that insures deposits in banks and thrift institutions. The FDIC directly examines and supervises banks and savings banks.

Federal Emergency Management Agency (FEMA) – A government agency involved with all the different aspects of emergency management from preparation to recovery and prevention.

federal Fair Housing Act – Title VIII of the Civil Rights Act of 1968 and the Fair Housing Amendments Act of 1988, taken together, constitute the Fair Housing Act. The Act makes it illegal for anyone to refuse to sell or rent a property to a person because of race or any other protected group.

federal funds rate – The interest rate the Fed charges to member banks on unsecured loans.

Federal Home Loan Banks (FHLB) – Manages and regulates savings and loan associations, as the Federal Reserve System regulates the commercial banking industry.

Federal Home Loan Mortgage Corporation – Federal Home Loan Mortgage Corporation (Freddie Mac) buys mortgages from lending institutions, pools them with other loans, and sells shares to investors.

Federal Housing Administration (FHA) – Created in 1934, the FHA provides mortgage insurance on loans made by FHA-approved lenders throughout the United States and its territories. FHA insures mortgages on single family, multifamily, and manufactured homes and has a stabilizing affect on the mortgage market.

Federal National Mortgage Association – The Federal Home Loan Mortgage Corporation (Fannie Mae) is a government-chartered corporation that buys qualified residential mortgage loans from the financial institutions that originate them, securitizes the loans, and repackages them to sell as investment securities.

Federal Open Market Committee (FOMC) – Directs and regulates the Federal Reserve System's open-market operations. Open-market operations consist of the bulk sale and purchase of government securities.

Federal Reserve System – The central bank in the United States that creates monetary policy to maintain healthy credit conditions nationwide, and to counteract inflation and deflation. Within the Federal Reserve System (Fed), there are 12 Federal Reserve District Banks, one in each of twelve defined geographic areas of the country.

federally related transaction – Any real estate transaction involving federal insurance or assistance.

federal tax lien – A lien placed on a taxpayer's real property, by the federal government, if the owner has not paid his or her taxes or is in violation of federal income tax or payroll tax laws.

fee appraiser – A professional appraiser who is not employed by a particular fiduciary lender; an independent appraiser. Also known as a field appraiser.

fee simple – The most complete form of ownership of real property, which one can sell, pass to another by will or inheritance, do any other thing with real property allowed by law. Also known as fee simple absolute or an estate of inheritance.

fee simple defeasible – A fee simple estate subject to being defeated, annulled, or revoked.

fee simple subject to condition subsequent – Any fee estate containing a condition that if violated, could lead to the termination of the estate and give the grantor a right of entry.

feedstocks – The raw material used in manufacturing a product, such as the oil or gas used to make a plastic.

felt – A flexible sheet or fibrous material that is saturated with asphalt and used as an underlayment for roof shingles or flashing for water resistance. Also known as tar paper.

fenestration – The arrangement, plan, and design of windows in a structure.

festival (themed) marketplace – Urban shopping center, featuring restaurant and entertainment associated with a place of historic or cultural interest.

fiberglass insulation – The most familiar type of insulation. It is spun from molten glass, and is pure white in its virgin state. Additives and binders often color the fiberglass, with pink and yellow being the most common. Fiberglass comes in rolls, batts, and as loose insulation that is blown into place.

FICO® – Credit scores calculated by the Fair Isaac Corporation. FICO® scores run from the 300s to above 900 and generated through complex statistical models created by the Fair Isaac Corporation.

fictitious business name – A business name that does not use the last name of the person who registered the business. Also known as DBA, doing business as, and assumed name.

fictitious deed of trust – A recorded deed of trust containing general terms and provisions, naming no specific parties, describing no property, and used for reference only.

fiduciary – A person who is required to act for the benefit of another person on all matters within the scope of their relationship.

fiduciary duty – That duty owed by an agent to act in the highest good faith toward the principal and not to obtain any advantage over the latter by the slightest misrepresentation, concealment, duress, or pressure.

fiduciary relationship – A relationship that implies a position of trust or confidence.

fief – Rights in the land that become heritable.

file – The act of placing an original document on public record.

filter – Any porous device that allows the passage of air but traps airborne particles, thus cleaning the air.

final value estimate – The appraiser's estimate of the defined value of the subject property, arrived at by reconciling the estimates of value, derived from the sales comparison, cost, and income approaches.

finance charge – The dollar amount a lender's extension of credit will cost, composed of any direct or indirect charges, such as interest, points, and fees incurred when borrowing money.

finance fee – The fee a mortgage brokerage charges to the borrower to cover expenses when creating a mortgage with their institution.

financial analysis – A study of a property's income producing performance and potential.

financial institution – An intermediary financial organization that collects funds and invests them in financial assets, or lends them back out in order to earn a profit.

Financial Institutions Reform, Recovery, and Enforcement Act (FIRREA) – A federal law passed in 1989 to provide guidelines for the regulation of financial institutions.

financial planning – Forecasting future repair and maintenance costs and includes deciding how much of the association's collected dues should be placed in reserves to accommodate these future needs.

financial service center – A center that provides customers with a variety of financial services, such as insurance, real estate sales, real estate loans, and banking services, in one location.

financial statements – A written report of the financial condition of a firm. Financial statements include income statement, balance sheet, and statement of cash flow.

financing – The act of loaning and borrowing money in order to buy an item. Also, the various fees and charges incurred when borrowing money.

financing statement – A written notice filed with the county recorder by a creditor who extended credit for the purchase of personal property. Establishes the creditor's interests in the personal property, which is security for the debt.

finder's fee – Money paid to a person for finding a buyer to purchase a property or a seller to list property. Also known as a referral fee.

finish flooring – The final covering on the floor (usually decorative hardwood).

finished area – The enclosed area in a home suitable for year-round use.

finish-out – New building shell that has been accommodated for a new commercial tenant.

fireplace – A wood-, gas-, or coal-burning appliance that is primarily used to provide ambiance to a room.

fire stop – A wooden block built between the wall studs or joists of a structure, with covered walls, closing off the passage of air and limiting the spread of fire.

FIRPTA – *See* Foreign Investment in Real Property Tax Act.

first deed of trust – A legal document pledging the collateral for a loan with first priority over all other claims against the property, except taxes and bonded indebtedness. The first deed of trust is superior to any other. *See* deed of trust.

firsthand data – Data from personal inspection or review.

first-hour rating – The ability of a water heater to meet peak-hour demands. It measures how much hot water the heater will deliver during a busy hour. The first-hour rating accounts for the effects of tank size, and how quickly cold water is heated.

first mortgage – A loan that takes priority over all other loans. Also called a senior loan.

fiscal year – 12-month accounting period unrelated to the calendar year.

five-ranked windows – Five rectangular windows equally spaced across the second story of Georgian colonial-style houses.

fixed assets – Assets not easily converted into cash. Fixed assets include land, buildings, furniture and fixtures, equipment, leasehold improvements, and vehicles.

fixed capital – Money invested in fixed assets or property.

fixed costs – Expenses occurring regularly, regardless of changes in business activity. Examples are property taxes, rent, insurance, and maintenance.

fixed expenses – Operating costs that are more or less permanent and vary little from year to year regardless of occupancy.

fixed-rate loan – A loan with two distinct features: (1) The interest rate remains fixed for the life of the loan. (2) The payments remain level for the life of the loan and are structured to repay the debt completely at the end of the loan term.

fixed split plan – A commission plan with no incremental increases or chargebacks.

fixed window – A window with no moveable parts, such as a picture window.

fixity-of location – The physical characteristic of real estate that subjects it to the influence of its surroundings.

fixture – Anything permanently attached to real property.

flag lot – A potential building site whose configuration looks like a flag on a pole. It is generally located behind another lot, with an access road or driveway extending through and to one side of the front lot, and reaches the main road. The access road represents the flagpole.

flagstone – A decorative, flat, slate-like stone, used in walkways and patios, and processed in a variety of colors.

flashing – Waterproof sheets of plastic or corrosion-resistant metal, installed along with exterior finishing materials for the prevention of water leakage in such places as the intersection of a wall and roof or the valley of a roof.

flat lease – A lease with equal payments made at set intervals throughout the life of the lease.

flat roof – This roof is popular in the Southwestern house styles, such as pueblo and Spanish eclectic, and modern styles such as international, art moderne, and art deco.

flexible payment mortgage – A loan with graduated payments.

flipping – Buying a property at one price and quickly selling it to another at an inflated price.

floating slab – A type of foundation composed of one section for the floor and another for the foundation wall, each poured separately.

flood (100-year) – Boundary indicating areas of moderate flood hazards.

flood hazard boundary maps – Maps identifying the general flood hazards within a community.

flood hazard zone – An area prone to flooding. In order to obtain any loan secured by a property in such a zone, the buyer must purchase flood insurance.

flood insurance – Insurance covering damage from floods or tidal waves. Primary and secondary lending institutions require flood insurance on any financed property within certain areas identified by the Federal Emergency Management Agency (FEMA) as being flood-prone. The insurance premium is a fixed amount.

floodplain – Land that is subject to periodic flooding, due to its proximity to a body of water.

floodwater – Water overflowing a defined channel.

floor duty (floor time) – A common practice in real estate offices of assigning agents, on a rotating basis, the responsibility of handling all walk-ins and phone calls from prospective buyers and sellers, who are not clients of a specific agent.

floor plan – Drawings showing the placement, layout, and size of rooms in a building.

flow hood – A device used to measure the amount of air flowing through a register.

flue – The opening or passageway in a chimney through which smoke, gases, and ash pass from a building.

fluorescent lighting – The light produced by a fluorescent tube is caused by an electric current conducted through mercury and inert gases.

fly-in community – Residential community built around airplane or jet runways.

FNMA – *See* Federal National Mortgage Association.

folk victorian style – The affordable version of a Queen Anne house. Symmetrical, rectangular, or L-shaped with white wood siding, steep gabled roofs, and a front porch with turned spindles.

footing – An extended part of the foundation at the base or bottom of a foundation wall, pier, or column.

forbearance – Forgiving a debt or obligation. Example: When a creditor refrains from action against a debt, after the debt has become due.

forced-air system – A type of heating system in which heated air is blown by a fan through air channels or ducts to rooms.

force majeure – A force that cannot be resisted or controlled. Includes acts of God, and acts of man (riots, strikes, arson, etc.). The term is primarily used in insurance and in any type of performance contract, such as construction.

forced sale – The sale of property, due to the debtor's inability or unwillingness to make payments on the loan.

foreclosure – A legal procedure by which mortgaged property is sold to satisfy the debt.

foreclosure sale – The sale of property given as security to secure performance of an obligation.

Foreign Investment in Real Property Tax Act (FIRPTA) – A federal law requiring non-resident aliens and foreign corporations to pay U.S. income tax on gains earned from the sale of U.S. real property interest.

forfeiture – Relinquishing rights to something, due to nonperformance of an obligation or condition. A delinquent borrower may lose the rights to property due to forfeiture.

forgery – The illegal falsification of a signature or document, making an entire contract void.

formaldehyde – A chemical, organic compound found in building materials, such as adhesives, plastics, preservatives, and fabric treatments. It is listed as a probable human carcinogen.

form report – Written appraisal report, presented on a standardized form or checklist.

for sale by owner (FSBO) – An owner who attempts to sell a property without listing with a broker. Many owners in this situation will cooperate and compensate a broker who ultimately represents a buyer.

fossil fuels – Non-renewable energy sources formed in the Earth's crust from decayed organic material. The common fossil fuels are petroleum, coal, and natural gas.

foundation – The base of a house; usually concrete.

foundation plan – Drawing showing foundation, sub-floors, footing, and pier placement.

foyer – A large entrance or reception area located just inside the front entrance of a building, such as in a theater or hotel; also found in many homes.

framing – Construction of the framework of a house, made up of studs, rafters, joists, and beams.

franchise – A right or privilege awarded by law to operate a business using another company's name and products. In real estate, there are franchised brokerages such as Century 21® and ERA®.

fraud – An act meant to deceive in order to get someone to part with something of value.

free and clear title – A title unburdened by any liens, clouds, or other encumbrances.

freehold estate – An estate or ownership rights in real property, continuing for an indefinite period of time. Also called fee estate.

freestanding store – Retail outlet not associated with a shopping center and may be located at a distance from congested shopping areas and downtowns.

French doors – Double doors hinged at either side.

French drain – A small trench that allows surface water to drain away from a building or area that is prone to surface water build up or flooding.

French Normandy style – This housing style has a round stone tower topped with a cone-shaped roof. Sometimes the tower is the entrance to the house. In addition, vertical half-timbering adds height to the house.

French provincial style – This style of house is large, square, and symmetrical with two floors and a distinctive steep, high, hip roof. Windows and chimneys are symmetrical and balanced.

frequency distribution – The arrangement of data into groups according to the frequency with which they appear in the data set.

fresco – A method of painting on wet plaster on a wall. As it dries, the paint becomes part of the wall and remains much longer than if simply painted on a dry plaster wall.

frontage – The width of a property on the side facing a street.

front-end ratio – The percentage of all housing expenses (including principal, interest, taxes, insurance, mortgage insurance, and homeowners' association fees) to gross income.

front foot – Measurement, in feet, of the width of a property on the side facing the street.

front money – The minimum amount of money necessary to initiate a new business venture.

frost line – The depth of frost penetration in the soil. Depths vary in different parts of the country. Footing placement should be below this depth to prevent movement.

fructus industrials – Annual crops produced by human labor, such as fruits, nuts, vegetables, and grains.

fructus naturales – Naturally occurring plant growth, such as grasses, trees, and shrubs as part of the real property.

fuel cell – A device that converts the energy of a fuel, (Hydrogen, natural gas, methanol, gasoline, etc.) and an oxidant (air or oxygen) into useable electricity.

fuel efficiency – The ratio of heat produced by a fuel for doing work to the available heat in the fuel.

fuel oil – A liquid petroleum product less volatile than gasoline, used as an energy source.

full disclosure – The requirement to reveal any and all relevant facts pertaining to a property. A broker is legally obligated to give full disclosure. Sellers are also legally obligated to provide full disclosure of any known defects of the property.

full reconveyance – The transferring of property by a lender, to a borrower, once the mortgage debt is completely repaid.

fully amortized note – A note that is fully repaid at maturity by periodic reduction of the principal.

functional obsolescence – A type of depreciation stemming from poor architectural design, lack of modern facilities, out-of-date equipment, changes in styles of construction, or changes in utility demand.

functional utility – The combined factors of usefulness with desirability.

funding fee – A fee charged to the veteran borrower when securing a DVA guaranteed loan.

fungi – One of a large group of thallophytes living in damp wood, which include mold, mildew, rust, mushrooms, etc. These parasites live on organisms or feed on dead organic material. They lack true roots, stems, leaves, and chlorophyll, and reproduce by means of spores.

furnace – A heating appliance that produces heat by facilitating the combustion of fuel and air.

fuse – A safety device in an electrical system, such as a strip of easily melted metal. The strip is set in a plug, which is placed in a circuit as a safeguard, and if the current is too strong, the metal melts and breaks the circuit, preventing a fire.

future benefits – The anticipated benefits the present owner will receive from the property in the future.

future interest – An interest in real property that will take effect at a future time.

future value – The estimated lump-sum value of money or property at a date in the future.

G

gable roof – A roof design using rafters cut to the same length and joined in the center to form a peak, with two sides of the roof sloping down from that peak.

galleria – Glass-roofed mall based on Victorian-era shopping arcades.

gallery – In architecture, a covered walkway, open on one side, running along an upper story of a building, either inside or outside.

gambrel roof – Typically seen in Dutch colonial architecture, is a curbed roof, with a steep lower slope and a flatter one above. A gambrel roof contains a gable at each end, just like a standard gable roof. This roof is often used on barns.

gap analysis – An analysis of the difference between a market's supply and demand.

gap financing – A short-term, high-interest loan that helps to bridge a gap between available bank loans and the total amount of required financing. Gap financing is used for machinery, equipment, leasehold improvements, inventory, or working capital for start-up or business expansion.

garden apartments – One to two-story walk-up buildings with one or two bedroom units.

garnishment – Attachment of personal property of a debtor in the possession of a third person.

gas-filled windows – An inert gas such as argon is used instead of air between the windowpanes. Inert gases have a much better insulation value than air.

gasification – A manufacturing process that converts any matter containing carbon (including biomass) into synthesis gas.

gasoline – An aliphatic hydrocarbon fuel used to power internal combustion engines.

gazebo – A small structure with a roof and open sides, usually in the garden, where one may sit and enjoy the view. Also called a belvedere.

GDP – *See* gross domestic product.

GEM – *See* growing equity mortgage.

general agent – A person authorized by a principal to perform any and all tasks associated with the continued operation of a particular project.

general contractor – A construction specialist who negotiates construction contracts with developers to construct a building or other real estate project. He or she must pass an examination to obtain a license from the state regulatory agency. Also called the prime contractor.

general index – A title company's record of matters affecting title to land maintained according to names of individuals and entities rather than by real property description.

general ledger – A report showing an accounting of all debits and credits passing through the business bank account for various periods of time.

general lien – A lien affecting all the property owned by a debtor, rather than a specific property. A general lien may be created either by the courts, by issuing a judgment, by creditors, or through federal and state tax liens.

general obligation bonds – A type of municipal bond funded from property taxes and used for public improvements, such as public utilities, prisons, or schools.

general partner – In a limited partnership situation, the individual or company who acquires, organizes, manages, and is primarily liable for the investment.

general partnership – Business entity established by two or more individuals or businesses, which join to operate a business for profit.

general plan – A comprehensive, master plan adopted by cities and counties that is used as a guide for long-term physical development. A general plan is implemented by decisions that direct the allocation of public resources and shape private development.

general-purpose buildings – Buildings used for assembly plants, light manufacturing, or storage facilities.

Generation X – The group of homebuyers born between 1961 and 1981.

gentrification – The process of purchasing, renovating, and rehabilitating properties in an older, run-down neighborhood.

geodetic survey system – A method of legal land description used for very large areas. A network of benchmarks located by latitude and longitude mark the entire country. It is a variation of the rectangular survey system.

geographic segmentation – Specialization of serving the needs of clients in a particular geographical area.

Georgian colonial architecture – A more formal and elaborate form of Georgian architecture.

Georgian style – A formal style house with symmetrical lines. It has paired chimneys (one on each side) and five windows across the front of the second story.

geotextiles – Cloth or cloth like materials intended for use in the soil, usually for filtering or containing soil water. Some types are used to prevent or control erosion.

geothermal energy – Energy (hot water and steam) extracted from geothermal reservoirs in the Earth's crust.

geothermal heat pump – A heat pump that uses underground coils to transfer heat from the ground to the inside of a building. Also known as a ground source heat pump.

geothermal power – Power generated by using geothermal energy.

ghostbox – Large, empty building where a big-box store was formerly located.

gift deed – Deed whose consideration is love and affection.

gift tax – A federal tax imposed on a donor making a gift. A gift is the transfer of any type of property for less than what the property is really worth.

gingerbread work – Ornamentation in a building's (usually residential) architecture, which adds to aesthetic appeal, rather than functional value.

Ginnie Mae – *See* Government National Mortgage Association.

girder – A heavy, horizontal wood or steal beam used to support other beams, joists, floors, and partitions.

glazing – Transparent or translucent material (glass or plastic) used to admit light and/or to reduce heat loss; used for building windows, skylights, or greenhouses.

global cooling – A decrease in the average temperature of the Earth's atmosphere, especially a sustained decrease resulting from climate change.

global positioning system – A device using satellite technology to track your location and map out driving directions.

global warming – An increase in the average temperature of the Earth's atmosphere, especially a sustained increase resulting from climate change.

goal – A measurable outcome or accomplishment.

goal setting – An activity requiring you to make a list of things you want to achieve, acquire, or attract in a certain amount of time.

going concern value – The value existing in an established business property, compared with the value of selling the real estate and other assets of a concern whose business is not yet established. The term takes into account the goodwill and earning capacity of a business.

good consideration – Terms that denote acceptable consideration include valuable, adequate, good, or sufficient consideration. Consideration is something of value given by one party to a contract to another party, in exchange for something of value. Gifts, such as real property given solely based on love and affection, are good consideration. These gifts meet the legal requirement that consideration be present in a contract.

good faith – A bona fide act or an act done honestly, whether it is actually negligent or not. Recording laws protect good faith purchasers. Acts committed in bad faith are often punishable as a crime.

good faith estimate – When a potential homebuyer applies for a mortgage loan, the lender must give the buyer a good faith estimate of settlement costs, which lists the charges the buyer is likely to pay at settlement and states whether the lender requires the buyer to use a particular settlement service.

good funds – Funds that have already cleared the bank, such as cashier's checks, certified checks, or wired monies.

goodwill – An intangible, salable asset arising from the reputation of a business; the expectation of continued public patronage.

governing documents – Documents that rule over an organization in conjunction with the association bylaws, restrictions, and rules and regulations.

Government National Mortgage Association (Ginnie Mae) – A division of HUD. It funds high-risk mortgages for high-risk borrowers, typically in areas approved for government construction projects that have no other funding sources.

governmental forces – One of four forces believed to affect real estate value in appraisal theory. Examples of governmental forces are government controls and regulations, zoning and building codes, and fiscal policies.

grace period – An agreed-upon time after the payment of a debt is past due, during which a party can perform, without being considered in default.

grade – Ground level at the foundation or perimeter of the building.

grading – A process used when the level or elevation of the ground has to be changed or altered, using bladed machines that scrape the earth.

graduated lease – A long-term lease with an escalation clause, allowing for a rent increase, based upon the occurrence of a certain event. Also called a step-up lease.

graduated payment mortgage – A loan with partially deferred payments of principal at the start of the term, increasing as the loan matures. Also known as the flexible rate mortgage.

grandfather clause – A clause in a law permitting the continuation of a use or business which, when established, was permissible but, because of a change in the law, is now not lawful. Commonly used in zoning ordinances.

grant – A technical legal term in a deed of conveyance bestowing an interest in real property on another. The grant in a deed is given by the grantor to the grantee.

grant deed – A type of deed in which the grantor warrants that he or she has not previously conveyed the property being granted, has not encumbered the property, except as disclosed, and will convey to the grantee any title to the property acquired later.

grantee – The person receiving the property, or the one to whom it is being conveyed.

granting clause – Words of purchase, such as grants, conveys, transfers, or sells contained in a deed or other instrument conveying the property.

grantor – The person conveying, or transferring, the property.

gratuitous agent – A person not paid by the principal for services on behalf of the principal, who cannot be forced to act as an agent, but who becomes bound to act in good faith and obey a principal's instructions, once he or she undertakes to act as an agent.

grayfield – A dying mall or other property becoming obsolete.

graywater – Any wastewater, except in the toilet, produced from baths and showers, clothes washers, and lavatories in a home.

gravitational energy – The energy stored in an object's height or the potential energy associated with gravitational force.

green building – The practice of creating structures and using processes that are environmentally responsible and resource-efficient throughout a building's life-cycle from siting to design, construction, operation, maintenance, renovation and deconstruction. Also known as a sustainable building.

green energy – Energy produced and used in ways that produce less air pollution and other environmental impacts.

greenfield – Undeveloped land.

green flooring – Sustainable flooring alternative made from grasses (bamboo) and trees (cork oak and eucalyptus) that mature in half of the time (or less) than it takes hardwoods to reach market size. These products are considered rapidly renewing.

greenhouse effect – The result of water vapor, carbon dioxide, and other atmospheric gases trapping radiant (infrared) energy, thereby keeping the Earth's surface warmer than it would otherwise be.

greenhouse gases (GHG) – Those gases, such as water vapor, carbon dioxide, nitrous oxide, methane, hydrofluorocarbons (HFCs), perfluorocarbons (PFCs) and sulfur hexafluoride, that are transparent to solar (short-wave) radiation but opaque to long-wave (infrared) radiation, thus preventing long-wave radiant energy from leaving Earth's atmosphere. The net effect is a trapping of absorbed radiation and a tendency to warm the planet's surface.

greenhouse gas intensity – A measure of gas emissions per pound of production.

green properties – Green properties are constructed with environmentally preferable building materials and embody the elements of green building, such as healthy indoor environment, energy efficiency, water stewardship, and waste reduction.

green roof system – A conventional roof that is covered with a layer of vegetation. Also known as a living roof.

green wash – To falsely claim a product is environmentally sound. Also known as faux green.

grid – *See* electric power grid.

gross area – Total space designed for occupancy and exclusive use of tenants, measured from outside wall surfaces to the center of shared interior walls.

gross building area (GBA) – All enclosed floor areas, as measured along a building's outside perimeter.

gross density – The average number of houses allowed per acre under density zoning ordinances.

gross domestic product (GDP) – A measure of the U.S. economy adopted in 1991; the total market values of capital and goods and services produced within the United States borders during a given period (usually 1 year).

gross income – Total income from property before any expenses are deducted.

gross income multiplier (GIM) – A gross income multiplier (GIM) is a figure which, when multiplied by the annual gross income, equals the property's market value. The gross income multiplier accounts for all possible potential income.

gross leasable area (GLA) – Total area designed for occupancy and exclusive use of tenants, measured from outside wall surfaces to the center of shared interior walls. The total leasable floor space does not include common areas or other areas not being leased by the tenant.

gross lease – A lease agreement in which the tenant pays an agreed-upon sum as rent and the landlord pays any other expenses such as taxes, maintenance, or insurance. Also called a flat, fixed, or straight lease.

gross living area (GLA) – The total living space of a home, generally represented by the habitable, finished, above-grade floor space. Calculated by measuring the building's outside perimeter. This generally excludes garages and screened patios or porches (Florida rooms).

gross rent – Income (calculated annually or monthly) received from rental units, before any expenses are deducted.

gross rent multiplier (GRM) – A figure which, when multiplied by the monthly rental income, equals the property's market value. The GRM must be obtained from recent comparable sales since it varies with specific properties and areas.

ground fault circuit interrupter (GFCI) – An electrical safety device that instantly shuts down the circuit when a short develops. Required for outlets used in bathrooms, kitchens, outdoors, or wherever electrical equipment might come into contact with water.

ground lease – A lease of land only, on which the lessee usually owns the building or is required to build as specified by the land lease. Such leases are usually long-term net leases. Also called pad leases.

ground rent – Earnings of improved property credited to earnings of the ground itself after allowance has been made for earnings of improvements.

groundwater – Water beneath the surface of the land filling the spaces and cavities between the rocks and soil.

grout – Mortar poured or troweled into the joints between tiles or other masonry components.

growing equity mortgage (GEM) – A mortgage that has a fixed interest rate and increasing monthly payments. The increased payments are paid toward the loan principal. GEMs allow you to pay mortgages off earlier, save in interest payments, and build equity quickly.

guarantee of title – A form of title insurance based solely upon public record disclosures.

gunite – Air-sprayed concrete.

gutter – Horizontal channels installed at the edge of a roof to carry rainwater away from the house.

guy wire – A strong steel wire or cable strung from an anchor to an antenna or tree, used for support purposes.

H

habendum clause – Clause begining with the words "to have and to hold", and defines or limits the ownership interest of the grantee. Typically included in a warranty deed, but not in a grant deed.

habitat – An area with certain physical characteristics which support a particular community of animals and plants.

half-timbering – A method of construction where the wooden frame and principal beams of a structure are exposed, and the spaces between are filled with stucco, brick, or stone.

handicap – Any physical or mental impairment substantially limiting one or more major life activities.

hard money loan – The debt is incurred in exchange for cash, such as a 2nd or 3rd mortgage.

hardscape – The structures and features such as retaining walls, pathways, pools, sidewalks, curbs, and gutters that are part of the landscaping.

hardwood – Wood used for interior finish, such as oak, maple, and walnut.

hazard insurance – A property insurance policy protecting the owner and lender against physical hazards to property, such as fires, wind, storms, and other similar risks.

hazardous household waste – Consumer products such as paints, cleaners, stains, varnishes, car batteries, motor oil, and pesticides that contain hazardous components.

hazardous waste – Materials, such as chemicals, explosives, radioactive, biological, whose disposal is regulated by the Environmental Protection Agency (EPA).

header – The top horizontal, load-bearing board over a doorway or window opening.

hearth – The area in front of, and around, a fireplace. Usually constructed of brick, stone, or tile.

heat gain – Amount of heat added or created in a designated area.

heating capacity – A measure of the ability of a unit to add heat to an enclosed space.

heating seasonal performance factor (HSPF) – An efficiency rating for heat pumps. It is a measure of the average number of BTU of heat delivered for every Watt-hour of electricity used by the heat pump over the heating season.

heat loss – Amount of heat subtracted from a designated area.

heat-pump – Equipment that, during the heating season, draws heat into a building from outside and, during the cooling season, ejects heat from the building to the outside.

hectare – A metric measurement of land equal to 100 acres (10,000 square meters) or 2.471 acres.

heir – A person entitled by law to inherit property of a decedent.

heliodon – A device used to simulate the angle of the sun for assessing shading potentials of building structures or landscape features.

heliostat – A device that tracks the movement of the sun used to orient solar concentrating systems.

hereditaments – Things capable of being inherited.

HERS – The Home Energy Rating System is a national standardized system used by HERS Raters for rating the energy-efficiency of residential buildings.

HERS Index – A scoring system established by the Residential Energy Services Network (RESNET). The higher a home's HERS Index, the more energy efficient it is.

HERS Rater – home energy rater or auditor and third-party verifier certified by RESNET. Most known for blower door and duct blaster testing.

HERS Rating – A detailed energy analysis of the home, and legal document, producing a number that expresses the energy efficiency of a home.

HIF – Abbreviation for the Home Inspection Foundation.

high-efficiency particulate air (HEPA) filter – A designation for very fine air filters typically used in surgeries, clean rooms, or other specialized applications.

highest and best use (HBU) – The use, from among reasonably probable and adequately supported alternative uses, that is physically possible, legally permitted, economically feasible, and maximally productive.

high-mass construction – Passive building strategy of constructing buildings of massive, heat-retaining materials (such as masonry or adobe) to moderate diurnal temperature swings, especially in arid climates.

high-rise apartments – Have multiple floors between 75-491 feet high.

hip roof – A roof with four sloping sides that rise to a ridge. Usually found on garages or church steeples.

hiring profile – A description of the character traits, skill sets, and experience a candidate has to fill for a specific position.

historical hotels and inns – Signifies a particular era in history and may include antique furnishings.

historic cost – Cost of a property at the time it was constructed or purchased.

historic district zoning – A zoning classification that refers to a geographic area recognized to have historical significance.

holdback – A portion of the loaned funds not advanced by a lender, until the borrower meets specific requirements and/or conditions. In construction lending, a percentage of the contractor's loan funds are withheld until the construction is completed.

holder – The party to whom a promissory note is made payable.

holder in due course – A person who has obtained a promissory note or other negotiable instrument, without knowledge that it is defective, or was dishonored at the time it was negotiated.

hold harmless clause – A condition in a contract that protects a party from liability. The party is relieved from liability as a matter of negotiated agreement, or if circumstances beyond the party's control prevent him or her from satisfying the terms of the contract.

holdover tenant – A tenant who retains possession of leased property after the lease has expired. The landlord agrees to the occupation by continuing to accept rent.

hollow wall – A wall constructed of brick or stone, which is actually two separate walls, joined only at the top and the ends, making it hollow. Also called a cavity wall.

holographic will – A will, written in the maker's own handwriting, dated, and signed by the maker. The will is not witnessed and is not recorded.

home energy rater – Trained energy specialist who performs a standardized evaluation of the energy efficiency of a home.

home energy rating – A measurement of a home's energy efficiency.

home equity line of credit (HELOC) – A home equity line of credit is a form of revolving credit, in which a borrower's home serves as collateral.

home equity loan – A cash loan made against the equity in the borrower's home.

home inspection – The process by which an inspector examines the readily accessible physical structure, systems, and condition of a home and describes those systems and components in a written report.

home inspector – A person who performs the service of making a physical inspection of homes.

homeowner's exemption – A property tax exemption available on owner-occupied dwellings.

homeowner's insurance policy – Combined property and liability insurance designed for residential property owners.

homeowners' association (HOA) – A group of property owners in a common interest development that manages common areas, collects dues, and establishes property standards.

home performance contractor – Contractor who analyzes the house as a whole system and installs improvements to make it more energy efficient.

homestead property – Home, occupied by a family, exempt from the claims of unsecured creditors.

home warranty program – Coverage purchased to protect the buyer and seller against future repair or replacement costs related to the failure of appliances, heating, air conditioning, and major systems in the purchased property.

hopper window – A window hinged at the bottom and opens in the room. Also known as an eyebrow window.

hose bib – An outdoor water faucet.

Hoskold Tables – A method used to value an annuity, based on reinvesting capital immediately, and used by appraisers to value income property.

hostile possession – Possession of real property by someone other than the rightful owner. Hostile means the possessor's claim does not recognize, nor stand subordinate to, the owner's title. Hostile possession is necessary to establish a claim to real property under adverse possession.

hot dry rock – A geothermal energy resource that consists of high temperature, impermeable, crystalline rock above 300°F (150°C) that may be fractured and have little or no water.

hotelling – Workspace is unassigned and used by sales associates when they are in the office.

houseboat – Barge designed and equipped for use as a dwelling.

household hazardous waste – Consumer products, such as paints, cleaners, stains, varnishes, car batteries, motor oil, and pesticides that contain hazardous components.

housing inventory – Housing units available for sale or in the process of being made ready for sale.

housing starts – The number of housing units currently under construction. Often used as an economic indicator.

HUD – *See* Department of Housing and Urban Development.

HUD-1 Settlement Statement – A disclosure before settlement (closing) occurs, providing estimates of all settlement charges that will be paid by both buyer and seller.

human comfort zone – A band of temperatures from 67.5° F to about 78° F and 20% to 80% relative humidity.

humidifier – A device that adds humidity, or moisture, to the air.

humidistat – Device for measuring relative humidity and turns the humidifier on or off.

humidity – Dampness in the air caused by water vapor.

humus – Decomposed organic material that is an essential component of fertile soil; produced through composting.

HVAC – An abbreviation for heating, ventilation, and air-conditioning system that regulates the distribution of fresh air and heat throughout a building.

hybrid loans – Loans that offer features from various loan types.

hydrocarbon – An organic chemical compound found in fossil fuels comprised of hydrogen and carbon atoms in the gaseous, liquid, or solid phase.

hydrochlorofluorocarbons (HCFCs) – Chemicals composed of one or more carbon atoms and varying numbers of hydrogen, chlorine, and fluorine atoms.

hydrogen – The lightest of all gases, occurring chiefly in combination with oxygen in water; exists also in acids, bases, alcohols, petroleum, and other hydrocarbons.

hydrogen sulfide (HS) – A very odorous, toxic, and explosive gas produced by some bacteria in the absence of oxygen. It produces acids on contact with water.

hydronic heating – A heating system using heated water pumped through a building.

hydroelectric power – Energy that is derived from the force of moving water, such as waterwheels and dams. Tidal power is a type hydropower that converts the energy of tides into electricity.

hypothecate – To pledge property as security for a debt, without delivery of title or possession.

hypothetical condition – Defined in USPAP as "that which is contrary to what exists, but is supposed for the purpose of analysis."

I

ice dam – Dam-like buildups of ice along the eaves of buildings and roofs. They can force water up and under shingles, causing leaks (even in freezing weather).

impact fees – Charges imposed by local governments on developers of new residential, commercial, or industrial properties to compensate for the added costs of public services created by the new building.

implied agency – An agency created and performed without written agreement, but through words, actions, inference, and deduction from other facts.

implied contract – An agreement shown by acts and conduct, rather than written words.

implied listing – A listing agreement created by the actions of the parties involved, rather than by written contract. In some states, this type of contract is enforceable.

implied warranty of habitability – The property will be maintained to meet basic living requirements.

impound account – A trust account in which funds are held, usually by a lender, for the payment of property taxes and insurance premiums required to protect the lender's security. These amounts are collected with the note payment.

improved real estate – Land upon which buildings have been erected.

improvement ratio – The value of the improvements, divided by the total value of the property.

improvements – Valuable additions made to structures, usually private, to enhance value or extend useful remaining life. The term typically refers to buildings and other structures permanently attached to the land.

imputed interest – Interest applied by law. An interest rate imposed by the IRS, when the mortgage or land contract does not set one, or states one that is unreasonably low.

incandescent lamp – A light bulb in which a filament is energized by electric current to make light. Approximately 90% of the energy used by an incandescent lamp is given off as heat rather than light.

incentive zoning – Allows a developer to exceed the limitations set by a zoning law, if the developer agrees to fulfill conditions specified in the law.

inclusionary zoning – Local zoning ordinances that require residential developers to include a certain percentage of units for low-income and moderate-income households. Compliance with these ordinances is a contingency for governmental approval of the building project.

income (capitalization) approach – The method by which the value of an income-producing property is estimated. The income capitalization approach is based on the premise that there is an identifiable relationship between the net income a property generates and the value of the property. The process of estimating the present worth of a property, based on its anticipated income, is capitalization. Capitalization converts income to capital value. The income approach generally involves a three-step process: (1) estimate net operating income, (2) select an appropriate capitalization rate, and (3) capitalize the income.

income property – Property purchased for its income-producing capabilities.

income ratio – The difference between a borrower's total income and the amount necessary to cover one month's mortgage payment.

income statement – A document containing a detailed summary of the income and expenses of a business.

income stream – Actual or estimated flow of net earnings over time.

incompetent – A person who is legally unfit to enter into a contract. A person may be deemed incompetent by reason of mental illness, physical disability, drugs, age, or other reason that causes them to lack sufficient understanding, or be incapable of making reasonable decisions.

increasing annuity – Regular, periodic payments that increase in amount.

incremental plan – A commission plan with increases based on pre-determined sales thresholds.

incurable depreciation – Building defects or problems that would cost more to repair than the anticipated increase in value from such repair.

indemnify – To protect against damage, loss, or injury, or to make compensation to for damage, loss, or injury.

independent brokerage – A real estate company not affiliated with another local, regional, or national company.

independent contractor – A person who is hired to do a particular job and is subject to the control and direction of the person for whom they work. Independent contractors pay for their own expenses and taxes, and are not viewed as employees with benefits.

independent living facility – Multi-unit development in which seniors can live independently, but without having to maintain a home.

index – A statistical indicator measuring changes in the economy or financial markets. When an interest rate is tied to an index, such as the six-month Treasury bill rate, the interest rate will adjust up or down, as changes in the index occur.

index lease – A lease with a base rent and an escalation clause that provides protection against inflation for the property owner.

index method – Method for estimating construction costs that adjusts the original costs to the current cost level, by use of a multiplier obtained from a published cost index.

indicated value – Value estimate calculated or produced by an appraisal approach.

indirect costs – All of the time and costs involved in a construction project that are not directly related to the construction itself. Examples are loan fees, interest, legal fees, and marketing costs.

indirect lighting – A method of illumination in which the light is reflected from the ceiling or other object outside the fixture.

individually metered – Utility company provides separate service to each individual unit within a building.

Indoor AirPlus label – A specification developed by EPA to address the indoor environment component of green building. Homes that achieve this level of excellence are first qualified as ENERGY STAR, and then also incorporate more than 60 additional home design and construction features to control moisture, chemical exposure, radon, pests, ventilation, and filtration.

indoor air pollution – The amount of contaminants in the air inside a building. Indoor air pollution can often be worse than outside air pollution due to poor ventilation.

indoor air quality – The temperature, humidity, ventilation and chemical or biological contaminants of the air inside a building.

induction – The production of an electric current in a conductor by the variation of a magnetic field in its vicinity.

industrial property – A property where products are manufactured or assembled.

infill development – The development of vacant parcels in existing urban and suburban areas.

infiltration – (1) The introduction of outside air into a building – called air leakage. (2) The entry of groundwater runoff into the soil.

inflation – The sustained increase in the general price level of goods and services.

inflation guard coverage – Automatically adjusts the limits of insurance to keep up with inflation.

infrared camera – An infrared camera (video or still) makes an image that shows surface heat variations that can be used to help detect heat losses and air leakage in buildings.

infrastructure – Services and facilities provided by a municipality or privately provided, including roads, highways, water, sewage, emergency services, parks and recreation, and so on.

ingress – The right to enter onto a property using an easement.

inheritance tax – A tax imposed on heirs who inherit property.

injunction – A court order forcing a person to do or not do an act.

innocent landowner defense – A legal defense used by an owner of property to avoid liability for environmental contamination. The defense may only be used if the property was acquired after the hazardous substance existed, and the owner did not know the contamination existed at the time he acquired the property. The owner must have taken certain measures to determine the environmental condition of the property prior to acquiring it.

innocent misrepresentation – When a person unknowingly provides wrong information.

inorganic growth – Business expansion achieved by mergers and acquisitions.

in perpetuity – Of endless duration; forever.

inspect – To examine readily accessible systems and components of a building in accordance with standards of practice, using normal operating controls and opening readily operable access panels.

inspection – A visit to, and review of, a particular site or building.

inspector – A person hired to examine any system or component of a building in accordance with specified standards of practice.

installed – Attached in such a way that it requires removal with tools.

installment – The regular, periodic payments a borrower agrees to pay a lender, in order to repay the loan.

installment note – A note which provides for a series of periodic payments of principal and interest, until amount borrowed is paid in full. This periodic reduction of principal amortizes the loan.

installment sale – An installment sale occurs when payments are made by the buyer to the seller, over a period of more than one year, because the seller takes a note for some or all of the purchase price of the property. If the seller provides any type of financing, it is considered an installment sale. The seller may save taxes, by receiving smaller amounts over a period of years.

institutional advertising – Advertising is designed to create an image, enhance the reputation, and promote the company rather than a specific product.

institutional lender – A financial institution such as a bank, insurance company, savings and loan association, or other lending institution. These institutions receive money from depositors and customers, and then reinvest those deposits in mortgages. The government closely regulates institutional lenders, in order to limit risk to investors.

instrument – A formal legal document, such as a contract, deed, or will, setting forth the rights and liabilities of the parties involved.

insulation – Materials, such as fiberglass, rock wool, and urethane foam, used to slow heat loss and protect wires and other electricity carriers, and placed in the walls, ceilings, or floors of a structure. Insulation comes in different forms: blanket, batt, rigid, fill, or reflective; and may be made of glass wool, cotton, or wood fibers.

insurable value – The highest reasonable value that can be placed on property for insurance purposes.

insurance – Policies that guarantee compensation to the policyholder, in the event of loss from certain causes.

intangible property – Intangible property is non-physical property, such as copyrights and the goodwill of a business.

intangible value – That value attributable to a property that is difficult to determine precisely.

integrated design – A holistic building approach that examines the interaction between design, construction, and operations, to optimize the energy and environmental performance of the project.

integrated pest management (IPM) – An environmentally sound system of controlling landscape pests.

intellectual property – Various legal rights, which attach to certain types of information, ideas, or other intangibles.

intelligent building – Type of building that incorporates healthier and more resource-efficient models of construction, renovation, operation, maintenance, and demolition.

intended use – The use or uses of an appraiser's reported appraisal, appraisal review, or appraisal consulting assignment opinions and conclusions, as identified by the appraiser based on communication with the client at the time of the assignment.

intended users – Per USPAP, parties intending to use an appraisal.

interest – (1) The charge for the use of money. (2) Various rights, privileges, powers, and immunities with respect to real property.

interest factor (IF) – A theoretical rate of interest used to calculate the theoretical present or future worth of a sum of money or an annuity.

interest only loan – A straight, non-amortizing loan in which the lender receives only interest during the term of the loan, and principal is repaid in a lump sum at maturity.

interest rate – A percentage of a sum of money, charged for the use of that money, on a yearly or monthly basis.

interim financing – (1) A short-term loan usually made to finance the cost of construction. The loan money is disbursed in increments as construction progresses. (2) A short-term, temporary loan used until permanent financing is available, e.g., a construction loan.

interim use – A short-term and temporary use of a property until it is ready for a more productive highest and best use.

interior lot – A lot surrounded by other lots, with a frontage on the street. It is the most common type lot and may be desirable or not, depending on other factors.

intermediaries – Financial institutions such as banks, savings institutions, and life insurance companies.

intermediate theory – Some states follow the intermediate theory that a mortgage is a lien, unless the borrower defaults. The title then automatically transfers to the lender. In any case, the borrower enjoys possession of the property during the full term of the mortgage, no matter who holds title.

intermediation – The process of transferring capital from those who invest funds to those who wish to borrow.

internal rate of return – The rate of return generated by an investment over the holding period, considering all future benefits, and discounting them to equal the present value.

international style – This asymmetrical housing style is modern and practical in its use of concrete, glass, and steel to create sleek lines. It has a flat roof and floor to ceiling window walls.

interpleader action – A court proceeding initiated by the stakeholder of property, who claims no proprietary interest in it, for the purpose of deciding who among claimants is legally entitled to the property.

inter vivos trust – Trust in which the trustor (settlor) is still alive when the trust is established.

intestate – Term describing a person who dies without leaving a valid will.

intestate succession – When a person inherits property, as the result of someone dying without a will.

intrinsic value – The value inherent in the property itself. The value given to a geographical area or property, based on its features and amenities and an individual's personal preferences or choices.

inverse condemnation – An action brought by a private party to force the government to pay just compensation for diminishing the value or use of his or her property.

investment conduit – A means of investing. Examples include real estate trusts such as REITs, REMTs, and combination trusts.

investment property – Property, or an interest in property, purchased for the purpose of earning a profit.

investment value – The value of a particular property to a particular investor.

involuntary alienation – Transfer of property against the wishes of the owner.

involuntary lien – A lien created by operation of law.

involuntary trust – A trust created when a person obtains title to property and/or takes possession of it and holds it for another, even though there is no formal trust document or agreement. The court may determine that the holder of the title holds it as a constructive trustee for the benefit of the intended owner. This may occur through fraud, breach of faith, ignorance, or inadvertence. Also called constructive trust.

Inwood Tables – A set of interest tables widely used by appraisers, before the popularity of calculators and computers, in computing the present value of an annuity for a number of years at various interest rates.

irrigation – The artificial application of water to soil to promote plant growth.

irrigation districts – Quasi-political districts created under special laws to provide for water services to property owners in the district.

issue – Descendants of the testator.

J

jalousie window – These windows do not slide and are not hinged. Instead, they have narrow glass slats, like Venetian blinds, that are opened and closed with a crank.

jamb – The side post or lining of a doorway, window, or other opening.

joint and several liability – A legal term used in reference to a debt or a judgment for negligence, in which each debtor or each judgment defendant is responsible for the entire amount of the debt or judgment.

joint appraisal – An appraisal performed by more than one appraiser, but stating one common conclusion.

joint tenancy – Form of concurrent ownership providing for undivided ownership interests and automatic survivorship to remaining cotenants upon death of one of the joint tenants.

joint venture – A form of business organization composed of two or more persons to conduct a single enterprise for profit.

joist – A horizontal, parallel beam directly supporting the boards of a floor or the laths of a ceiling.

joule – Basic unit of thermal energy. One joule is equal to the energy transformed by the power of one watt operating for one second.

judgment – The final legal decision by a judge in a court of law, regarding the legal rights of parties to an action or proceeding.

judgment creditor – Party to a lawsuit who obtains a money judgment against the other party.

judgment lien – A statutory lien created by recording a judgment, or an abstract, ordering the payment of a sum of money.

judicial foreclosure – Foreclosure by court action.

jumbo loans – Loans above the maximum loan limit set by Fannie Mae and Freddie Mac.

junior lien – A lien of inferior priority.

junior loan – A loan that has a subordinate or inferior priority to another loan.

jurat – The portion of a certificate or affidavit stating when, where, and before whom it was sworn.

jurisdiction – The power to adjudicate concerning the subject matter in a given case.

JURISDICTIONAL EXCEPTION RULE – The JURISDICTIONAL EXCEPTION RULE preserves the remainder of USPAP, if one portion is contrary to a jurisdiction's law or public policy.

just compensation – Fair and reasonable payment due to a private property owner, when his or her property is condemned under eminent domain.

K

key lot – A lot resembling a key fitting into a lock and surrounded by the back yards of other lots. It is the least desirable, because of the lack of privacy.

kerosene – A light petroleum distillate that is used in space heaters, cook stoves, and water heaters and is suitable for use as a light source when burned in wick-fed lamps.

key performance indicators – Metrics used to measure the worth of the effort by a business or individual in reaching goals.

kickback – An illegal payment made in return for a referral that resulted in a transaction.

kicker – An additional feature, such as a bonus, which makes a loan more attractive to an investor or lender.

kick-out clause – *See* early termination clause.

kilowatt (kW) – A unit of power equal to 1,000 watts. It is usually used as a measure of electrical power.

kilowatt hour (kWh) – A measure of energy equal to the amount of power multiplied by the amount of time the power is used. It is most often used to describe amounts of electrical energy. A 100-watt light bulb burning for 10 hours uses one kilowatt-hour of power.

kinetic energy – Energy possessed by virtue of an object's motion. Kinetic energy varies directly in proportion to an object's mass and the square of its velocity.

kiosk – A small structure, usually constructed with one or more sides open, often used as a newsstand or other small vending operation.

kit house – A house-in-a-box, complete with blue prints and all the materials needed to build a home.

L

labor-extensive industries – Industries with a low level of employees per acre. Labor-extensive industries generally need plant facilities with an area of at least 100,000 square feet.

labor-intensive industries – Industries with a high level of employees per acre and may need up to 25,000 square feet of floor space.

laches – A legal doctrine stating that those who take too long to assert a legal right lose their entitlement to compensation.

lagoon – (1) a body of comparatively shallow salt or brackish water separated from the deeper sea by a shallow or exposed sandbank, coral reef, or similar feature. (2) In wastewater treatment or livestock facilities, a shallow pond used to store wastewater where sunlight and biological activity decompose the waste.

laissez-faire – A French term meaning, let do. A laissez-faire market system is a free market system.

lamp – The lighting industry uses the term lamp to refer to the source of light, the light bulb itself, not the fixture where the light bulb is located.

land – A three-dimensional area consisting of a parcel of the earth's surface, limited quantities of airspace above the surface, the materials and minerals beneath the surface to the center of the earth (subsurface).

LAND – The mnemonic for the four elements of a valid lease: Length of time, Amount of rent, Names of parties, and Description of the property.

land bank – Land purchased and held for future development. Scenic property is sometimes land banked to prevent its development, in an effort to contain urban or suburban sprawl.

land capitalization rate – The rate of return in investment and return of investment for the land only.

land contract – A contract for the sale of real property, where the seller gives up possession, but retains the title until the purchase price is paid in full; also known as a contract of sale or agreement of sale.

land description – A description of a piece of real property. The description may be informal, such as a street address or a legal description using a metes and bounds survey, recorded lot, block and tract system, or a Public Lands Survey method to describe its location.

landfill gas – A methane gas byproduct of landfills.

landlocked – Property surrounded by other property, with no access to a public road, street, or alley.

landlord – Property owner. Under a lease, the property owner is termed a lessor.

land residual method – A method of determining the value of land in which the net income remaining to the land, after income attributable to the building has been deducted, is capitalized into an estimate of value for the land.

landscaping – The art of arranging rocks, lumber, and plants around the outside of a property for an aesthetic purpose, such as an appealing look, or for practical purposes, such as to prevent erosion or provide parking areas. Landscape may include softscape and hardscape.

land trust – A trust created by the owner of real property, in which the property is the only asset.

land-use intensity – Local zoning codes regulating the density of land development, including living space and recreation space requirements. Important considerations in the construction of planned unit developments.

large-lot zoning – Zoning used to reduce residential density, by requiring large building lots. Also called acreage zoning or snob zoning.

late charge – An added fee a borrower is charged for failure to pay a regular loan installment when due.

latent defect – Defects in a home that may be hidden from a buyer, but known by a seller, and must be disclosed.

lateral support – Landowners' right to have their land in its natural condition held in place from the sides by adjoining land so that it will not fall away.

law – Body of rules and principles that every member of society must follow.

lawful object – A requirement of a valid contract. The purpose, object, or action of a contract must be legal in order to make it valid.

leaching field – An array of trenches containing aggregate and distribution pipes, through which septic-tank effluent seeps into the surrounding soil. Also known as an absorption field.

lead (Pb) – A heavy metal that is hazardous to health if breathed or swallowed. Its use in gasoline, paints, and plumbing compounds has been sharply restricted or eliminated by federal laws and regulations.

lead flashing – When working with tile roofs, lead flashing is used. In the case of plumbing vent flashing, the lead flashing is molded to the shape of the tile's surface. Then the next tile covers the top of the lead flashing, in order to prevent water from seeping under the flashing.

lead poisoning – An illness caused by high concentrations of lead in the blood. Lead poisoning can cause major health problems, especially learning disabilities in children. Lead is commonly found in lead-based paint and water contaminated by lead pipes. By law, purchasers of houses built prior to 1978 must receive a lead disclosure detailing the dangers of lead.

lease – An agreement, written or unwritten, transferring the right to exclusive possession and use of real estate for a definite period of time.

lease abstract – Summary of the terms of an existing commercial lease.

lease concessions – Incentives offered to a tenant, by a landlord, in order to attract the tenant to sign a lease. Enticements include such things as free rent for the first month (or longer, in the case of commercial property) or improvements made to the property at the landlord's expense.

leased fee estate – The interest of the lessor in property.

lease estoppel certificate – Signed statement by the tenant verifying that the lease information contained in the estoppel certificate is true and correct.

leasehold estate – The lessee's interest in the leased property during the term of the lease. The duration of leasehold is known as a tenancy.

leasehold value – Market value of the excess of economic rent over contract rent.

lease option – A clause in a lease agreement giving the tenant the option to purchase the property, under certain conditions. Lease options may give a tenant the right to renew or extend the lease, under certain conditions, as stated in the original lease agreement.

lease-up time – Time from the date maintenance gives the keys back to management for rental to the effective date of the new lease.

leasing agent – An agent who secures qualified tenants for leases on residential, commercial, or industrial property.

leasing plan – Should be developed in concern with the marketing plan. Its goal is to organize the leasing process and reduce vacancy rates.

LEED – Leaders in Energy and Environmental Design (LEED) is a building environmental certification program developed and operated by the U.S. Green Building Council.

legacy – A gift of personal property by will.

legal description – A formal description of real property recognized by law, by which property can be definitely located by reference to metes and bounds, the Public Lands Survey method, or recorded maps.

legally permissible – One of the requirements in highest and best use analysis. Land uses that are allowed under current zoning and other land use regulations.

legal notice – The legally required notification of others, as a result of property possession or document recordation. Legal notice may be a registered letter, advertisement in a designated newspaper, telegram, or other such method. Also known as constructive notice.

legal title – Title that is complete and perfect regarding right of ownership.

legatee – A person to whom personal property is given by will.

leichtlehm – Straw and clay mixture, moistened and pressed between forms, which hardens into a strong material. Typically used for making walls. An old and durable technique. (German for light loam).

lender – A company or person that makes mortgage loans, such as a mortgage banker, credit union, bank, or savings and loan.

lender pressure – A lender directly or indirectly pressuring an appraiser to estimate a property's value at a certain amount.

lessee – The person acquiring an estate for years in a lease.

lessor – The person transferring an estate for years in a lease.

less-than-freehold estate – *See* non-freehold estate.

lethe – A measure of air purity that is equal to one complete air change in an interior space.

letter of intent (LOI) – Preliminary offer that proposes basic terms and conditions for the lease.

leverage – The utilization of borrowed funds to increase purchasing power, or using a smaller, borrowed investment to generate a larger rate of return.

levy – Seizure of property by judicial process.

liability – A financial obligation; a debt. Also a responsibility.

liability indemnity clause – A clause in a lease that holds a landlord harmless from the actions of his or her tenants.

liability insurance – Insurance that provides protection from the negligent acts and omissions of an individual, business, or organization that causes bodily injury and/or property damage to a third party.

LIBOR – The London Interbank Offered Rate (LIBOR) is the rate banks charge to borrow funds from other banks in the short-term international interbank market. The loans are made in dollar-denominated Eurodollars, and a small number of large London banks establish the LIBOR rate daily.

license – Permissive use of land, which may be revoked at any time by the grantor.

Licensed Real Property Appraiser – An individual who has met specific education, experience, and examination requirements. He or she may appraise any non-complex 1-4 unit residential property, with a transaction value less than $1 million and any complex 1-4 unit residential property with a transaction value less than $250,000.

licensee – A person who holds a valid real estate or appraisal license.

license laws – The laws that authorize states to license and regulate real estate licensees, appraisers, and home inspectors.

lien – A legal right, interest, or claim in the property of another for the payment of a debt.

lien theory – One of the theories of mortgage security. Under lien theory, the lender creates a lien on a borrower's real property, but the borrower retains the legal rights, as opposed to the lender gaining title to the property under a title theory. In the event of a loan default, the lender has no right of possession, but must foreclose the lien and sell the property.

lien waiver – A legal document many property owners require contractors to sign, in order to protect their property. In signing the document, the supplier or contractor relinquishes their right to place a lien on the owner's property. The waiver is signed upon receipt of payment for the goods and services provided by the contractor.

life cycle assessment (LCA) – LCA is a method used to determine the impact a product or building has on the environment and available resources during its entire life cycle.

life-cycle cost (LCC) – The total cost of a product over the full life of the product.

life cycle of a product –All stages of a product's development from extraction of fuel for power to production, marketing, use, and disposal.

life estate – An estate, limited in duration to the life of its owner or the life of a designated person.

life tenant – A person whose interest in real property lasts as long as they (or some other person) lives.

lifestyle center – Open-air shopping center often located near affluent residential neighborhoods.

lifting clause – A provision included in a junior mortgage document allowing the underlying senior mortgage to be replaced or refinanced, as long as the amount of the new senior loan does not exceed the amount of the first lien outstanding at the time the junior loan was made.

light – Visually perceived radiant energy (a small part of the electromagnetic spectrum).

light and air easement – Negative easement created by grant preventing servient landowner from building a structure or planting trees that would prevent sunlight or air from reaching the dominant estate.

light construction – Construction of a building using materials which have low densities (like wood or aerated concrete). The lower densities of these materials reduce their capacity to store heat.

light industrial businesses – Light manufacturing, assembly, or storage facilities.

lighting fixture – The physical item referred to as a lamp (table lamp or floor lamp) is called the fixture by the lighting industry.

light pipe – A device that gathers incoming sunlight sometimes using a solar tracking system. The light is concentrated using lenses or mirrors and is then transmitted to the interior of a building by special tubes. A special luminaire is required to provide distribution of the light within the building.

light shelf – A horizontal reflective surface, at or above eye level, used both to passively channel natural daylighting into an occupied space and provide shading.

lignite – The softest type of coal, is brownish in color, and has a 30-40% carbon content.

like-kind property – In a real estate exchange, properties that are similar in nature or character, even if they differ in grade or quality. Per IRS rules, real properties are of like-kind, regardless of whether they are improved or unimproved. Therefore, a bare lot may be exchanged fairly for an apartment house.

limited appraisal – An appraisal developed under and resulting from invoking USPAP's SCOPE OR WORK RULE.

limited liability company (LLC) – A business that has characteristics of both corporations and limited partnerships. The LLC offers its owners the benefits of limited liability and pass through taxation, much like an S corporation.

limited partnership – A partnership comprising a general partner and limited partners. The general partner operates the partnership and is fully liable for the debts of the firm. The limited partners are liable only to the extent of their investments.

limited power of attorney – A power of attorney that is limited to a specific situation or job.

limiting conditions – In an appraisal report, conditions that restrict the assumptions contained in the report to certain situations. For example, the date and use of the appraisal.

linear – Linear configuration is three or more contiguous stores in a line. It is the most common configuration for shopping centers.

linear foot – A measurement meaning one foot or twelve inches in length as opposed to a square foot or a cubic foot.

linear regression – Statistical technique used to calculate adjustment value or estimate sales price.

line-of-sight easement – An easement prohibiting the use or modification of land within the easement area in any way that interferes with the view.

line-trees – Trees or hedges whose trunks grow on the boundary line.

lingua franca – Any language widely used beyond the population of its native speakers so people of different backgrounds can communicate clearly.

linoleum – A durable, natural flooring material (may be used for other purposes, such as countertops) made primarily of cork.

lintel – A horizontal board that supports the load over an opening, such as a door or window.

liquefied natural gas (LNG) – A natural gas that has been cooled to about -260°F for shipment and/or storage as a liquid.

liquid assets – Assets that can be promptly converted into cash.

liquidated damages – An amount specified in advance of entering into an agreement, that must be paid as a penalty in the event of a breach of the contract.

liquidation value – The value that can be received from the marketplace when the property has to be sold immediately.

liquidity – The amount of cash an individual, business, or financial institution has on hand or that is readily available. The ability of an asset to be converted into cash quickly, without discounting the price.

lis pendens – A recorded notice that indicates pending litigation on a property, preventing a conveyance or any other transfer of ownership, until the lawsuit is settled and the lis pendens removed.

listing agent – A broker who obtains a listing from a seller to act as an agent for compensation.

listing agreement – A written contract by which a principal, or seller, employs a broker to sell real estate.

listing presentation – A thorough, professional presentation given by a real estate licensee to persuade the prospective seller that he or she is the specialist who will sell the home.

listing price – The amount of money a seller agrees to accept from a buyer, as stated in the listing agreement. The listing price may be negotiable during the listing period.

litigation – Process of bringing a lawsuit against someone.

littoral – Land bordering a lake, ocean, or sea.

load – The power required to run a defined circuit or system, such as a refrigerator, building, or an entire electricity distribution system.

loan assumption – A buyer assumes the existing loan when a property is sold. The buyer takes over primary liability for the loan, with the original borrower secondarily liable, if there is a default.

loan constant – The annual mortgage payments divided by the mortgage balance. Used to calculate the annual payment needed to pay off a loan.

loan portfolio – The loans that a financial institution, or another lender, holds at any given time.

loan processing – The steps taken by a lender from the time the application is received to the time the loan is approved.

loan-to-value ratio (LTV) – The ratio of the amount of the mortgage loan to the appraised value of the real property, generally expressed as a percentage.

loan transfer – The transfer to, or assumption of, existing financing by the new owner when a property is sold.

local area network (LAN) – A system that allows the various computers in the office to share data and communicate with each other.

location – A particular area on earth defined by a legal description.

locational obsolescence – Depreciation caused by the physical location of the subject property and its proximity to a negative influence. *See* external obsolescence.

lockbox – A special locking box the broker places on the door of a listed property. Lockboxes are used to secure the property, control entry, and facilitate showings to prospective buyers.

lock-in clause – A clause in a loan agreement that prohibits repayment of the loan prior to a specified date.

loft building – A building with large un-partitioned floor areas often used for storage. They are also popular as contemporary residential units.

loft conversion – Industrial, warehouse, or commercial space that has been converted to an apartment.

logo – A mark or symbol used as an identifier for an individual, company, or organization.

long-lived – Structural components that need replacement infrequently, and sometimes never.

loss control – The policies and procedures put in place to reduce the possibility of things going wrong.

loss payee – Party named to receive benefits when a claim on an insurance policy is filed.

lot and block system – A system to legally describe land by identifying the registered lot and then block on a recorded subdivision plat or survey. Also known as subdivision system or recorded map system.

lot split – Sale of a portion of a parcel of land.

louvers – A series of horizontal slats set at an angle to let in light and air, allow ventilation of fumes, and keep out rain.

low-e window glazing – A special window coating that helps prevent the warmth inside a building from escaping through the glass in the winter (pyrolitic). A variation (solar control) is designed to block heat from the summer sun. Low-E coating can reduce energy use by up to 35%.

low- or no-VOC paint – Paints that release no, or minimal VOC pollutants, is virtually odor free, and is safer for people with chemical sensitivities.

low rise – A building with fewer than seven stories above ground level.

L-shaped – L-shaped center has two linear strips of stores connected at right angles, forming the letter L. Usually, the anchor tenants are located on the two ends. Parking is in the area formed by the L-shape. This shape is commonly used for community-sized centers.

lumen (lm) – The luminous flux emitted (within a unit solid angle or one steradian) by a point source having a uniform luminous intensity of one candela.

lumen method – A method of estimating the interior luminance from window daylighting at three locations within a room, based on empirical studies. Also called daylighting.

luminaire – A complete electric lighting unit, including housing, lamp, and focusing and/or diffusing elements; informally referred to as fixture.

luminous ceiling – A type of ceiling emitting light from its entire surface, through the use of fluorescent light above translucent glass or plastic.

lump-sum contract – A construction contract in which the contractor agrees to perform a specific amount of work for a fixed price. The inflexible nature of the contract can create problems, as well as advantages for the contractors and the employers.

lux – The unit of illuminance equivalent to one lumen per square meter.

M

maintenance – The general costs of operation and upkeep of a property, including employee wages, repairs, supplies, and services.

maintenance expenses – Costs incurred for day-to-day-upkeep, such as management, employee wages and benefits, fuel, utility services, decorating, and repairs.

maintenance fee – An amount charged to property owners to maintain their property in an operational and productive state. This fee is charged especially to condominium owners.

maintenance supervisor – Person responsible for the maintenance of the buildings he or she manages.

maker – The borrower who executes a promissory note and becomes primarily liable for payment to the lender.

mall – Large, enclosed, climate-controlled shopping center with adjacent parking and out buildings.

mall manager – Person employed by the owner or a management company to supervise daily operations of the shopping center.

Management – Per USPAP, the Management section of the ETHICS RULE discusses "the disclosure of certain fees and commissions, identifies prohibited compensation arrangements, and discusses certain prohibited advertising and solicitation issues."

management contract – A contract that states the terms of the agreement between the owner and the property manager.

management plan – A plan for future management based on financial reports and projections, and accepted by ownership.

management pricing worksheet – Method of pricing the fee the management company charges by itemizing the activities to be performed, determining the direct cost related to each activity, and adding overhead, anticipated marketing, and a profit margin.

manager – An executive who oversees a firm's real estate resources and sets goals and strategies to protect the interests of owners. Also called an asset manager.

manometer – An instrument that measures the pressure differences between two locations.

mansard roof – A four-sided roof that slopes upward from the edge of the roof to a square peak. The roof has two different slopes around all sides of the structure, the upper of which may be nearly horizontal and the lower nearly vertical. This type of roof is featured in Second Empire and other French-inspired housing styles.

mansionization – Oversized extravagant homes built in an existing tract of modest homes.

mantel – The decorative facing around a fireplace. Mantels are usually constructed of wood or stone and topped with a shelf.

manufactured home – A home built in a factory after June 15, 1976 and must conform to the U.S. Government's Manufactured Home Construction and Safety Standards.

margin – In an adjustable-rate loan, the amount added to the index rate that represents the lender's cost of doing business (includes costs, profits, and risk of loss of the loan). Generally, the margin stays constant during the life of the loan.

marginal land – Land whose value has been diminished due to some internal defect or external condition. In most cases, the cost to correct the flaw or condition is as much or more than the expected return from the property.

margin of security – The difference between the amount of the mortgage loan(s) and the appraised value of the property.

MARIA – The mnemonic for the five tests of a fixture: Method of attachment, Adaptation, Relationship of the parties, Intention, and Agreement of the parties.

marina – Facility that offers service to the public or members for docking, storage, watercraft, and as a permanent residence.

marital property – A general term for property owned by married people. Married people may have a special status as property owners; forms of ownership vary from state-to-state.

market – A place or condition suitable for selling and buying.

market analysis – (1) A study of the economic factors existing in and affecting the local marketplace that relates to the subject property. (2) To identify, research, and analyze the particular market in which the appraised property operates.

market characteristics – Property types, sizes, styles, ages, and quality.

market comparison approach – An appraisal method using the principles of substitution to compare similar properties, which have recently sold, to the subject property. Also called market data approach and sales comparison approach.

market conditions – Features of the marketplace, including, but not limited to, interest rates, employment levels, vacancy rates, demographics, and absorption levels.

market exposure – Making a reasonable number of potential buyers of a property aware that the property is available.

market extraction – Method of estimating depreciation, in which building values abstracted from sales are compared to current costs new.

market indicators – Statistical measures of the construction and real estate industry, using industry activity such as number of permits issued, indices of building costs, deeds recorded, and homes for sale. Analysts use the indicators to forecast the market's direction.

market price – The price paid regardless of pressures, motives, or intelligence.

market rent – The rent a property should bring in the open market as determined by current rents on comparable properties.

market segmentation – The process of identifying and analyzing submarkets within larger markets.

market survey – A report generated by a property manager using computer software that compares the subject property in various categories of performance to competing properties in the area.

market trade area – The geographic area from which a retail center draws its customers.

market trend analysis – An analysis of data that exhibits an ongoing upward or downward pattern that is not due to seasonal changes.

market value – The price a property would bring, if freely offered on the open market, with both a willing buyer and a willing seller. Also called objective value.

marketable title – Good or clear saleable title, reasonably free from risk of litigation over possible defects.

marketing – The process involved in promoting a service or product.

marketing budget – An allocation of resources for the marketing strategies and tactics.

marketing pieces – Items used to market a business, such as business cards, stationery and envelopes, flyers, door hangers and brochures, promotional or giveaway items, newsletters, and presentation binders. Also known as marketing collateral.

marketing plan – A detailed written document of actions necessary to achieve the goals described in the marketing strategy.

masonry – Construction made from brick, cement block, or stone, which provides structural support as well as a decorative finish.

mass appraisal – Appraising more than one property, using standard computerized techniques (statistical analysis, regression, automated valuation models, etc.). Neighborhoods, subdivisions, and large groupings of similar properties are appraised at one time.

mass transit – Conveyance of persons or goods from one place to another on a local public transportation system such as light rail, bus, or subway.

master metered – Refers to a utility company that provides service to one customer, who redistributes the utilities to the occupants within the building.

master plan – A city or county's overall plan for physical development. *See* zoning.

material fact – Any fact likely to affect the judgment of the principal, when giving consent to the agent to enter into a particular transaction on the specified terms.

matrix – *See* adjustment grid.

maturity – The date on which an agreement expires; the termination of a promissory note when the full amount is due.

maximally productive – The property use that produces the greatest return on investment. One of the tests of highest and best use.

maximum allowable rent – The maximum legal rent a landlord may charge for a controlled rental unit.

mean – A measure of central tendency which is calculated by adding the average prices or numeric values of a statistical sample and dividing that by the number of values in the sample. Also known as the average.

meander – To follow a winding course.

mean high tide line – The average height of certain high waters.

measurement tables – A table of unit conversions from U.S. measurements to their metric equivalents.

mechanical energy – The energy stored in objects by tension.

mechanical ventilation – The active process of supplying or removing air to or from an indoor space by powered equipment such as motor-driven fans and blowers, but not by devices such as wind-driven turbine ventilators and mechanically operated windows.

mechanic's lien – A statutory lien in favor of persons contributing labor, material, supplies, etc. to a work of improvement upon real property.

median – A measure of central tendency that equals the middle value in a statistical sample. The middle value in a statistical sample.

median income – This is the middle income in a series of incomes ranked from lowest to highest.

mediation – Process in which a neutral, uninterested third party helps the parties involved in a dispute to negotiate a settlement or other resolution.

Mediterranean style – Home style consisting of a blend of Italian, Moorish, Byzantine, and California mission styles. It is characterized by white or light-colored stucco on the exterior and a red tiled gable roof with very little or no overhanging eaves.

meeting of the minds – Agreement between the parties in a contract situation. There can be no contract unless there is a meeting of the minds. A meeting of the minds may be enforceable if the actions and words of the parties indicate agreement.

mega center – An oversized shopping center that may attract shoppers from hundreds of miles around. Also called a super mall.

megalopolis – A large, densely-populated metropolitan area made up of several major urban areas.

menace – (1) Using the threat of violence to get agreement in accepting a contract. (2) The illegal practice of using the threat of violence in order to get agreement in accepting a contract.

mentor – A person who provides quality support, advice, and counseling.

mercury vapor lamp – The oldest type of high-intensity discharge lighting, used primarily for street lighting.

merger – A transaction between two companies joining, which results in a wholly new firm.

merger of title – The absorption of a lesser estate into a larger estate.

meridian – In the Public Land Survey System, imaginary north-south lines intersecting base lines to form a starting point for measurement of land.

metes and bounds – A metes and bounds land description measures the dimensions of a property using direction and distance between landmarks and monuments. The metes and bounds description is the oldest method used to describe real property. Metes mean measurements in length (measured in feet) from one monument to another. Bounds refer to the direction. The direction of the boundary lines are given in degrees, minutes, and seconds.

methane (CH4) – An odorless, colorless gas, nearly insoluble in water, which burns with a pale, faintly luminous flame to produce water and carbon dioxide (or carbon monoxide if oxygen is deficient).

metrics – A prescribed set of measurements that quantify results.

mezzanine – A small floor between two regular floors of a building.

MGIC – *See* Mortgage Guaranty Insurance Corporation.

microclimate – The small scale climate of a building site, affected by site geography, site topography, vegetation, and proximity to bodies of water, etc., which may very slightly from the prevalent regional climatic conditions.

micro wind turbine – A very small wind turbine designed to provide electric power to a home or other local site for a variety of applications.

mid-rise – A building with between 7 and 25 stories above ground level.

mildew – A common name for mold or fungi, which is often used in reference to fungal growth on bathroom tiles and fixtures.

mile – A linear measurement of distance. Equals 1,760 yards or 5,280 feet.

mill – One-tenth of one cent. In property tax assessment, the tax rate is expressed as a number of mills. Equals one-thousandth of a dollar and is numerically expressed as $0.001.

millage rate – Expresses the property tax rate in terms of tenths of a cent per dollar of property value. The rate varies from district to district and county to county.

Millennium Generation – The children of Generation X, born between 1982 and 2000. Also known as Generation Y.

MIMO form – The move-in/move-out form; detailing inventory and initial condition of a rental space upon move-in, and inventory and condition upon move-out. The MIMO form helps to determine whether or not, and how much of, the rental deposit will be returned.

mineral rights – The legal interest in the valuable items found below the surface of a property (i.e., gold and coal).

minerals – Land elements found beneath the ground, such as gold and coal, and owned as real property. Once these elements are taken from the ground, they become personal property.

minimum lot size – The smallest dimensions allowed for a building lot, specified by zoning ordinance.

minimum rent – The fixed minimum rent amount paid under a percentage lease. Also known as base rent.

mini-storage facility – A commercial property that allows individuals to lease empty space for storing personal items or excess inventory. Also known as a self-storage facility.

minor – A person under 18 years of age and thus, not of legal capacity to enter into any legal contract.

MIP – *See* mortgage insurance premium.

mirror offer – An offer that matches all terms in the listing.

misplaced improvement – An improvement on a piece of real estate, whose highest and best use does not match that of the property.

misrepresentation – Making a false statement or concealing a material fact, causing someone loss or harm.

mission statement – The purpose or reason for the company's existence.

mission style – This housing style has round parapets on the roof that resemble those found on Spanish colonial churches. They are one to two stories, rectangular-shaped, with flat roofs with red tile accents.

mistake – (1) An error or misunderstanding. (2) The parties to an agreement have a misunderstanding about a fact that is material to the transaction.

mixed-use center – Complex that in addition to retail stores, integrates offices, restaurants, movie theaters, hotels, and residences.

mixed-use property – A property that may have more than one use. For example, a retail store with an apartment upstairs.

MLS – *See* multiple listing service.

mnemonics – Memory aids, using the first letters of words significant to the definition of a term in a form that can be easily remembered. For example, DUST is the mnemonic for the four elements of value: Demand, Utility, Scarcity, and Transferability.

mobilehome – A factory-built home manufactured prior to June 15, 1976, constructed on a chassis and wheels, and designed for permanent or semi-attachment to land.

mobilehome loan – A mortgage loan made on a mobile home; usually created for a shorter period than a conventional real estate mortgage.

mobilehome park – Any area or tract of land where two or more mobilehome lots are rented or leased or held out for rent or leased to accommodate manufactured homes or mobile homes used for human habitation.

mode – (1) A measure of central tendency that equals the most frequently occurring price or value in a statistical sample. (2) The most frequent value in a set of numbers. If the set is very small, and there are no duplicate numbers, then there is no mode.

modified age/life method – A method of calculating depreciation. Curable physical and functional items of accrued depreciation are identified. The cost-to-cure all these items is deducted from the reproduction or replacement cost of the improvements. The ratio derived from the age/life method is then multiplied by the remaining cost to arrive at an estimate of accrued depreciation from all other causes.

modular home – Building composed of modules constructed on an assembly line in a factory. *See* manufactured home.

modular housing – A system for the construction of dwellings and other improvements to real property through the on-site assembly of component parts (modules) that have been mass-produced away from the building site.

mold – A fungus produced especially on damp or decaying organic matter.

molding – Long, narrow strips of wood or synthetic material, used as a finish piece to cover the crack between the meeting of a wall with a floor or ceiling. Used for decoration only.

monetary default – Defaulting on, or breaching the terms of, a loan by not making the agreed-upon payments.

monetary policy – Monetary policy is carried out by the Federal Reserve System's actions to influence the availability and cost of money and credit, as a means of helping to promote national economic goals. Monetary policy is made by the Federal Open Market Committee, which consists of the Board of Governors of the Federal Reserve System and the Reserve Bank presidents.

money encumbrance – An encumbrance that affects the title. Also called financial encumbrance.

money market certificate – A type of certificate of deposit or savings account offered by financial institutions, in which a minimum balance is deposited and left until a specified date. The amount of interest earned on the deposit is specific to the type of account, amount deposited, and length of time the funds must remain on deposit.

money market fund – A type of mutual fund which is uninsured and unregulated.

monolithic slab – A slab foundation poured in one piece.

monopoly – Person or group with exclusive control over a product or service within a given region.

Monterey style – The most distinguishing feature of the Monterey style house is the second-story balcony on the front of the house. These houses often have a courtyard, wrought iron trim, and fencing.

month-to-month tenancy – A periodic tenancy in which no lease agreement exists, or where one has expired, and the tenant pays rent for one period at a time. The tenancy continues until either the lessor or lessee gives notice of termination. To terminate a month-to-month tenancy, advance notice equal to one rental period is generally required.

monument – A fixed landmark used in a metes and bounds land description.

moratorium – (1) A temporary prohibition against building in certain areas to control the rate of development. (2) A temporary suspension by statute of the enforceability of a debt.

mortgage – A two party security instrument pledging land as security for the performance of an obligation.

mortgage backed security (MBS) – An investment instrument, a security, guaranteed by a mortgage pool. The securities are pooled together and sold to other institutions or the public.

mortgage banker – A person whose principal business is the originating financing, closing, selling, and servicing of loans secured by real property.

mortgage broker – A person or entity who has access to many lenders and can locate and negotiate the best rates, terms, and conditions for borrowers, thereby earning a commission.

mortgage constant – The total annual debt payment divided by the loan amount (principal). It is the ratio of annual debt service to the principal amount of the mortgage loan.

mortgagee – The lender under a mortgage.

Mortgage Guaranty Insurance Corporation (MGIC) – The nation's largest private mortgage insurance provider.

mortgage insurance premium (MIP) – A fee charged for either an FHA or private mortgage insurance policy. It may be a one-time payment at closing or included in the monthly payments.

mortgage lien – A lien or claim against a mortgaged property, created by the property owner, that secures the underlying debt obligation.

mortgage pool – A group of mortgages or other related financial instruments, combined for resale to investors on a secondary market.

mortgage release document – A document filed when a loan has been repaid in full, releasing the borrower of all obligations and the lender of all rights to the property.

mortgage revenue bond – A type of industrial development bond offered by state and local governments through their housing financing agencies. The interest rates are low and the bond is tax-exempt.

mortgage yield – The amount received or returned from an investment, expressed as a percentage.

mortgagor – The borrower under a mortgage.

mud sill – The lowest horizontal component of a structure, such as a foundation timber placed directly on the ground or foundation.

mullion – A non-structural, vertical strip separating the panes of a window or panels of a door. Also an upright framing member of panels or wainscoting.

multi-family units – Residential structures intended to house more than one family unit, such as duplexes or apartment buildings.

multiple-glazed window – Windows with two or more layers of glazing. Some windows use glass only, others use plastic film as an inner layer.

multiple listing service (MLS) – A marketing organization composed of member brokers who agree to share their listing agreements with one another in the hope of procuring ready, willing, and able buyers for their properties more quickly than they could on their own. In exchange for a potentially larger audience of buyers, the brokers agree to share commissions. The service also provides members with information on mortgage loans, competitive market analysis data, and worksheets for qualifying buyers and estimating ownership and closing costs. The public can now obtain much of the information through various real estate websites.

multiple regression analysis – A statistical technique for estimating a particular variable, such as probable sales price, using more than one other known variables.

multiplier – A number that, when multiplied by the income, gives an estimate of value. Also called gross income multiplier or gross rent multiplier.

municipal bond – A county or state bond issued and sold in order to finance public improvements, such as schools, parks, and renewal projects.

municipal solid waste (MSW) – Urban refuse collected from households and businesses in a community for landfilling. Includes paper, organic matter, metals, plastic, etc., but not certain agricultural or industrial wastes. It is not regulated as hazardous.

municipal waste – Defined in the Energy Security Act as "any organic matter, including sewage, sewage sludge, and industrial or commercial waste, and mixtures of such matter and inorganic refuse from any publicly or privately operated municipal waste collection or similar disposal system, or from similar waste flows (other than such flows which constitute agricultural wastes or residues, or wood wastes or residues from wood harvesting activities or production of forest products)."

municipal waste-to-energy plant – A facility that produces fuel or energy from municipal solid waste.

muntin – A non-structural, horizontal strip that divides the panes in a window.

mutual assent – The offer and acceptance of a contract. Mutual assent is one of the essentials of a valid contract. Also known as meeting of the minds or mutual consent.

mutual funds – Investment vehicles sold and managed by investment companies.

mutual mortgage insurance (MMI) – A fee for an insurance policy charged to the borrower to protect the lender under an FHA loan, in the event of foreclosure on the property.

mutual rescission – All parties to a contract agree to cancel the agreement and put themselves back where they started.

mutual water company – A water company organized by or for water in a given district with the object of securing an ample water supply at a reasonable rate.

mutually exclusive – When two or more events have no data or sample points in common.

N

NACHI – An abbreviation for the National Association of Certified Home Inspectors.

NAHI – An abbreviation for the National Association of Home Inspectors.

naked legal title – Title lacking the rights and privileges commonly associated with ownership, that may be held by a trustee under a deed of trust.

NAR – *See* National Association of REALTORS®.

narrative appraisal report – A detailed, formal written report of the appraisal and the value conclusion.

National Apartment Leasing Professional (NALP) – A designation offered by the National Apartment Association (NAA).

National Association of REALTORS® (NAR) – The largest and most prestigious real estate organization. It is made up of local boards and state associations, and only members may use the trademark REALTOR®. Members must adhere to a strict Code of Ethics.

National Environmental Policy Act (NEPA) – A law passed by Congress in 1970 that requires an environmental impact statement to be prepared and released prior to any federal action that would affect the environment. Some state and local governments require an environmental impact study before private developments or improvements commence.

native vegetation – A plant whose presence and survival in a specific region is not due to human intervention.

natural cooling – Use of environmental phenomena to cool buildings, e.g., natural ventilation, evaporative cooling, and radiative cooling.

natural gas – A hydrocarbon gas obtained chiefly from underground sources, often in association with oil and coal deposits.

negative amortization – A gradual increase in the principal of the loan that occurs when the monthly payment is not large enough to cover the entire principal and interest due. The unpaid amount is added to the remaining principal due.

negative annuity – An investment resulting in a regular series of losses.

negative cash flow – Cash flow is negative when money goes from the investor to the investment.

negative declaration – A finding by state or local agency that a proposed project will not have the potential to cause significant impacts to the environment.

negative easement – An easement preventing a servient lanndowner from using or improving the land in a certain way, because of the effect it would have on the dominant estate.

negative pressure – Condition that exists when less air is supplied to a space than is exhausted from the space, so the air pressure within that space is less than that in surrounding areas.

negligent misrepresentations – Untrue statements made without facts to back them up.

negotiable – Capable of being negotiated, assignable, or transferable in the ordinary course of business.

negotiable instrument – Any written instrument that may be transferred by endorsement or delivery.

negotiation – The act of bargaining, in order to reach a meeting of the minds between parties in a business transaction. Negotiation is a necessary part of the real estate sales process.

neighborhood – An area delineated by geographical or political boundaries that is comprised of properties that have complementary land uses. A neighborhood may be defined by physical boundaries, a change in land use, or intangible factors like school district boundaries.

neighborhood barrier – Any natural or man-made features separating one neighborhood from another.

neighborhood center – A retail center, usually anchored by a grocery store and supported by a dozen other stores. This type of center is usually financially feasible when there are approximately a thousand households in the area to sustain sales.

neighborhood cycle – The process of neighborhood change, including four phases of change: development, maturity, decline, and renaissance.

neo-eclectic style – A postmodern housing style combining a variety of details from different styles to produce a harmonious look.

neotraditional planning – Planning based on nineteenth-century American town prototypes, this type of planning minimizes automobile use and encourages a sense of community with a town center and open public areas.

net effective rent – The net income derived from a lease, after deducting all costs incurred by the landlord for procuring the lease, such as leasehold improvement allowances, real estate fees, free rent, etc. The resulting figure is generally expressed as an annual dollar amount per square foot.

net energy production – The amount of useful energy produced by a system less the amount of energy required to produce the fuel.

net income – Gross annual income, less income lost due to vacancies and uncollectible rents, less all operating expenses.

net income ratio – Net income divided by the effective gross income.

net lease – In a net lease, the tenant makes the rental payment and reimburses the landlord for certain agreed upon expenses. Net leases are categorized as single net (N), double net (NN), and triple net (NNN) leases. With each type of net lease, beginning with the single net lease, additional expenses are added to the tenant's obligation.

net listing – A listing agreement in which the commission is not definite. The broker receives a commission calculated by deducting the list price and the seller's closing costs from the selling price. For example, if the house listed at $500,000, with closing costs of $10,000 and sells for $525,000, the commission would be $15,000. A net listing agreement is discouraged in most states and is illegal in some because of the high danger of unethical practices.

net operating income (NOI) – The annual gross income from all revenues (rent, laundry facility, late fees, parking fees, etc.) from an investment property, less an annual vacancy factor or any rental losses, less operating expenses. Also called net annual income.

net operating income ratio – The ratio between the net operating income of a property and its effective gross income.

net rate – The rate of interest given to an investor, after servicing fees have been deducted from the gross rate.

net sheet – A line-by-line description of the fees associated with the sale of a home, including commission. It shows the approximate net amount of money the seller can expect to receive for a specified sales price.

net worth – An individual or company's total assets, less their total liabilities. Net worth is calculated to determine the creditworthiness and financial strength of an individual or company.

neural networks (NNs) – Network or circuit of biological neurons, which mimic human reasoning as part of a decision-making process.

neutral depository – A third party, generally an escrow company, which holds the documents and funds related to a real estate transaction until the conditions of the agreement are fulfilled. The neutral depository becomes the trustee for the money and papers until they are distributed according to the escrow instructions.

new urbanism – A city planning movement that focuses on revitalizing the inner city and reforming the American suburb within an integrated regional structure.

niche market – A market that consists of consumers with the same specialized needs.

nit (nt) – Unit of luminance equal to one candela per square meter. No-build option scenario against which the true environmental cost-effectiveness of building concepts can be evaluated.

nitrogen – A colorless, tasteless, odorless gas which makes up 78.1 percent the atmosphere.

nitrogen oxides (NOx) – Oxides of nitrogen that are a chief component of air pollution. Mainly produced by the burning of fossil fuels.

noise criteria (NC) – Series of curves of octave-band sound pressure levels from 63 to 8000 Hertz. They are commonly used in the United States to rate interior noise levels.

noise reduction (NR) – The simple loss of sound level that occurs in passing through a medium. Most often noise reduction refers to a single octave or one-third octave-band noise.

nominal interest rate – The interest rate named or stated in loan documents. Also called the contract rate.

nominee – A person designated to act in the place and stead of another.

non-amortizing loan – A loan with no payments. Principal and interest are due at the end of the term.

non-conforming building – An existing building that does not conform to the latest building or zoning codes.

non-conforming loan – A loan that does not meet the conventional lending standards of Fannie Mae and Freddie Mac. Jumbo loans and sub-prime loans are types of non-conforming loans.

non-conforming use – A property whose use was legal, according to the zoning requirements at the time of construction; however, the zoning has since changed, technically making the current property use illegal. When the use is still allowed, although does not conform to current zoning law, it is identified as a non-conforming use of property.

non-economic highest and best use – A type of highest and best use that focuses on contribution to the community and community developmental goals, rather than income-production.

non-fiduciary – Refers to certain lenders who provide funds for real estate finance. They owe no duty to others and can maintain complete discretion over their activities, because they invest their own funds. Non-fiduciaries include title insurance companies, private loan companies, and individuals.

non-freehold estate – An estate in real property for the temporary and limited right of use in the real property, such as a tenancy for years, from period to period, at will, or at sufferance. It is an estate with a fixed or determinable duration. Also known as a leasehold estate.

non-judicial foreclosure – The power to foreclose on a property without court approval. The sale of property is pursuant to the power of sale provisions contained in a security instrument.

non-monetary default – A loan default that is the result of something other than non-payment. The default comes from failure to perform some other condition of the loan agreement.

non-profit corporation – A corporation formed for a purpose other than making a profit. Examples include charities, as well as political and educational organizations. These corporations do not have shareholders, but are controlled and maintained by a board of directors.

non-refundable fee – A fee that will not be returned to the tenant under any circumstance, and this fee cannot legally be called a deposit.

non-renewable fuels – Fuels that cannot be easily made or renewed, such as oil, natural gas, and coal.

non-renewable resources – Natural resources that are consumed faster than can be produced eventually leading to depletion.

normal wear and tear – Deterioration or loss in value caused by the tenant's normal and reasonable use.

notarize – To prove execution of a document by means of a notary public's certificate of acknowledgment.

notary public – A public officer who is authorized to function as an official witness to contracts, administer oaths, take acknowledgments of deeds and other conveyances, and to perform other official acts.

note – A loan document signed by the borrower, serving as evidence of a debt. The document states the loan amount, the terms of the loan, the interest rate, the obligation to repay, and method of repayment. Also called promissory note.

note of action – A lis pendens.

notice – An announcement of an event or fact. Notice may be written or oral. Most contracts contain a paragraph that defines proper notice and tells the parties how to give notice.

notice of belief of abandonment – If the evidence is strong that the property has been abandoned, the property manager should follow state laws and issue a notice of belief of abandonment.

notice of cessation – A recorded notice shortening the time for filing mechanic's liens if work ceases prior to completion.

notice of completion – A notice filed by the owner or general contractor after completion of work on improvements, limiting the time in which mechanic's liens can be filed against the property.

notice of default – A notice to a defaulting party that there has been a nonpayment of a debt.

notice of delinquency – When junior and senior loans exist, the borrower may authorize the senior lender to send a notice to the junior lender in the event of a default.

notice of lien – A written notice of the creation of a mechanic's lien, required in some states. A copy of the notice must be delivered to the owner and other parties affected by the lien.

notice of non-responsibility – A recorded notice by an owner of real property that he/she will not be responsible for payment of costs of improvements contracted for thereon by some other person.

notice of trustee's sale – Notice given, and published, that a trustee's sale will be held to sell a property to satisfy a debt.

notice to pay rent or quit – A written notice from the landlord to the tenant informing him or her to meet the landlord's requirements or move out of the property within a specific number of days, as specified by law. Also known as an eviction notice.

notice to quit – A step in the eviction process. A written notice given by a landlord to a tenant, stating that the landlord intends to retake possession of the property and that the tenant must leave. The notice may indicate whether the tenant must vacate at the end of the lease term, or earlier.

notorious possession – Open and active possession of a property. The possession must be open and notorious, so that the owner is presumed to know and understand it exists. One of the requirements for adverse possession.

novation – The substitution of a new obligation for an old one.

nuclear energy – Energy that comes from splitting atoms of radioactive materials, such as uranium, and which produces radioactive wastes.

nuclear fuel – Fissionable materials that have been enriched to such a composition that, when placed in a nuclear reactor, will support a self-sustaining fission chain reaction, producing heat in a controlled manner for process use.

nuclear power – Electric power or motive power generated by a nuclear reactor.

nuclear waste – Radioactive waste that is produced by those activities needed to produce nuclear fission (splitting of the atom).

nuisance – An activity remaining outside the property or a land use that is incompatible or that interferes with surrounding land uses.

nuisance per se – Nuisance by statute or based on case law.

nuisance value – The value reflected in the price that a buyer would be willing to pay to eliminate an objectionable situation.

null and void – Of no legal validity or effect.

nuncupative will – An oral will.

O

100% commission plan – Plan in which agents receive 100% of the commission, but pay their brokers a desk fee.

obligee – One to whom a promise to pay or other legal obligation is owed.

obligor – A person or entity who is responsible for the payment of a debt or other legal obligation. The promise to pay or legal obligation is owed to the obligee.

observed condition method – *See* breakdown method.

observed conditions – The condition of a property, determined by observation.

observed depreciation – The decrease in a building's utility, resulting in a loss of value. Depreciation that is identified through physical inspection.

obsolescence – Loss in value, due to reduced desirability and usefulness of a structure, because its design and construction became obsolete. Loss in value, because a structure is old and has not been maintained. Obsolescence may be functional or economic.

ocean energy systems – Energy conversion technologies that harness the energy in tides, waves, and thermal gradients in the oceans.

occupancy rate – The percentage of total rental units occupied and producing income.

offer – A presentation or proposal to obtain acceptance and form a contract.

offer and acceptance – Two elements of a valid contract.

offeree – The party receiving an offer.

offer to purchase – The proposal made to an owner of property by a potential buyer to purchase the property under stated terms.

offeror – The party making an offer.

off-gassing – The process by which volatile organic compounds (VOCs) evaporate and release chemicals into the air. Also known as out-gassing.

office-layout – The diagram, usually drawn to scale, of a room or office. It shows the permanent walls and placement of cubicles, furnishings, and equipment.

Office of Thrift Supervision (OTS) – The primary regulator of all federally chartered and many state chartered thrift institutions, which include savings banks and savings and loan associations. OTS is funded by assessments and fees levied on the institutions it regulates.

offset statement – Statement customarily furnished an escrow holder as to the current status of rental accounts, security deposits, and balance due on liens and encumbrances.

offsite improvements – Improvements made outside the property's boundary line, such as the installation of streets, sidewalks, and sewers that add to the site's utility.

ohm – The unit of electric resistance. It equals the resistance of a circuit in which the potential difference of one volt produces a current of one ampere.

oil – A mixture of hydrocarbons usually existing in the liquid state in natural underground pools or reservoirs. Oil in its natural state is called crude oil.

OLD CAR – The mnemonic for the fiduciary duties an agent owes a principle: Obedience, Loyalty, Disclosure and Confidentiality, Accounting, Reasonable care.

oliogolopy – A market dominated by a small number of participants who are able to collectively exert control over supply and market prices.

ongoing expenses – Expenses that recur at regular intervals—weekly, monthly, quarterly.

on-site improvements – Buildings, structures, or other amenities erected on a property and contributing to its value.

on-site manager – A property manager who lives on-site, handles day-to-day activities, and interacts with tenants on a regular basis.

open-air shopping centers – Shopping centers in which stores are not enclosed under a single roof.

open bid – A real estate transaction where the bids are accessible to all potential buyers. In open bidding, the potential buyers know what other bidders have offered, and can alter their bid accordingly. The sellers can also see the bids as they are presented and choose or negotiate the best one.

open-end loan – A loan that is expandable by increments, up to a certain amount. The total amount is secured by the same mortgage or deed of trust.

open house – A house that is open-to prospective buyers or tenants for inspection, during certain hours and days of the week, without an appointment.

open listing – A listing agreement giving any number of brokers the right to sell a property. The first broker to obtain a buyer earns the commission. Unlike an exclusive listing agreement, an open listing does not necessarily require a specific termination date.

open loop recycling – A recycling system in which a particular material is remanufactured into the same product (e.g. glass bottles into glass bottles).

open market operations – The buying and selling of government securities in the open-market by the Fed, in order to increase or decrease the amount of money in the banking system and influence the amount of available credit. When the Fed buys securities, more money is available for banks to lend. When the Fed sells securities, the opposite is true. The open-market operations process is the most flexible and widely used technique for expanding or slowing the economy.

open space – Land that has not been improved or built upon.

operating budget – An itemized statement of income, expenses, and net operating income before debt service and cash flow. A basic tool used by the property manager to help in planning for future operations. The operating budget gives the property owner an idea of the cash yield expected from the property during a period of time, generally a typical year.

operating expense ratio – Relationship of a property's expenses to income, found by dividing total operating expenses by effective gross income.

operating expenses – Expenditures necessary to the operation of an income-producing building, such as employee salaries. Operating expenses are subtracted from effective gross income to arrive at net operating income.

operating statement – Written record of a property's gross income, expenses, and resulting net income for a given period of time.

opportunity cost – The value differential between alternative investments with differing rates of return.

option – A contract to keep open, for a set period of time, an offer to purchase or lease real property. The option holder is not obligated to exercise the right.

optionee – The person who wants to purchase or lease the property (lessee).

option listing – This listing gives the broker the right to purchase the property that is listed. A broker with an option is acting as a principal, as well as an agent.

optionor – The person who owns the property (seller, lessor).

oral contract – A contract made verbally. Real estate and lease contracts should not be oral. They should be written, in order to avoid conflict and misunderstandings.

oral report – An appraisal report communicated to the client verbally, rather than in writing.

ordinance – A law adopted by a local governing body.

organic growth – The business expansion by increasing sales and output.

organic matter – Materials of animal or vegetable origin.

oriel window – A window projecting outward, similar to a bay window. However, unlike a bay window that is supported by the foundation, an oriel window is supported by brackets or a cantilever.

orientation – The placement of a building on its lot, in relation to exposure to sun, prevailing wind, traffic,and privacy from the street. The relation of a building and its associated fenestration and interior surfaces to compass direction and, therefore, to the location of the sun.

origination fee – The fee charged by a lender for creating a mortgage. The fee is generally a percentage of the total loan amount and covers initial costs such as preparation of documents, credit fees, inspection fees, and appraisal fees.

or-more clause – A clause in a mortgage or deed of trust that allows a borrower to pay it off early with no penalty.

OSHA – An abbreviation for the federal Occupational Safety and Health Administration, which regulates workplace safety.

ostensible – That which is apparent or that which seems to be.

ostensible agency – An agency relationship created by the actions of the parties, rather than by an express agreement.

outcome – Result of a single trial of an experiment.

outlawed – A claim, right, or cause of action unenforceable due to lapse of time.

outlet center (factory outlet) – Shopping center with national brand-name retailers selling high quality merchandise with well-known brands at discounted prices.

overage – The rent paid in addition to the fixed base rent. Under a percentage lease, overage is usually based on an index or percent of sales. It is discounted at a higher rate, because it is less certain than the fixed base rent.

overall rate – A capitalization rate measuring income attributable to both land and improvements—the whole property.

overhang – An extension of a roof beyond the exterior walls, used as shading or protection from rain.

over-improvement – An improvement that is not the highest and best use for the site on which it is placed, by reason of excess size or cost. Also called superadequacy.

overriding deed of trust – A method of financing in which a new loan is created that includes both the unpaid principal balance of the first loan and whatever new sums are loaned by the lender. The new loan is in a secondary position to the original loan. Also called an All-Inclusive Deed of trust (AITD).

overt – Open.

owner's title insurance policy – A policy of title insurance insuring the title of an owner.

ownership – The right of one or more persons to possess and use property to the exclusion of all others.

ownership in severalty – Property owned by one person or entity.

ozone (O3) – A molecule made of three oxygen atoms instead of the usual two. At ground level, ozone is an air pollutant; however, in the stratosphere, ozone is a protective layer that shields the planet from harmful ultraviolet radiation.

ozone depletion – Destruction of the stratospheric ozone layer which shields the Earth from ultraviolet radiation harmful to life.

ozone layer – Protective layer in the atmosphere that absorbs some of the sun's ultraviolet rays, reducing some of the radiation that reaches the Earth's surface.

P

package loan – A type of loan on real property used in home financing covering land, structures, fixtures and other personal property.

packed sale – A type of mortgage fraud, in which excessive points, fees, and interest rates are charged to unsuspecting buyers.

pad tenant – Freestanding retailer or service located on a separate parcel in front of a shopping center.

paired sales analysis – An appraisal method of estimating the amount of adjustment for the presence or absence of any feature by pairing the sales prices of otherwise identical properties with and without that feature. Also known as paired data set analysis, matched pairs analysis, and direct market method.

palladian window – A window that is divided into three parts, with rectangular panes on each side of a wide arch. They are placed at the center of an upper story as a focal point in Colonial or Queen Anne houses.

PAM – *See* pledged account mortgage.

PANCHO – The mnemonic for the six requirements for adverse possession: **P**ossession, **A**dverse, **N**otorious, **C**ontinuous, **H**ostile, and **O**pen.

panel box – A box, usually containing breakers or fuses, located at the point of entry of electric service conductors. Also known as the service panel.

panelized home – A type of factory-built housing. A panelized home arrives at the construction site in small units, usually as completed walls with all the wiring and plumbing intact.

panic peddling – Making written or verbal statements that cause fear or alarm, in order to gain sales or rental listings. Panic peddling is often associated with sales or rentals to minorities. It is illegal.

parameter – A statistical term for a single number or attribute of the individual things, persons, or other entities in a population.

paramount title – Title which is superior or foremost to all others.

parcel – Any area of land contained within a single description.

parcel map – Map showing a parcel of land that will be subdivided into less than five parcels or units, and shows land boundaries, streets, and parcel numbers.

parol – Oral.

parol evidence rule – In a dispute over a real estate transaction, the parol evidence rule refers to any evidence that is not written. Thus, any agreement between buyer and seller, made prior to or outside of the written sales contract, is inadmissible.

parquet floor – A floor constructed with short pieces of hardwood laid in various patterns, as opposed to a strip floor in which the pieces are laid end to end.

partial eviction – A situation in which a landlord's negligence renders a portion of the property unusable to a tenant.

partial reconveyance – A provision in a land contract, deed of trust or mortgage for a conveyance of a portion of the property to the buyer upon satisfaction of specified conditions. Also called a partial release.

partial interest – An interest in real estate that represents less than the fee simple estate (i.e., a leased fee or leasehold estate).

partially amortized installment note – A promissory note with a repayment schedule that is not sufficient to pay off the loan over its term. At maturity, the remaining principal balance is due in full.

partial taking – The process by which a governmental agency acquires only a portion of a property through condemnation.

participating broker – A brokerage company or one of its agents who finds a buyer for a property that is listed with a different brokerage company.

participation financing – Financing in which the lender is also a partner. This enhances the profitability and safety of the lender's position in the arrangement.

participation loan – A large loan created by more than one lender, thus enabling the borrower to obtain more financing than from an individual lender; a loan in which the lender receives partial ownership in the financed project.

particulates – Fine liquid or solid particles such as dust, smoke, mist, fumes, or smog, found in air or emissions.

partition action – A court action to divide a property held by co-owners.

partnership – A form of business ownership in which two or more persons join their money and skills to conduct the business.

party wall – A wall erected on the boundary line between two adjoining properties, which are under different ownership, for the use of both parties.

passive building design – Resource (like sunlight, cooling breezes, etc.). Passive design strategies typically do not involve any moving parts or mechanical processes.

passive cooling – Using passive building strategies to relieve the cooling load of a building by capitalizing on such things as predictable summer breezes or by shading windows from direct summer sunlight.

passive solar design – Designing a building's architectural elements to collect, store, and distribute solar resources for heating, cooling, and daylighting.

passive solar system – Systems that collect, move, and store heat using natural heat-transfer mechanisms, such as conduction and air convection currents.

pass-through expenses – Common area maintenance charges initially paid by the landlord that are passed on to the tenants.

pass-through securities – Fixed income securities that are pooled and backed by packages of assets, like mortgages. The purchaser of these securities receives principal and interest payments. The proceeds from the sale of securities in the secondary market are passed on to the securities buyer.

patent deed – The legal document that transfers real property from the state or federal government to a person.

patent defect – Observable defects in a home that must be disclosed by a seller.

payback period – The time estimated for a capital investment to pay for itself, calculated by relating the cost of the investment to the profit it will earn or savings it will incur.

payoff – The final payment of a debt.

payoff demand – A statement, issued by a lender, showing the unpaid principal balance, accrued interest, outstanding late charges, legal fees, and all other amounts necessary to pay off a debt in full.

payroll taxes – State and federal taxes that an employer, (the property management company) is required to withhold and/or pay on behalf of the company's employees.

PCAM – *See* Professional Community Association Manager.

peak-hour demand – The maximum water usage, in gallons/hour, during the time of day when the greatest amount of hot water is used.

peak phase – The point at which the economy has reached its highest level of demand, price, and value (the upper turning point of a business or real estate cycle).

pedestrian pocket – A simple cluster of housing, retail space, and offices within a quarter-mile radius of a transit system. Smaller scale than new towns or Planned Unit Developments.

pedestrian scale – An urban development pattern where walking is a safe, convenient, and interesting travel mode.

pellet stove – A stove that burns compressed wood or biomass pellets to create heat.

penthouse – A condominium or apartment at the highest point of a building that is used as a residence. In addition, a small building on a rooftop, which houses elevator machinery, ventilating equipment, etc.

PEPS – The mnemonic for the four forces influencing value: Physical and environmental characteristics, Economic influences, Political (Governmental) regulations, and Social ideals and standards.

per capita income – Total income of an area divided by its total population.

percentage adjustment – Type of sales adjustment, where the estimated difference between the comparable sale and the subject is first calculated as a percentage of the sales price of the comparable, and then applied as an upward or downward adjustment to the price.

percentage fee increase – Manager improves the income of the property and decreases if the property revenue drops.

percentage lease – A type of lease in which the rent is determined, in whole or in part, from the volume of business.

percentage of base and percentage on gross over minimum method – Tenant pays an agreed upon percentage of gross sales based on a pre-determined minimum gross sales amount and pays an additional percentage amount on the gross receipts that exceed the minimum.

percolating water – Underground water not flowing in a defined channel.

percolation test – A test performed by a hydraulic engineer to determine the ability of soil to absorb water.

perfecting title – The process of eliminating any claims, flaws, or defects affecting a title.

performance-based retrofit – Evaluating the whole house through tested results and achieving measured energy efficiency through multi-measure planned implementation.

performing loan – A loan that has, and continues to fulfill, all of the terms and conditions required under the mortgage.

perimeter heating – Heating systems that deliver warm air to rooms by means of registers or baseboards located along exterior walls.

periodic tenancy – Tenancy for successive periods of equal duration.

perlite – A lightweight, expanded mineral bead; highly flame-resistant and with good insulating value.

permanent financing – A long-term loan ranging from 20 to 30 years, with fixed or variable interest rates.

permeability – The time rate of water vapor transmission through unit area of a material of unit thickness induced by unit vapor pressure difference between two specific surfaces, under specified temperature and humidity conditions.

personal guarantee – Promise to repay business debts from personal assets if the business is unable to pay.

personal income – An individual's gross income from all sources.

personal marketing – Marketing designed to remind people to think of a specific individual rather than the company.

personal property – Anything movable that is not real property.

personal selling – Any form of direct communication (usually face-to-face) between a salesperson and a customer.

PETE – The mnemonic for four types of government controls: Police power, Eminent domain, Taxation, and Escheat.

phenolic laminate – A high-pressure laminated sheet made from paper and phenol formaldehyde resin, commonly used for furniture and kitchen cabinet surfaces.

phenols – Organic compounds that are byproducts of petroleum refining, tanning, and textile, dye and resin manufacturing. Low concentrations cause taste and odor problems in water; higher concentrations can kill aquatic life and humans.

phosphorus – An essential chemical food element that can contribute to the eutrophication of lakes and other water bodies.

photocells – Light-sensing cells used to activate controllers at dawn or dusk.

photometer – An instrument for measuring photometric quantities, such as luminance, luminous intensity, luminous flux, and illuminance.

photovoltaic – Generation of electricity from the energy of sunlight, using photocells.

physical assets – Physical assets of an association include buildings, common areas, and other common features of the CID.

physical deterioration – A type of depreciation that came from wear and tear, negligent care, damage by dry rot or termites, or severe changes in temperature. Also known as deferred maintenance.

physical life – The length of time a structure can be considered habitable, without regard to its economic use.

physically possible – One of the four criteria for determining highest and best use. For a use to be considered the highest and best, the size, shape, and terrain of the property must be able to accommodate the use.

pier and beam foundation – A type of foundation using piers which rest on footing support beams or girders, which in turn support the superstructure. It is a relatively inexpensive form of foundation, rarely used for residential homes.

pier(s) – Columns designed to support a concentrated load. Pier columns are made of steel, steel reinforced concrete or wood, and transfer the building load to the ground.

piggyback loan – Two loans are made to finance a home, where a bank or other institutional lender finances the first, for example at 80% of the purchase price, and a private lender finances the remaining 20% of the purchase price. The 20% loan is a piggyback loan. The private lender is in secondary (subordinate) position on the loan, and is termed a piggyback lender.

pitch – The slope, incline, or rise of a roof.

pitch control – A method used to control the speed of a wind turbine by varying the orientation or pitch of the blades.

placement fee – A fee charged by a mortgage broker for bringing together a borrower and a lender who subsequently negotiate a loan agreement.

plaintiff – Person filing the civil suit in a court of law.

planned development – A type of common interest development with clustered single-family detached residences, townhouses, garden apartments, and other types of residences, with ample open space, community recreational facilities, and sometimes local shopping and employment centers.

planning commission – An agency of local government charged with planning the development, redevelopment, or preservation of an area.

plasticity – The range of moisture content within which the soil will remain plastic.

plat – A plot, map, or chart.

plate – A horizontal board used to support vertical posts or studs.

platform frame construction – A type of framing used in residential construction, in which the building is constructed one story at a time, so that each story serves as a platform for the next. Platform is the most common type of framing.

plat map – A surveyor's map of land, showing natural and man-made boundaries, buildings, and other improvements.

pleading – The formal writing filed in court containing the various claims and defenses of plaintiff and of defendant.

pledge – The transfer of property to a lender, as security for repayment of a debt.

pledged account mortgage (PAM) – A type of loan under which a sum of cash paid by the owner is set aside in an account. The account is drawn upon during the initial years of the loan, to supplement periodic mortgage payments. This reduces the payment amounts in early years.

plottage increment – The increase in value when two or more contiguous properties are joined together and made available as a single unit.

plumbing system – The system of pipes and fixtures for the distribution of clean water and the disposal of sewage in a building.

ply – The number of layers of roofing (i.e., one-ply, two-ply).

plywood – Wood made of three or more layers, or plies, of veneer joined with glue, usually laid with the grain of adjoining plies at right angles to one another. This arrangement makes plywood strong and highly resistant to movement from expansion and contraction. It comes in many grades with ratings from A to D.

pocket door – A special type of sliding door that is suspended overhead on tracks and slides into a pocket in the wall, when open.

pocket listing – A listing kept by the listing agent that is not shared with other brokers in the office or other multiple listing service members. This is discouraged by the real estate profession and is prohibited by many broker's offices.

point estimate of value – The final value indication reported as a single dollar amount.

point of beginning – Starting place for a legal description of land, using the metes and bounds method.

points – A factor used in rate adjustment. One point is equal to 1 percent of the principal conventional loan amount. Points are a one-time charge paid for the use of money.

police power – The power of the state to enact laws, within constitutional limits, to promote the order, safety, health, morals, and general welfare of our society.

policy – A predetermined course of action established as a guide toward accepted objectives and strategies of an organization.

policy and procedures manual – The document that contains all the policies, procedures, and work instructions that make up the way a company carries out all the functions of its business.

policy of title insurance – A contract indemnifying against loss resulting from a defect in title to the interest or lien in real property insured.

pollutants – Any substance introduced into the environment that adversely affects the usefulness of a resource.

pollution – Contamination of air, land, or water with substances that compromise the ecosystem; threaten human, animal or plant health; or adversely affect use of natural resources.

polynomial – Expression used in mathematics, constructed from one or more variables and constants, using only the operations of addition, subtraction, multiplication, and constant positive whole number exponents.

polyvinyl phloride (PVC) – A tough, environmentally indestructible plastic that releases hydrochloric acid when burned.

population – (1) The total number of people inhabiting a specific area. (2) In statistics, the entire set of data from which a statistical sample is drawn.

porte cochere – A roofed structure that extends from the entrance of a building to a driveway, offering shelter to people getting into or out of vehicles.

positive cash flow – Income generated by the property flows toward the owner.

possession – Possessing or occupying property, whether actually or constructively. Actual possession is physically occupying the land. Constructive possession is legally possessing title to a property.

possessory interest – Present right to physically occupy land and to exclude others from that same land.

post-consumer recycled content – Material that has been used by consumers, such as used newspaper, and has been diverted or separated from waste management systems for recycling.

postmodern style – *See* neo-eclectic style.

potable water – Fresh water that is safe and agreeable for drinking.

potential energy – Stored energy, which is also described as the stored energy of position possessed by an object.

potential gross income – A property's total potential income, from all sources, during a specified period of time.

power of attorney – A legal document that gives a person the legal authority to act on behalf of another person.

power of sale – A clause in a deed of trust or mortgage that gives the holder the right to sell the property, in the event of default by the borrower.

prairie style – This housing style is much larger than the craftsman bungalows and is designed with low horizontal lines that require larger lots. These houses have low-pitched hip roofs with large overhanging eaves, casement windows, and rows of small, high windows.

pre-appraisal lease clause – Rental rate method that is enacted at the expiration of a lease.

preapproval letter – A written commitment from a lender to loan a certain amount, based on a buyer's written application.

pre-approved loan – A pending loan in which all the necessary documents and information have been filed, and there are no outstanding credit or income issues to prevent the loan from being granted.

precedent – Concept of looking back at cases previously decided and following those decisions for the sake of consistency and fairness.

precut home – A type of factory-built housing. A precut home is like a house in a box. All the materials are delivered to the construction site unassembled, but precut to fit exactly in place.

prefabricated house – A house manufactured and sometimes partly assembled before delivery to building site.

preliminary notice – A written notice that must be given to the owner by anyone eligible to file a mechanic's lien. The notice must be given after labor or materials are first provided for a job, within the time from specified by law.

preliminary title report – An offer to issue a policy of title insurance in the future for a specific fee.

premises liability – Insurance that covers liability for accidental injury or property damage that results from either a condition on the premises or operations in progress.

premium – A fee paid for an insurance policy, paid in one lump sum, or in monthly installments.

prenuptial agreement – An agreement made between a man and woman before they wed, establishing property rights of each during the marriage, and in the event of their divorce or a death. Also called an antenuptial agreement.

prepaid interest – Interest charged on a loan that is paid before it is incurred.

prepaid items of expense – Prorations of prepaid items of expense which are credited to the seller at closing.

prepayment – Paying all or part of a debt, before it is due.

prepayment clause – A clause in a deed of trust or mortgage that allows a lender to collect a certain percentage of a loan as a penalty for an early payoff.

prepayment penalty – The fee or charge imposed upon a debtor, who desires to pay off their loan before its maturity.

prepayment privilege – The right given to a borrower to repay all or part of a mortgage debt prior to its maturity, without penalty.

prequalified loan – The status of a loan decision in its preliminary stage. A lender provides a prequalification letter based on a credit report and initial information provided by the buyer to the lender.

prescription – The process of acquiring an interest, not ownership, in a certain property. Examples include an easement or right of way. Similar to adverse possession, except that title is not acquired, as it is through adverse possession. Adverse possession also requires the payment of property taxes, where prescription does not.

prescriptive building retrofit – Making an energy efficient implementation to reduce energy in the home.

prescriptive easement – Using someone else's property, without his or her permission.

present interest – Interest in land that can be exercised by the owner today.

present worth – The value of today's money, projected into the future. Using a mathematical equation that factors the amount of money, the interest rate per period, and the number of periods, the future value of today's money may be calculated.

pressure dose – A method of pumping wastewater to subsurface leaching fields in which soils or slopes are a limiting factor. Typical leach fields operate with gravity.

pre-tax cash flow – The portion of net operating income after debt service is paid, but before income tax is deducted. Also called before-tax cash flow or equity dividend.

preventive maintenance – Maintenance of the property necessary to prevent future defects or repairs.

price – The amount of money, or other consideration, paid for a specific good or service.

price fixing – Act of conspiring with the competition to set prices for selling goods or services.

price point – Point on the scale of possible prices at which a property might be marketed.

prima facie – Latin meaning first sight, a fact presumed to be true until disproved.

primary lenders – Originators of real estate loans.

primary mortgage market – The term for the market made up of financial institutions, such as commercial banks or mortgage companies, that originate mortgage loans and lend directly to borrowers. The primary lender may hold the loans to maturity or sell the loans to second owners in the secondary mortgage market.

prime loans – *See* "A" paper loan.

prime rate – The minimum interest rate charged by lenders on loans made to borrowers with the best credit rating.

principal – (1) In a real estate transaction, the buyer or seller who hires the broker to represent him or her in the sale or purchase of a property. (2) The amount of money borrowed.

principal meridian – An imaginary line running true north and south used in the Public Land Survey System as a survey reference point. This imaginary line intersects a base line.

principle of:

anticipation – States that value is created by the anticipation of benefits derived in the future.

balance – States that the greatest value of a property will occur when the type and size of the improvements are proportional to each other as well as to the land.

change – Holds that it is the future, not the past, which is of prime importance in estimating value. Real estate values are constantly changed by environmental, economic, political, and social forces.

competition – States that real estate values are affected by supply and demand because of competition. Typically follows three steps: (1) Market demand generates profits. (2) Profits generate competition. (3) Competition stabilizes profits.

conformity – States that maximum value results when properties in a neighborhood are relatively similar in size, style, quality, use, and/or type.

consistent use – Requires that land and improvements be appraised, based on the same use.

contribution – Calculates the worth of a particular component in terms of its contribution to the value of the whole property, or an item's worth is calculated as the amount that its absence would detract from the value of the whole.

increasing and decreasing returns – The idea that income and other benefits available from real estate may be increased by adding capital improvements only up to the point of balance in the agents of production, beyond which the increase in value tends to be less than the increase in costs. Also known as law of increasing and decreasing returns.

opportunity cost – The economic principle that recognizes competing investments, usually in different industries, that may have a greater return.

progression – States that the worth of a lesser valued residence tends to be enhanced by association with higher valued residences in the same area.

regression – States that higher-valued properties tend to suffer when placed in close proximity with lower-valued properties.

substitution – Affirms that the maximum value of a property tends to be set by the cost of acquiring an equally desirable and valuable substitute property, assuming no cost delay is encountered in making the substitution. The foundation for the appraisal process. It is the basic principle used to create a comparative market analysis (CMA) to determine value.

supply and demand – States that market value is affected by the intersection of supply and demand forces in the market, as of the appraisal date. Prices and rent levels tend to increase when demand is greater than supply and decrease when supply exceeds demand.

surplus productivity – States that the net income that remains, after the ownership expenses of labor, capital, and management have been paid, is surplus income that is attributable to the land. This is also called land rent and is used as the basis for residual land valuation techniques.

priority – The order in which deeds and other instruments are recorded.

priority lien position – The relative superiority of competing liens and encumbrances.

private grant – The granting of private property to other private persons.

private mortgage insurance (PMI) – Mortgage guarantee insurance available to insure a first position conventional, high-risk loan. A first loan is considered high risk, if the loan-to-market value exceeds 80%. Private mortgage insurance is required on the portion of the loan amount that exceeds 80% of the loan-to-market value.

private nuisance – Nuisance affecting only a few people.

private restrictions – Created at the time of sale or in the general plan of a subdivision.

privity – Closeness; mutuality of relationship.

probabilistic model – Input can only estimate or approximate the output.

probability theory – Model of those conditions under which a specific occurrence will or will not happen.

probate – The legal process to prove a will is valid.

probate sale – A court-approved sale of the property of a deceased person.

procedure – A particular or specific way of accomplishing an objective.

procuring cause – (1) A broker who produces a buyer ready, willing, and able to purchase the property for the price and on the terms specified by the seller, regardless of whether the sale is completed. (2) Person responsible for the ultimate sale of real property so as to be entitled to a commission.

product advertising – Advertising is designed to promote a specific product or service.

Professional Community Association Manager (PCAM) – An advanced designation offered by the Community Associations Institute (CAI).

proffer – To offer an opinion or advice up for approval.

profit and loss statement – *See* income statement.

profit-à-prendre – Right to enter another's land to remove soil, substances of the soil, or other resource.

pro-forma statement – A financial statement of the future income and operating expenses of a real estate property, based on a certain set of assumptions. A pro-forma is used to create budgets and determine economic feasibility.

programmable thermostat – Thermostat for heating and/ or cooling equipment that can record different temperature settings for varying times. Programmable thermostats can be electronic, or mechanical.

projection – A statement of anticipated income and expenses from operations, used to aid in planning or budgeting.

promissory note – The evidence of the debt, which states the amount of the money borrowed, the terms of repayment, and the date due.

promotional mix – The combination of promotional methods.

promotional strategy – The plan describing the best way to employ the different promotional methods—advertising, direct marketing, sales promotion, personal selling, and public relations.

promulgate – To publish or make laws known.

propane – A manufactured, liquid petroleum gas (LPG), typically used for cooking or heating.

property – Anything that may be acquired and owned lawfully.

property analysis – An on-site inspection and study of the subject property, so that the entire physical plant is thoroughly understood.

property insurance – Insurance covering the loss of the building, loss of personal property, or the loss of its use.

property management – A specialty in which real estate brokers or property managers lease and manage properties, including homes, apartments, condominiums, commercial and industrial complexes, shopping centers, and a variety of specialty properties. Management of property involves leasing, marketing, operations, maintenance, and financial planning and reporting for the property being managed.

property management agreement – Contract between the owner of real property and the property manager.

property marketing plan – Organized marketing efforts designed to create interest in a property, causing it to sell at a top price.

property portfolio – The number and type of investment properties (residential and commercial) owned by an investor.

property profile – A report about a specific piece of property, usually provided by a title company.

property report – Monthly report prepared by the property manager for the owner that establishes current and projected costs, and gives recommendations for capital expenses.

property residual technique – A method of value estimation by capitalizing the income to the whole property.

property supervisor – A property manager who is responsible for several properties and supervises the on-site managers of these properties.

property tax – Tax that is charged on either real or personal property. Only the state and local governments have the constitutional right to tax land.

proprietary lease – The lease used in co-op apartment buildings.

pro rata – In proportion; according to a certain percentage or proportion of a whole.

prorate – To divide and distribute expenses and income, such as homeowners' association fees, taxes, interest, and rent, between the buyer and seller of property, as of the date of closing or settlement.

prospect – A potential buyer or seller in a real estate transaction. A prospect does not become a client, until a fiduciary relationship is established, most often by signing a listing or sales contract.

prospect equal service report – A report provided by the National Association of REALTORS® can be used as a guideline for service and documentation of nondiscrimination.

prospecting – The process of identifying potential customers.

prosperity – A stage in the business cycle when unemployment is low and consumers have strong purchasing power.

protected class – A class of people who are protected from discrimination by federal or state law.

public dedication – When private property is intended for public use. There are three types of public dedication: common law dedication, statutory dedication, or deed.

public grant – The transfer of title by the government to a private individual.

Public Housing Authority (PHA) – Local public agency under the control of HUD that administers HUD's Low-Income Public Housing Program and other HUD programs.

Public Land Survey System (PLSS) – A method of legal land description, using east-west lines (base lines) and north-south lines (principal meridians). Additional lines, drawn six miles apart, are known as township lines (east-west) and range lines (north-south). Also called the U.S. Government Survey System and Rectangular Survey System.

public nuisance – Nuisance annoying the whole community in general.

public record – A document disclosing all-important facts about the property.

public relations – The activities used to create goodwill toward a company.

public restrictions – Limitations on use of real property associated with government intervention.

pueblo revival style – A version of the Santa Fe style, characterized by roof beams which protrude through the walls and help support the roof.

puffing – An exaggerated statement of opinion about property, that is not factual.

pull advertising – Advertising that attracts customers to a company.

pur autre vie – For another's life. A life estate created on the life of a designated person.

purchase agreement – A written agreement between a buyer and seller, detailing the price and terms of the purchase.

purchase money loan – A loan used for the purpose of purchasing real property.

purchase offer – A written offer for the purchase of a property.

purchasing power – The value of money, as measured by the amount of goods it can buy.

push advertising – Advertising that is sent to potential customers to attract the few who may have interest in the company or products.

pyramid roof – A roof with four sloping sides that rise to a ridge. Usually found on garages or church steeples. Also called a hip roof.

pyramiding through refinancing – A method of acquiring additional properties through refinancing of existing mortgages, then reinvesting the proceeds in new property.

Q

qualified buyer – A buyer who is financially capable of paying for a property. Some buyers are pre-qualified by a lender, before submitting an offer to buy property.

qualifying rate – The initial interest rate, as determined by the current rate of the chosen index.

qualitative analysis – Compares data on properties to obtain relative comparisons between properties in the same market.

quality control – The procedure used to check loan quality throughout the application and funding process.

quantitative analysis – Compares data on properties to obtain results that are then applied to other properties in the same market.

quantity survey method – The most in-depth and detailed method used to estimate reproduction or replacement cost of a building. This method requires a detailed estimate of all labor and materials used in the components of a building. Items such as overhead, insurance, taxes, cost of labor for assembly of the building, and contractor's profit are added to the direct costs of building. This method is time consuming, but very accurate. Also called a price take-off method.

quasi-contract – A contract implied by law; based on conduct.

Queen Anne style – A house with multiple stories, projecting wings, a complicated roofline with very steep cross-gabled roofs, towers, turrets, vertical windows, and balconies, multiple chimneys with decorative chimney pots, scrollwork, bric-a-brac, gingerbread, and gingerbread with frosting.

quiet enjoyment – Right of an owner or tenant to the use of the property, without interference from the acts or claims of third parties.

quiet title action – Court proceeding to establish a title to property or to remove a cloud on the title.

quitclaim deed – A deed containing no warranties and conveying the current right, title and interest of the grantor, if any, to real property.

R

radiant barrier – Radiant barriers are thin sheets of highly reflective material, like aluminum, that reduce heat transfer from thermal radiation across the air space between the roof and the attic floor.

radiant energy – Energy traveling outward in all directions from its source in the form of electromagnetic waves. It is measured in units of energy such as joules, ergs, or kilowatt hours.

radiant heating – A method of heating, usually consisting of coils or pipes placed in the floor, wall, or ceiling.

radiation – Transfer of heat by means of the straight-line passage of electromagnetic waves through space (including vacuums) from a warmer object to a cooler one. Sunlight is a form of radiation.

radioactive waste – Byproduct of creating energy from nuclear fission.

radon – Colorless, odorless, gas that is a carcinogen detected by a spectrometer.

rafter – One of a series of boards of a roof designed to support roof loads.

rain forest – A tropical or subtropical forest with a vast leaf canopy that requires an average annual rainfall of approximately 2,000 millimeters. Rain forests absorb large quantities of carbon dioxide and shelter a large percentage of the world's plant and animal species.

rainscreen – A method of constructing walls in which the cladding is separated from a membrane by an airspace that allows pressure equalization to prevent rain from being forced in.

rammed earth – A wall-building technique, by which a certain mixture of earth, water, and usually a small amount of cement, is very forcibly tamped inside formwork. The resulting wall has high mass, so it works well in hot climates.

ranch style house – A house style that is rambling, with low-pitched gable roofs and an open, airy interior design, commonly describing any one-story house.

random sample – Selection of an item in a population or group to be sampled by chance.

range – column of townships running north and south in a row parallel to, and east or west of a principal meridian.

range lines – Used in the Public Land Survey System, imaginary vertical lines, six miles east and west of the meridian that form columns.

range of value – The difference between the highest and lowest variant.

rate – The percentage of interest charged on the loan principal. *See* interest rate.

ratification – The approval or adoption of a previously unauthorized act.

ratified – Approved after the fact.

rating exposures – Variables that affect the rating formula.

ratio capitalization – Describes any capitalization method that uses the typical ratio of income to value to convert projected income into a value estimate for the property (or property component) under appraisal. Includes direct capitalization, as well as land, building, and equity residual capitalization methods, when sales price-income ratios are used.

RCF number – Unique number used to track the amount of calls from a specific ad.

ready, willing, and able – A phrase that refers to a prospective buyer's legal capacity and financial ability to purchase property.

real estate – Land and anything permanently attached to the land, including buildings and structures. The terms real property and real estate are often used interchangeably. Real property includes all real estate, plus the legal bundle of rights inherent in the ownership of real estate.

real estate broker – Someone holding a broker license issued by the state, who is permitted by law to negotiate real estate transactions between principals and to employ persons holding real estate licenses.

real estate cycle – The cycle of supply and demand in real estate that is affected by the business cycle. The changing cycle results in changes in the level of activity for building, lending, purchasing, and leasing real estate. The cycle swings between the extremes of a buyer's market and a seller's market.

real estate investment trust (REIT) – A special trust arrangement under federal and state law, whereby investors may pool funds for investments in real property and avoid corporate taxes. The investors in the REIT purchase certificates of ownership. The profits are passed to individual investors and are taxed as normal income.

real estate mortgage investment conduit (REMIC) – A tax entity created by the Tax Reform Act of 1986 that issues multiple classes of investor interests (securities) backed by a pool of mortgages. It avoids the double taxation generally imposed on similar corporations.

real estate mortgage trust (REMT) – A type of REIT that buys and sells real estate mortgages, rather than the real estate itself.

Real Estate Professional Assistant (REPA) – The designation of a real estate assistant who has completed the course offered by the National Association of REALTORS®.

Real Estate Settlement Procedures Act (RESPA) – A 1974 federal law requiring disclosure to borrowers of settlement (closing) procedures and costs by means of a pamphlet and forms prescribed by the United States Department of Housing and Urban Development.

real estate syndicate – An organization of investors, usually in the form of a limited partnership, who have joined together for the purpose of pooling capital for the acquisition of real property interests.

real property – Real property includes the land, anything permanently attached to the land, anything appurtenant to the land, or anything immovable by law. Real property includes all real estate, plus the legal bundle of rights inherent in the ownership of real estate. Current use of the term real property makes it synonymous with real estate.

Real Property Administrator (RPA) – The most widely used designation in the asset and property management fields. It applies to overall property management and administration. The designation is offered by the Building Owners and Managers Institute (BOMI).

real property sales contract – An agreement to purchase real property for a certain price and under certain conditions. Usually, the buyer makes a down payment and pays the rest in installments over a period of time. The buyer usually gains possession of the property, but takes title only when the purchase price has been paid in full.

Realtist – A member of a national organization, generally composed of African-American real estate brokers, known as the National Association of Real Estate Brokers (NAREB).

REALTOR® – A real estate broker or agent holding active membership in a real estate board affiliated with the National Association of REALTORS®. To acquire this designation, the broker or agent must adhere to a strict Code of Ethics, and the rules and regulations adopted by NAR.

recapture – The recovery by an owner of invested money, which is known as return of investment, not to be confused with interest, which is a return on investment. Also known as capital recapture.

recapture rate – The rate at which invested capital is returned to the investor, from a wasting asset, or one that is depreciating.

recasting – The act of redesigning an existing loan balance, in order to avoid a default. The loan period may be extended, payments reduced, or the interest rate periodically adjusted to help the distressed borrower.

receiver – An impartial person appointed by the court to manage properties that are involved in foreclosure or other litigation. The receiver collects the property's rents and profits, and applies or disposes of them as directed by the court.

recession – A stage in the business cycle when production and supply surpass demand, resulting in unemployment and declining prices.

reciprocal easements – Easements created as covenants, to limit the use of the land for the benefit of all the owners in an entire tract. Typically at the site of a planned subdivision.

recognition clause – A clause included in a blanket loan contract, used to purchase a tract of land for subdivision and development. It protects the rights of buyers of small parcels, in case of default by the developer.

reconciliation – The adjustment process of weighing results of all three appraisal methods to arrive at a final estimate of the subject property's market value. Also known as correlation.

reconstructed operating statement – The process of eliminating the inapplicable expense items for appraisal purposes and adjusting the remaining valid expenses, if necessary.

reconveyance – The act of transferring title of property back to the original owner. In the case of a deed of trust, the borrower conveys title to a third-party trustee as security for the debt. When the debt is paid off, the property is reconveyed to the owner.

reconveyance deed – A deed that is issued to convey the property to the original owner, once the loan is repaid. Conveys title to property from a trustee to the borrower (trustor), upon payment in full of the secured debt.

Record Keeping – Per USPAP, the Record Keeping section of the ETHICS RULE "identifies the record keeping requirements appraisers must follow."

recorded map system – *See* lot, block, and tract system.

recording – The act of filing written documents affecting the title to real property with the county recorder.

recovery – A stage in the business cycle following a recession when consumers once again buy goods at reduced prices, increasing demand in relation to supply.

recovery fund – A fund used to compensate individuals who have suffered losses due to fraudulent acts or misrepresentation by a real estate licensee. The fund is created and maintained with fees paid by real estate licensees, as part of their registration process with the state.

recovery plan – A detailed outline of what needs to be done and by who after a disaster occurs.

recovery rate – The rate at which water can be heated from 50° F to 140° F (or 90° temperature variance, taking into account starting temperature and maximum allowable temperature for the water).

recruiting – The process of attracting, qualifying, and hiring for a business.

recuse – Disqualify someone from an assignment.

recycled material – Material that would otherwise be destined for disposal but is diverted or separated from the waste stream, reintroduced as material feed-stock, and processed into marketed end-products.

recycling – The practice of collecting reusable waste materials for reprocessing into new products. Glass, metal, paper and plastics can be recycled, as can salvaged construction materials.

red flag – A warning. Something that indicates a potential problem and deserves further investigation.

redemption – The legal right of a debtor to reacquire title to property sold through judicial foreclosure, within a statutory period of time.

redemption period – A period of time established by state law, during which a property owner has the right to recover real estate after a foreclosure or tax sale, by paying the sales price plus interest and costs.

redlining – The illegal use of a property's location to deny financing or insurance.

referral – A client who is obtained through the recommendation of another.

refinancing – Paying off an existing obligation and assuming a new obligation in its place.

reflectance – The ratio of reflected light flux to incident light flux.

reflected glare – Glare resulting from specular reflection of high luminances in polished or glossy surfaces in the field of view. See also Veiling reflection.

reflection – The process by which incident light flux leaves a surface, or medium, from the incident side, without a change in frequency.

reflective insulation – A metallic foil material (usually aluminum) designed to block radiant heat transfer across open spaces. Also called a radiant barrier.

refrigerant – A chemical that condenses from a vapor to liquid and, in the process, decreases in temperature.

regional analysis – An analysis that considers the physical, economic, political, and social aspects of the region.

regional center – A large retail shopping center (sometimes called a mall) with 400,000 to 800,000 square feet, a dozen major department stores, and 100 to 150 general merchandise and specialty shops. Customers are drawn from a distance of 5 to 15 miles.

regional manager – A property manager who works for a large property management company and oversees the work of property supervisors or on-site managers.

Registered Property Manager (RPM) – A property management designation offered by the International Real Estate Institute (IREI).

regression analysis – Statistical technique for calculating sales price or adjustments, or for estimating probable sales prices, or other variables.

Regulation Z – This regulation is issued by the Board of Governors of the Federal Reserve System to implement the federal Truth-in-Lending Act, which is contained in Title I of the Consumer Credit Protection Act.

rehabilitation – The restoration of a property to its former or improved condition, without changing the basic design or plan.

reinforcing bar – Steel bars that are placed in concrete slabs, foundations, footings, piers, etc., to provide reinforcement. Also called rebar.

reinstate – To bring current and restore.

REIT – *See* real estate investment trust.

relative humidity – The percentage of water vapor in the air in relation to the amount of water vapor the air could hold at that given temperature before condensing to liquid form.

release clause – A provision found in mortgages or deeds of trust that enables the borrower to obtain partial release of specific parcels of land that are no longer required as security for the loan.

release of liability – An agreement that releases the borrower from obligation for repayment of a loan.

reliction – The exposing of previously covered land by receding water.

relief valve – A valve that is set to open at a certain pressure level, in order to prevent the pressure in a container or system from reaching unsafe levels. Used in plumbing systems.

relocation company – A firm that administers all aspects of moving individuals to a new community.

remainder depreciation – The possible future loss in value of an improvement to real property.

remainder estate – A future estate, other than a reversion, taking effect upon termination of a prior estate.

remainderman – An individual who owns an estate in remainder estate.

remaining economic life – The number of years between the structure's estimated economic life and its effective age.

remediation – The removal of contaminants from a building or land.

remedy – The means by which a right is enforced or by which the violation of a right is prevented or compensated. The four basic types of judicial remedies are (1) damages; (2) restitution; (3) coercive remedies; and (4) declaratory remedies.

REMIC – *See* real estate mortgage investment conduit.

remodeling – Changes the basic design or plan of the building to correct deficiencies.

REMT – *See* real estate mortgage trust.

renewable – A renewable product can be grown or naturally replenished or cleansed at a rate that exceeds human depletion of the resource.

renewable energy – Energy produced from regenerative or virtually inexhaustible resources such as biomass, solar radiation, the wind, water, or heat from the Earth's interior.

renewable resources – Resources that are created or produced at least as fast as they are consumed, so that nothing is depleted.

renovation – Bringing back a property to its normal condition.

rent – Payment for the use or possession of a property, generally under a lease agreement.

rent abatement – A free rental period.

rentable area – The total square footage of a building that can be rented, which excludes elements of the building that penetrate through the floor to areas below and their enclosing walls, such as stairs, elevator shafts, and vertical ducts.

rental income – The total of the economic, or fair, rent for each of the units.

rental period – Length of time (days, weeks, months) between the rent payments.

rental survey – An analysis of competitive rents used to identify the amount of income the subject property might generate.

rent concessions – Reduce rental rates or up-front costs, such as security deposits. Concessions are offered by the property owner to entice tenants to a property. Rent concessions may be given to a tenant for any type of property, and are sometimes necessary to attract tenants when demand is low.

rent control – A collection of law that limits or prohibits rent increases in some communities. Also called rent stabilization.

renters insurance – Insurance covering the tenant's personal property that is stolen or damaged, and pays the expenses of finding a different place to rent while the property is being restored.

rent roll – List of tenants.

rent-up – The requirement of a lender, that the developer prove a certain percentage of the commercial space will be rented. The developer may have to do this in order to obtain financing, and the percentage required usually represents the rental income needed to break even.

repairs – Alterations and improvements made to a property to maintain its condition or restore it to its original condition. Repairs are made to extend the useful life of the property.

replacement cost – Cost of constructing a building or structure that would have a similar utility to the subject improvement, but constructed with modern materials and according to current standards, design, and layout.

replacement reserves – Funds set aside by the property owner to pay for the replacement of certain building components and fixtures that periodically wear out.

replacement value – The dollar amount required to replace any improvements that have been lost to fire, flood, wind, or other natural disasters.

replevin – A form of action for the recovery of personal property.

report – Any communication, written or oral of an appraisal, appraisal review, or appraisal consulting service that is transmitted to the client upon completion of an assignment.

reproduction cost – The current cost of building a replica of the subject structure, using similar quality materials.

request for notice – A notice that is sent, upon request, to any parties who have an interest in a deed of trust, informing them of a default.

rescission – Legal action taken to repeal a contract, either by mutual consent of the parties, or by one party when the other party has breached a contract.

reservation – A right or an interest retained by a grantor in a conveyance.

reserve requirements – The amount of money and liquid assets the Federal Reserve requires member banks to set aside as a safety measure. The amount is usually a percentage of deposits.

residential brokerage – The business of helping homeowners sell and homebuyers purchase homes.

Residential Lead-Based Paint Hazard Reduction Act of 1992 (Title X) – Effective on September 6, 1996 for owners of property with four or fewer units. A lead-hazard information brochure and disclosure form must be provided to a lessee by a landlord. In addition, the presence of any known lead-based paint must be disclosed.

residential lease – A lease used for one to four dwelling, single-family residences.

residential property – A property where people reside, including single-family residences, condominiums, and apartment buildings.

resident-manager – A person employed to manage an apartment building on a part-time or full-time basis.

residual – In appraising, the income or value remaining after all deductions have been made.

residual techniques of capitalization – Capitalization techniques that attribute income to a component of the property, such as land or building, or debt or equity, to analyze its value contribution to the total property.

RESNET – Residential Energy Services Network. National association that certifies HERS raters and whose standards are recognized by the federal government for verification of a building's energy performance.

resource oriented industries – A business located near the supplies or raw material source in order to minimize transportation costs.

resource recovery – The process of obtaining matter or energy from materials formerly discarded.

resources – Materials found in the environment that can be extracted economically. Resources are abiotic resources (non-renewable) and biotic resources (renewable).

RESPA – *See* Real Estate Settlement Procedures Act.

respondent superior – The superior is responsible for the acts of the subordinate.

restricted license – Probationary license issued when a license has been suspended, revoked, or denied after a hearing.

Restricted Use Appraisal Report – The briefest presentation of an appraisal and contains the least detail. Called restricted use because the client is the only intended user of the report.

restrictions – Limitations or prohibitions respecting use of real property imposed in deeds or in a declaration.

restrictive covenant – A clause in a deed or lease that restricts the way the property may be used or occupied, such as lot size, building lines, type of architecture, and land uses.

retail – Consumer goods and services from a fixed location such as a store or shop.

retail property – Property used for retailing.

retail trade area – Geographical area from which customers are attracted to the retail establishment.

retaining walls – Walls constructed to hold back soil and prevent erosion.

retaliatory actions – Raising the rent, reducing services provided to the tenant, or evicting the tenant.

retaliatory eviction – An eviction that occurs in revenge for some complaint made by the tenant.

retirement community – Planned community for residents who either have retired from an active work life or have reached a set age.

retrofit – Modification of an existing building or facility to include new systems or components.

retrospective appraisal – An appraisal that looks at the value of a property, at a point of time in the past.

return – Profit from an investment; the yield. *See* return on investment.

return air – Air that has circulated through a building as supply air and has been returned to the HVAC system for additional conditioning or release from the building.

return of investment – Recapture or conversion of the investment in real estate to cash or other valuable assets.

return on investment (ROI) – The income derived from an investment in one year, usually expressed as a percentage of the total amount invested. Also called return or yield.

reverse annuity mortgage (RAM) – A loan that enables elderly homeowners to borrow against the equity in their homes by receiving monthly payments from a lender, that are needed to help meet living costs.

reverse directory – A directory from which you can obtain a subscriber's name and address, when only a telephone number or e-mail address is known.

reversion – The right to future possession or enjoyment by a person, or the person's heirs, creating the proceeding estate.

reversionary interest – A future interest, for example, the right of a landlord to reclaim the property at the end of the lease.

reversionary value – The estimated value of a property at the expiration of a certain time period.

revocation – The canceling of an offer to contract by the person making the original offer.

revoke – Recall and make void.

rezoning – A change or amendment made to the zoning in a geographic area.

rider – A supplement to; an addition to; an endorsement to a document.

ridge board – The highest horizontal member of a roof, running along the ridge, and meeting the rafters at right angles.

ridgeline – The peak of a roof.

right of appropriation – The act of the government to divert water for public use.

right of first refusal – The right of a person to have the first opportunity to purchase or lease real property. The holder of the right cannot exercise the right to purchase, until the owner actually offers the property for sale or entertains an offer to purchase from a third party. If the holder of the right decides not to exercise his/her right, then the owner is free to accept the offer made by the third party or any other party at that price or higher.

right of replevin – The tenant has a legal right to recover personal property unlawfully taken by the landlord.

right of survivorship – The right of a surviving tenant or tenants to succeed to the entire interest of the deceased tenant, which is the distinguishing feature of a joint tenancy.

right-of-way – The right to use or pass over a certain portion of another's property.

rigid board insulation – Fibrous materials or plastic foams shaped into board-like forms to provide thermal and acoustical insulation.

riparian rights – The rights of a landowner, whose land is next to a natural watercourse, to reasonable use of whatever water flows past the property.

rise – The vertical distance from the eaves line to the ridge.

risk – The possibility of incurring loss or misfortune.

risk averse – Extremely cautious.

risk avoidance – The conscious act of not doing something that might have a risk.

risk management – The practice of selecting cost effective ways to minimize the effect of risks to the business.

risk management plan – The analysis of likely risks with both high and low impact, as well as mitigation strategies.

risk reduction – The methods that reduce the severity of the loss or the likelihood of the loss from occurring.

risk retention – Accepting the loss when it occurs because the cost of insuring against the loss would be greater over time than the total losses sustained.

risk transfer – Transferring the risk to someone or something else, i.e. purchasing insurance.

rockwool insulation – Dirty grey insulation spun from the slag from refining metals.

rod – A length measuring the equivalent of 5 ½ yards or 16 ½ feet.

ROI – *See* return on investment.

rollover mortgage – A loan that allows the rewriting of a new loan, at the termination of a prior loan.

rotunda – A room or building, shaped in a circle, usually with a domed roof.

rounding – Expressing an amount as an approximate number.

routine maintenance – Maintenance work planned and performed on a regular basis.

row houses – A method of construction of individual houses, with common side walls and a common roof. Also referred to as townhouses.

RPA – *See* Real Property Administrator.

RPM – *See* Registered Property Manager.

RSI – A unit of measurement of resistance to heat flow in m2 ° C/W per 25 mm. R = 0.17.

Rules – In appraisal, the rules in USPAP include: the ETHICS RULE, the COMPETENCY RULE, the SCOPE OF WORK RULE, and the JURISDICTIONAL EXCEPTION RULE.

run – (1) The width of a single stair tread as measured from front to back. (2) The horizontal distance covered by a flight of stairs.

runs with the land – The transfer of rights or covenants, affecting property, to successive owners.

runoff – Water from rainfall or irrigation that flows off of land, instead of soaking in. It effectively becomes a lost resource, and contributes to non-point source pollution.

rural – An area outside of an established urban area or metropolitan district.

R-value – A rating that measures how well insulation resists heat. The higher the better.

S

safety clause – Clause protecting listing broker's commission, if the owner personally sells the property to someone who was shown the property or made an offer during the term of the listing.

sale and leaseback – A transaction in which a grantee in a deed leases the same property back to the grantor without a change in its possession.

sale-resale analysis – A method for determining adjustment or depreciation amounts that is useful when a property sells and is resold in a relatively short period of time. Assuming both sales are arm's-length, open market transactions, and assuming that there have been no significant changes to the property during the time between the two sales, the difference in price could be a basis for a time adjustment.

sales comparison approach – An appraisal method based on the principles of substitution that compares similar properties, which have recently sold, to the subject property. Also called the market data approach, market approach, or comparison approach.

sales contract – A contract for the sale and purchase of real property.

sales price – The actual price that a buyer pays for a property.

salesperson – A person who is employed by a licensed real estate broker to perform a variety of acts in the business of real estate. Salespeople may be either employees of, or independent contractors to a broker. In some states, the salesperson is called a sales associate.

sales promotion – The various short-term marketing activities used to supplement traditional advertising.

sales tax – A tax paid by consumers, collected by a retailer as a percentage of the retail sales of a product and forwarded to the appropriate state collecting authority.

salvage value – (1) For accounting purposes, the anticipated fair market value of the property at the end of its useful life. (2) For appraisal purposes, the value imputable to a house, structure, or object if it were to be moved to another location.

sample – A defined group within the whole that appraisers work with when analyzing statistical data.

sandwich lease – A lease agreement in which a tenant sublets the property to another person, thus creating a sublessor-sublessee relationship.

Santa Fe style – A housing style with thick, earth-colored adobe walls and a flat roof with rounded parapets. Windows and heavy wooden doors are set into deep openings. The roof has red clay tile accents, and the enclosed patios add a Spanish influence.

sash – Wood or metal frames containing one or more window panes.

satellite office – Small office used for maintaining corporate management offices off-site.

satisfaction – The performance of the terms of an obligation.

saturation – In marketing, saturation occurs when a product is widely distributed in the market area as the result of widespread competition to market and sell the same product (supply exceeds demand).

saturation zone – The area below the water table.

savings and loan association (S&L) – A lending institution created as a mutual organization or as a stock institution . Deposits are insured by FDIC's Deposit Insurance Fund.

saw-tooth roof – A series of single-pitched roofs, resembling the sharp edge of a saw. Usually used in factories, this roof contains windows in each facing to allow maximum lighting. Not used in modern construction.

scab – A gusset plate or other flat brace used for bolting, nailing, screwing, or otherwise connecting two framing components.

scarcity – Less availability of a commodity in the marketplace resulting in increased value when demand exceeds supply.

scattered-site rentals – Rentals that are more time consuming and costly to manage because they are owned by different investors and spread over a large geographic area.

scenic easement – An easement created to preserve a property in its natural state and prevent its development.

scheduled gross income (SGI) – All of the income a property is scheduled to produce.

scheduled rent – Rent paid by agreement between lessor and lessee. Also called contract rent.

schematics – Preliminary drawings and sketches by an architect, such as site plans and elevations.

scholarly voice – Learning to think and write clearly using specific, concise, and polished language like a scholar.

SCI – The mnemonic for three approaches to value: Sales comparison approach, Cost approach, and Income approach.

SCOPE OF WORK RULE – The SCOPE OF WORK RULE requires the appraiser to do all the analysis necessary to complete the appraisal assignment and provide reliable and credible results. The SCOPE OF WORK RULE requires the appraiser to identify the problem to be solved (Problem Identification), determine and perform the scope of work necessary to develop credible assignment results (Scope of Work Acceptability), and disclose the scope of work in the report (Disclosure Obligations).

S corporation – A corporation that operates like a corporation, but is treated like a partnership for tax purposes.

scrap value – The value imputable to components of a structure, such as lumber, copper, roofing materials, or bricks, if they are removed from the existing premises for use elsewhere.

scrubber – An air pollution control device used to remove airborne particulates and water-soluble vapors and gases from gaseous emissions. The process used may be wet scrubbing or dry scrubbing.

seasonal energy efficiency ratio (SEER) – SEER measures the average cooling efficiency over the entire cooling season for an air conditioner or heat pump. The higher this number the better.

second deed of trust – A junior, subordinate deed of trust because it is recorded after a first deed of trust.

secondary financing – A loan that is subordinate to a primary loan and cannot be satisfied until the primary loan is paid. Most governmental loan programs permit secondary financing, but place restrictions on its use.

secondary mortgage market – The financial market in which primary mortgage lenders sell the mortgages they make to obtain more funds, in order to originate more loans. This process provides liquidity for lenders.

second empire style – Symmetrical, boxy, vertical two-to-three story houses. Typical ornamentation includes paired columns and elaborate wrought iron along the rooftop, and a high, boxy mansard roof with a trapezoid shape.

secondhand data – Data from reliable sources such as title companies, multiple listing services, and appraiser's files.

second mortgage – A junior, subordinate mortgage because it is recorded after a first mortgage.

secret profit – Undisclosed profit made by a broker at his or her principal's expense.

section – An area of land, as used in the Public Land Survey System of land description, that is one square mile, 640 acres, or 1/36 of a township.

Section 8 program – One program of the U.S. Department of Housing and Urban Development (HUD). The Section 8 program subsidizes the rent of low- and moderate-income tenants.

securitization – The pooling of traditional bank assets, loans, mortgages, or other non-tradeable financial transactions for the purpose of converting them into tradeable securities.

security – Collateral; property pledged or hypothecated to secure performance of an obligation.

security agreement – A document commonly used to secure a loan on personal property.

security deposit – Refundable deposit of money made to assure performance of an obligation.

security instrument – A legal document, given by the borrower to the lender, pledging the title of the property to the lender as collateral for the loan.

security interest – The interest of a creditor (lender) in the property of a debtor (borrower).

SEER – *See* seasonal energy efficiency ratio.

seisin – The possession of land under a claim of freehold.

sealed combustion – A combustion appliance, such as a furnace, water heater, or fireplace, acquires all air for combustion though a dedicated sealed passage from the outside; combustion occurs in a sealed combustion chamber, and all combustion products are vented to the outside through a separate dedicated sealed vent.

Self-Contained Appraisal Report – Contains the most detailed information. Self-contained means that everything the user of the report needs to understand the appraisal results is contained within the report.

self insurance – Another phrase for risk retention.

seller's market – The market condition that exists when a seller is in a more commanding position than a buyer and controls the price and terms of a sale. This occurs when market demand exceeds supply.

seller's statement – A record of the financial proceeds the sellers will receive, upon the closing of a real estate transaction.

selling price – The actual price that a buyer pays for a property.

semiannual – Twice per year, at six month intervals.

semimonthly – Twice a month.

senior loan – A real estate loan that has first priority.

sentimental value – The value imputable to a property because of a close personal interest or relationship by the owner or potential owner.

separate property – Property owned by a married person in his or her own right outside of the community interest including property acquired by the spouse before marriage or by gift or inheritance.

septic system – An underground, self-contained sewage treatment system that has a storage tank where waste is decomposed through bacterial action. Septic systems are usually used in rural areas without sanitary sewer systems.

septic tank – A watertight sewage settling tank, designed to accommodate liquid and solid waste, which must be at least five feet away from the improvements.

server – A powerful computer that can store and handle requests for data, email, file transfers, and other network services from other computers.

service entrance – Electric service components from the point of utility company supply to the service equipment or service panel.

service income – Income derived from laundry facilities, vending machines, video/DVD/CD rentals, and selling utility services to tenants.

service of process – The official act of notifying a defendant of an upcoming lawsuit, and the delivery of his or her summons. Service is usually performed by the sheriff.

servicing fee/rate – The fee earned by a servicer for administering a loan for an investor, usually expressed as a percentage of the unpaid principal balance of the loan and deducted from the monthly mortgage payment.

servicing loans – Supervising and administering a loan after it has been made. This involves such things as collecting the payments, keeping accounting records, computing the interest and principal, foreclosure of defaulted loans, and so on.

servient tenement – The property that is burdened by an easement.

setback – The distance a building must be set back from the property line, street, or curb; usually determined by local building codes.

settlement – Process by which ownership of real property or title to the property is passed from seller to buyer.

settlor – One who creates a trust.

severalty – Ownership of real property by one person or entity.

severance damage – In eminent domain actions, the damage to the remainder of a property resulting from a part take of the whole property and the construction of the improvements as proposed.

sewage system – Pipelines or conduits, pumping stations, force mains, and all other structures, devices, and facilities used for collecting or conducting wastes to a point for treatment or disposal.

sewer – A channel or conduit that carries wastewater and storm water runoff from the source to a treatment plant or receiving stream.

SFR – *See* single-family residence.

SGI – *See* scheduled gross income.

shading coefficient (SC) – The amount by which the window reduces heat gain. The lower the shading coefficient, the less solar heat is admitted.

shake – A thick wooden shingle, hand cut from logs, used for roofing or siding.

shared appreciation mortgage (SAM) – A mortgage in which the lender and borrower agree to share a certain percentage of the increase in market value of the property.

shed roof – This roof has a streamlined shape, which is one-half of a gable roof, and is popular for Contemporary styles.

shed style – This housing style is modern and is characterized by its asymmetrical style and multiple roofs sloping in different directions.

shell – Building being leased that has walls, concrete floor, lighting, HVAC, standard plumbing, bathrooms, and electrical outlets.

sheriff's deed – A deed given to a buyer when property is sold through court action, in order to satisfy a judgment for money or foreclosure of a mortgage.

Sherman Antitrust Act – Federal law created to protect consumers from price fixing.

shopping center – A classification of retail stores, characterized by off-street parking and clusters of stores, subject to a uniform development plan. A careful analysis should be made to determine the proper merchant mix for maximum profitability.

shoreline – The intersection of the land with the water (mean high water line).

shoring – The use of timbers to prevent the sliding of earth at a construction site.

short-lived – Structural components that are expected to be replaced or repaired on a consistent basis, throughout the life of the structure.

short sale – A sale of encumbered real property that produces less money than is owed to the lender. The lender essentially decides to accept a loss and release the property from the mortgage or deed of trust, allowing the property to be sold free and clear. This is an alternative to foreclosure.

short-term fluctuations – Changes in business and economic activity that occur within the year.

sick building syndrome (SBS) – The EPA defines SBS as situations in which building occupants experience acute health and/or comfort effects that appear to be linked to time spent in a particular building, but where no specific illness or cause can be identified. The complaints may be localized in a particular room or zone, or may be spread throughout the building. Occupants experience relief of symptoms shortly after leaving the building.

sidelights – Tall, narrow windows that flank the entry door. These windows are characteristic of Greek Revival and are found in Neo-Eclectic houses.

side yard setback – The distance a building must be set back from the lot line at the side of the property.

siding – Any variety of materials used as final covering on the exterior of a house. Materials such as aluminum, wood, or vinyl siding eliminate the need for repeated painting.

signature – A mark or name upon a document or instrument, in order to make it valid. In real estate, to be acceptable for recordation, a signature generally must be in black ink and be one's full legal name.

significant digits – Those that go from the first numeral on the left over to the last numeral on the right that is not a zero.

signs – Any printed displays used to advertise the availability of real estate. The REALTOR® Code of Ethics states that signs should be placed on listed property only with the consent of the owner.

sill (mud sill) – The lowest horizontal member of the house frame, which rests on top of the foundation wall and forms a base for the studs. It is used to connect the exterior wall studs and floor joists. The term can also refer to the lowest horizontal member in the frame for a window or door.

simple interest – Interest computed on the principal amount of a loan only, as distinguished from compound interest.

single agency – The representation of only one party in a real estate transaction.

single-family residence (SFR) – A building that is designed for, and occupied by, one family.

single net lease – An arrangement whereby the tenant pays the rent, plus utilities, property taxes, and any special assessments on the property.

single-glazed window – A window frame with only one layer of glass offering very little insulating value, which accounts for considerable heat loss or gain.

single-hung windows – The bottom portion of the window slides up; commonly found in Ranch and modern style houses.

sinking fund – A fund set aside from the income derived from property, which, with accrued interest, will eventually pay for replacement of the improvements.

site – Land that has been prepared for use with grading, utilities, and access.

site assessment – Environmental analysis conducted as a stage in planning to assess a variety of measures from soils, topography, hydrology, environmental amenities such as wetlands, wind direction, solar orientation, animal and plant habitat, connections to community, etc.

situs – The position, situation, or location of a piece of land in a neighborhood.

six functions of $1 – Compound interest factors that are used in finance to adjust present or future payments for the time value of money.

skylight – A roof window that allows natural light into a room. Some skylights open and close to provide ventilation.

skyscraper – Tall, steel-framed structures that are used for offices, residences, or hotels.

slab-on-grade – A type of foundation where the structure sits directly on the ground. Monolithic slabs, floating slabs, screeded slabs, and post-tensioned slabs are all types of slab-on-grade foundations.

slander of title – False unjustified statements regarding another person's title to property.

slogan – A motto expressing the goals or nature of a business.

slope – (1) The degree of roof incline, expressed as the ratio of the rise, in inches, to the run, in feet. (2) The degree to which a piece of land deviates from level. It may be expressed in degrees of an angle, as a ratio of vertical rise to horizontal run, or as a decimal.

sludge – A semi-solid residue from any of a number of air or water treatment processes.

sludge composting – Process of composting treated municipal sewage waste with organic matter for use as a soil amendment.

SMA – *See* Systems Maintenance Administrator.

small wind turbine – Wind turbine with 100 kilowatts or less of rated power to meet the demands of a home, farm, or small business.

smart building – A type of building that incorporates new technologies and systems in its structural aspects. At the time of construction, builders incorporate energy-saving and technology-ready systems to reduce operating costs and benefit the environment.

smart grid – Advanced electricity transmission and distribution network (grid) that utilizes digital information and controls to improve reliability, security, and efficiency.

smart growth – Reconciling the needs of development with the quality of life. Smart growth focuses on revitalizing older suburbs and older city centers.

smart meter – Advanced electricity meter that utilizes sensors to provide information on power consumption and price.

SMART objectives – Objectives should be specific, measurable, attainable, relevant, and timely.

smart sprinkler controller – A water sprinkler control system that automatically adjusts the level of lawn watering based on weather and seasonal conditions.

smog – Air pollutants — dust, smoke, factory emissions and vehicle exhausts — usually centered on urban areas. Typical chemical components of smog include ozone, sulfur dioxide, nitrogen dioxide, and carbon monoxide.

snob zoning – Zoning used to reduce residential density, by requiring large building lots.

sodium silicate – A liquid used in asbestos encapsulation, concrete and mortar waterproofing, and high-temperature insulations (also called water glass). This substance is nontoxic when cured but caustic when wet.

soffit – The external area under the roof overhang, or the covering over the space under the eaves of a structure, frequently with an opening for attic ventilation.

softscape – The planting and maintenance of vegetation around a house to prevent erosion and improve its aesthetic appearance.

soil – The upper layer of ground that supports plant life.

soil pipe – A pipe that carries waste from the house to the main sewer line.

solar access – Access to the sun's rays by, for instance, restricting the location of shade trees or laying out the building so as to maximize the usefulness of solar energy.

solar altitude – In solar analysis, the vertical angular distance of a point in the sky above the horizon. Altitude is measured positively from the horizon to the zenith, from 0 to 90 degrees.

solar array – A number of solar modules connected together and appropriately mounted so as to provide a single substantial electrical output from the solar radiation falling on them.

solar azimuth – In solar analysis, the horizontal angular distance between the vertical plane containing a point in the sky (usually the sun) and true south.

solar collector – Device which uses the sun's energy to perform some kind of mechanical advantage which would normally be supplied by a non-renewable energy source. Photovoltaic panels (PVs) which convert the sun's energy directly into electricity, and solar hot water panels, which heat pre-heat water before sending it into a hot water heater are two examples.

solar easement – Easement for the purpose of receiving sunlight across real property of another for any solar energy system.

solar energy – Energy received from the sun in the form of electromagnetic radiation in the wavelength region from 0.3 to 2.7 microns. This includes all visible light as well as some ultraviolet and infrared radiation.

solar heat gain coefficient (SHGC) – The measure of the amount of solar energy that passes through the window.

solar power – Converting sunlight into electricity.

solar radiation – The full spectrum of electromagnetic energy including visible light from the sun. When solar radiation strikes a solid surface or a transparent medium such as air or glass, some of the energy is absorbed and converted into heat energy, some is reflected, and some is transmitted. All three of these effects are important for effective passive solar design.

Soldier's and Sailor's Relief Act – A federal law designed to protect persons in the military service from loss of property when their ability to make the payment has been affected by their entering military service.

sole plate – A horizontal board, usually 2" x 4", on which wall and partition studs rest.

sole proprietorship – A business owned and operated by one person.

solid waste – Non-liquid, non-soluble materials ranging from municipal garbage to industrial wastes that contain complex and sometimes hazardous substances. Solid wastes also include sewage sludge, agricultural refuse, demolition wastes, and mining residues.

SOP – *See* standard operating procedure.

space loss factor – The difference between the number of square feet (SF) in the lease and the actual measurable square footage within the demising walls.

spalling – The chipping, scarring, crumbling, or splitting of concrete, that is often the result of the rusting of the reinforcing steel in the concrete.

span – The horizontal distance from eaves to eaves.

Spanish architecture – An architectural style that copies the houses of Spain and Mexico. The homes have a courtyard, tiled roof, and are constructed of adobe or stucco.

Spanish colonial revival style – Houses that are rectangular, symmetrical, and two stories. They have low-pitched gable roofs with ceramic tiles, eaves with little or no overhang, stucco walls, wrought iron, and windows and doorways with round arches.

special agent – A person employed to perform a specific task.

special assessment – Any tax or special charge levied against real property for specific, local public improvements.

Special Information Booklet – When a potential homebuyer applies for a mortgage loan, the lender must give the buyer a *Special Information Booklet*, which contains consumer information on various real estate settlement services.

special power of attorney – A written instrument, where a principal confers limited authority upon an agent to perform certain prescribed acts on behalf of the principal.

special purpose property – Properties with unique and limited purposes within a community, such as mini-storage facilities, churches, and schools, making it difficult to convert to other uses.

special-use permit – *See* conditional-use permit.

specific lien – A lien placed against a certain property, such as a mechanic's lien, mortgage, deed of trust, attachment, property tax lien, or lis pendens.

specific market – For real estate, the specific markets are residential property and commercial property.

specific performance – A court action brought about by one party to force the other (breaching) party to fulfill the conditions of the contract.

special flood hazard area – Flood-prone area identified by FEMA. For appraisals, if the subject property is within a flood hazard zone, it needs to be noted in the appraisal report.

specific plan – A particular development site or area of the general plan.

spectrophotometer – An instrument for measuring the transmittance and reflectance of surfaces and media as a function of wavelength.

sphere of influence – A group of individuals whom you already know, who may choose to give you their business, or may refer you to someone who is in need of your services.

spite fence – Fence exceeding 10 feet in height erected for the purpose of annoying a neighbor.

split financing – A method of real estate financing in which land and improvements are financed separately. Often used by developers to obtain more financing than would be available with conventional financing.

split-fee financing – Separate financing for land and improvements.

split-level ranch style – This housing style, also known as the raised ranch style, usually has three levels at varying heights. These houses are asymmetrical, with a rectangular, L-shaped, or U-shaped design.

split-run ad – Two ads, one directory, separate RCF phone number for each ad type. Each ad is designed differently, as a method of testing the number of responses to each type of ad. The phone company sends a list to the advertiser each month of the number of calls resulting from each ad.

spot zoning – Zoning changed for a single parcel without considering the larger planning context.

square-foot method – A method for calculating reproduction or replacement cost by multiplying the cost per square foot by the building's area in square feet. The most common method used by appraisers and real estate agents to estimate the cost of construction.

stack effect – The upward flow of warm air, creating a positive pressure area at the top of a building and negative pressure at the bottom.

staging – Preparing a home for maximum appeal to buyers.

standard depth – Generally, the most typical lot depth in the neighborhood.

standard deviation – A measure of the extent of variability in a sample, that is, whether the observations are clustered near the mean or scattered throughout the range. Standard deviation is calculated by taking the square root of the sum of the squared differences between each observation and the mean of all observations, divided by the total number of observations.

standard operating procedure (SOP) – A procedures that has been established to increase efficiency, whenever specified, regularly occurring events take place.

standard policy – A policy of title insurance covering only matters of record. It does not cover against clouds that are off record, such as encroachments, unrecorded easements, and boundary-line discrepancies.

Standards – There are ten Standards within USPAP, and each Standard includes a series of Standards Rules.

Standards Rules – A series of rules within USPAP that specify what the appraiser must do.

standard subdivision – A land division with no common or mutual rights of either ownership or use among the owners of the parcels created by the division.

standby commitment – A letter from a lender that promises to fund a long-term loan, in order to buy out (or take out) the construction lender, once the building is successfully completed.

standby losses – The loss of heat by conduction through the walls of the storage water tank and through the first few feet of water pipes. To reduce standby losses, insulate the tank, the first two feet of the cold-water inlet pipe, and the first three feet of the hot water outlet pipe.

stare decisis – The legal doctrine that past decisions of courts stand as precedents for future decisions.

startup budget – Budget prepared to determine the costs of starting the business.

startup costs – One time costs or expenses for your business— advertising, computer equipment, etc.

statement of cash flow – Cash flow is the net spendable dollars remaining after paying all operating expenses. This report shows changes in the cash position of the company over a specific period.

Statement of Information – A brief statement of facts relied on by title insurers to assist in the proper identification of persons.

Statements on Appraisal Standards – Part of USPAP, these statements clarify, interpret, explain, or elaborate on a Rule or Standard.

statistic – A sample.

statistical significance – Degree to which a value is greater or smaller than is expected by chance.

statistics – The science of collecting, classifying, and interpreting information based on the number of things.

satus – The legal position of an individual; i.e., adult, minor, etc.

statute – A law.

statute of frauds – A state law that requires certain contracts to be in writing and signed, in order to be valid and enforceable and also to prevent fraud in the sale of land or an interest in land.

statute of limitations – A statute limiting the period of time during which legal action may be taken on a certain issue. The statute attempts to protect against outdated claims, about which a true and just outcome may be difficult to determine.

statutory – Regarding laws created by the enactment of legislation, as opposed to law created by court decisions.

stop notice – A notice given a construction lender by an unpaid contributor to a work of improvement for the purpose of intercepting loan funds.

straight note – A promissory note calling for payment of principal in one sum rather than in installments.

statutory disclosures – Disclosures that are required by law.

statutory redemption period – A limited period of time in which a debtor, whose property has been foreclosed upon and sold, may repay the debt and regain his or her property.

steering – The illegal practice of directing people to specific locations for housing accommodations, depriving them of choice. Steering is a violation of fair housing laws.

step-up basis – For income tax purposes. For capital gains calculations, the taxable gain is the difference between the basis of the property and the sales price. The step-up basis is the new value for a property, at fair market value, at the time of death of a co-owner, not at the time the property was purchased. For example, in community property, upon the death of one spouse, the value of the property becomes market value. Later, when the property is sold, the taxable gain for the entire property is the difference between the sales price and the new market value of the property.

step-up lease – Sometimes called a graduated lease. Usually, a long-term lease with smaller payments in the beginning that is stepped-up to larger payments, upon the occurrence of a certain event or passage of a period of time.

stigmatized property – Property that buyers or tenants may avoid, for reasons which are unrelated to its physical conditions or features. Also known as psychologically impacted property.

stock cooperative – A common interest development (CID) in which a corporation or trust holds title to the residential property and sells rights of tenancy, through the sale of stock. Stockholders in the corporation receive the right of exclusive occupancy of one of the units. Right of occupancy must be transferred with the stock.

stocks – Shares of ownership in a company or corporation.

storage capacity – The gallons of hot water a storage water heater can hold in the storage tank.

storm window – An extra window on the outside of an existing window, as additional protection against cold weather.

straight lease – Lease agreement in which rent is a fixed amount that stays the same over the entire lease term.

straight note – A promissory note in which payments of interest only are made periodically during the term of the note, with the principal payment due in one lump sum at maturity.

straight-line depreciation – A method of depreciation under which property is depreciated at a constant rate, throughout its estimated useful life.

straw man – One who purchases property for another, in order to conceal the identity of the true purchaser.

strip center – A small retail center located in the suburbs, containing half-a-dozen to a dozen stores of various kinds.

stucco – A wet plaster finish made of cement, sand, and lime, specifically designed for exterior use. Stucco is very popular as an outside wall surface in warm, dry areas.

studio apartment – Small self-contained, low rental apartment. Also known as a bachelor or efficiency apartment.

studs – In wall framing, the vertical members to which horizontal pieces are attached. Studs are placed 16 to 24 inches apart and serve as the main support for the roof and/ or the second floor.

subagent – A broker delegated by the listing agent (if authorized by the seller) who represents the seller in finding a buyer for the listed property.

subdivision – The division of land into separate parcels.

subdivision development method – A method of valuing land used for subdivision development. It relies on accurate forecasting of market demand, including both forecast absorption (the rate at which properties will sell) and projected gross sales (total income that the project will produce). Also called the land development method.

subdivision system – Also known as a recorded map system. *See* lot, block, and tract system.

subfloor – A wood floor, typically unfinished plywood, which is attached to a room's floor joists and to which the finished floor is attached.

subjacent support – Absolute right of the property owner to have his or her land supported from beneath its surface.

subjective-probability – Individual personal judgment about how likely a particular event is to occur. Also known as opinion probability.

subjective-value – Value given for personal reasons.

subject property – The property that is being appraised.

subject to clause – A buyer takes over existing loan payments or an encumbrance but does not assume personal liability therefore.

sublease – A lease given by a lessee that transfers less than the entire leasehold interest, with the original lessee being primarily liable for the rental agreement.

sublessee – New person who has possession of a leased property.

sublessor – The original tenant of a leased property. They are still primarily liable for paying the rent to the owner for the sublease.

subletting – The process by which an original tenant gives up use or possession of all or part of the property to another, but receives payment from the sub-lessee and remains fully responsible to the landlord for all lease payments.

submarket – Geographic, economic, or specialized subdivision of a specific market.

subordinate – To make inferior in priority.

subordinate lien – A lien on a property, whose priority is inferior to another lien on the same property.

subordination agreement – An agreement changing the priority of interests.

subordination clause – A clause in a contract, in which the holder of a deed of trust permits a subsequent loan to take priority.

subpoena – A written order to appear in court.

subprime loans – Loans that do not meet the borrower credit requirements of Fannie Mae and Freddie Mac. Also known as B and C paper loans.

subrogate – To substitute one person in place of another with reference to an obligation.

substitution – The appointment of a person to act in the place and stead of another.

substitution of liability (novation) – The substitution by agreement of a new obligation for an existing one. Also known as novation.

substructure – In construction, the structural support materials of a building, usually located underground. Refers to all the below grade improvements. Examples include piers, footings, beams, and slabs.

subsurface rights – Rights to the natural resources, such as minerals, oil, and gas below the surface.

suburban hotels – Hotels on the outskirts of the downtown district.

suburbs – The area within reasonable driving distance of a city's downtown.

succession – The legal transfer of a person's interest in real and personal property to his or her named heirs or beneficiaries, under the laws of descent.

sulphur dioxide – A colorless, irritating gas that is a primary cause of acid rain. It is a by-product of coal combustion.

Summary Appraisal Report – The most commonly used appraisal report option. It fulfills the minimum requirements for lenders to process their loans.

summation – A method of determining the capitalization rate in which various risk factors are weighted and combined.

summons – Written request that establishes the plaintiff's position in filing a complaint and calls for the defendant to answer or appear in court.

superadequacy – A type of functional obsolescence caused by a structural component that is too large or of a higher quality than that which is needed to obtain the highest and best use of the property. An item whose cost exceeds its value. Also called an over-improvement.

superfund – Officially known as the Comprehensive Environmental Response, Compensation and Liability Act (CERCLA), passed by Congress in 1980. It established two trust funds to help finance the cleanup of properties that have been impacted by the release of hazardous wastes and substances.

superior lien – A lien on real property, whose priority is superior to another claim on the same property.

superstructure – Refers to all the above-grade improvements.

superwindows – Double or triple-glazed window sandwiches which contain a center sheet of coated mylar low-emissivity film and are filled with argon or krypton gas.

supply – The total amount of a given type of property for sale or lease, at various prices, at any given point in time.

supply air – The total quantity of air supplied to a space of a building for thermal conditioning and ventilation. Typically, supply air consists of a mixture of return air and outdoor air that is appropriately filtered and conditioned.

supply and demand – A basic economic principle in which the greater the supply of an item, the lower its value. When an item is scarce in relation to demand, the value is high. The value of a property will increase as demand increases, and/or supply decreases.

surety – One who guarantees the performance of an obligation by another.

surface rights – The rights to use the surface of land, including the right to drill or mine through the surface when subsurface rights are involved.

surface water – Open expanses of water, such as rivers, lakes, reservoirs, ponds, streams, seas, estuaries, wetlands, springs, and wells.

surrender – When a tenant voluntarily gives up a lease, before the expiration of its term.

survey – The process by which a parcel of land is measured and its area is ascertained.

suspend – Temporarily make ineffective. A real estate license may be suspended for violation of the licensing law.

sustainable agriculture – Farming methods that conserve the environment by minimizing damage to soil, water sources, species habitat, and other natural resources.

sustainable development – Development that meets the needs of the present without compromising the ability of future generations to meet their own needs.

sustainably-sourced materials – Materials that are acquired in an environmentally sound manner emphasizing efficient and appropriate use of natural resources.

sweat equity – The value added to a property due to physical work done by the owner, such as do-it-yourself improvements.

swing loan – A short-term loan used to enable the purchaser of a new property to buy that property on the strength of the equity from the property the purchaser is selling. Also known as a bridge loan.

SWOT Analysis – Developed in the 1960s, by Albert Humphrey of Stanford University, it is a simple way to analyze a company's Strengths, Weaknesses, Opportunities, and Threats.

syndicate – A pooling arrangement or association of persons investing in real property by buying shares in an organization.

system – A combination of interacting or interdependent components, assembled to carry out one or more functions.

system capacity – System capacity is a measurement of the total amount of heat or cooling a furnace, heat pump, or air conditioner can produce in one hour.

Systems Maintenance Administrator (SMA) – A property management designation offered by the Building Owners and Managers Institute (BOMI), with emphasis on supervision of systems and personnel.

Systems Maintenance Technician (SMT) – A property management designation offered by the Building Owners and Managers Institute (BOMI), with emphasis on the technical maintenance of various systems, such as heating and air conditioning.

T

1031 exchange – As permitted in the Internal Revenue Code, exchanges of like-kind properties that postpone the payment of taxes on capital gains. The properties must be held for business use or as an investment.

takeout loan – Long-term, permanent loan to replace a short-term interim construction loan.

takeover – Property management company takes over an owner's property.

tandem plan – An investment plan that provides low-interest rate mortgages to low-income, qualified buyers. The Federal National Mortgage Association (FNMA) purchases low interest rate mortgages at a discount from the Government National Mortgage Association (GNMA).

tangible property – Physical items, such as equipment, land, buildings, and minerals.

tankless water heater – A water heater that heats water before it is directly distributed for end use as required. Tankless water heaters include demand water heaters and tankless coil water heaters.

target market – Group of people who are most likely to seek your services or buy your product.

target marketing – Marketing to a precise group of consumers.

tax and insurance participation clause – Lease clause that requires the tenant to pay rent, plus a pro rata share of both the property taxes and the insurance.

tax deed – A deed given to a successful bidder following a sale necessitated by the non-payment of real property taxes.

tax-deferred exchange – *See* 1031 exchange.

tax delinquent property – Property that has unpaid taxes.

tax-exempt bonds – Bonds issued to finance public or private improvements. The interest derived from the bonds may be exempt from federal, state, and local income taxes.

tax-free gifts – Gifts that are free from federal gift taxes.

tax increment financing – Financing established to stimulate community growth and generate increased tax revenue. State and local industrial development boards arrange the financing.

tax lien – A lien placed on property when income or property taxes are not paid. A tax lien remains with the property until the taxes are paid, even if the property is conveyed to another person.

Tax Relief Act of 1997 – A law enacted in 1997 that decreased the capital gains tax rate, thereby decreasing the high taxes charged to people after selling their investment or personal property.

tax roll – A list of all taxable property, showing the assessed value of each parcel. The tax roll establishes the tax base. Also called an assessment roll.

tax sale – Forced sale of real property by the county to satisfy delinquent taxes.

tax shelter – A strategy or technique of reducing income tax liability.

temperature – The degree of hotness or coldness.

tenancy – (1) The interest of a person holding property by any right or title. (2) A mode or method of ownership or holding title to property.

tenancy at sufferance – The interest of a tenant has when he or she continues to occupy the property after the expiration of a lease.

tenancy at will – A written or oral agreement, allowing a tenant to use or occupy property with the permission of the owner. The term of the tenancy is unspecified and the tenant may leave at any time, or at the request of the owner.

tenancy by the entirety – A special co-ownership by a husband and wife, which is characterized by the inability of one spouse alone to convey or encumber and by the incident of survivorship.

tenancy for life – A life estate.

tenancy for years – A tenancy created by a lease for a fixed period of time. If the tenancy is for more than one year, the agreement must be in writing according to the statute of frauds in most states.

tenancy in common – A form of co-ownership of property by two or more persons, each of whom has an undivided interest, without the right of survivorship.

tenancy in partnership – Ownership by two or more persons, who form a partnership for business purposes.

tenancy in severalty – Ownership of property by one person alone.

tenant – The person who possesses or occupies a property under a tenancy agreement.

tenant mix – The composition of tenants and the range of goods and services they provide.

tenant mix report – Used primarily for commercial properties.

tender – An unconditional offer to pay a debt or to perform an obligation.

tenement – Traditionally, tenement refers to real property rights, which pass with the land, such as buildings and improvements. In modern times, tenement may refer to run-down apartment buildings in urban areas.

term – The time duration of a lease or of a loan also, any provision of a contract or lease.

term loan – A loan for a specific period of time, usually two to ten years, repaid by regular installments, with the entire principal amount due at the end of the term.

termination of listing – The cancellation of a broker-principal contract.

terminus – The ending point in a metes and bounds survey that returns to the point of beginning. By terminating the boundary line at the point of beginning, the surveyed land area is enclosed.

termite – Ant-like insect, which feeds on wood and is highly destructive to wood surfaces.

termite inspection – A visual inspection of a property for the presence of termites. A licensed exterminator usually performs the inspection. Buyers may include a special condition in a sales contract that requires the sellers to provide a clean termite report.

termite report – A report of an inspection for wood-destroying pests by a person licensed by the state.

termite shield – A shield, usually of non-corrodible metal, placed on top of the foundation wall or around pipes to prevent passage of termites.

terrazzo – Flooring made by embedding small pieces of marble or granite into cement and polishing to a high gloss.

territorial style – A housing style that is a more angular, with square corners. In addition, the windows of are framed with straight, unpainted, wooden moldings, and brick detailing is present in the parapets.

testament – True declaration of a person's last will.

testamentary trust – A trust created by the last will and testament of a decedent.

testate – A person who dies leaving a valid will.

testator/testatrix – A person who has made a will.

The Appraisal Foundation – An entity created by the appraisal profession to regulate its own industry. Empowered by the Financial Institutions Reform, Recovery, and Enforcement Act of 1989 to set minimum standards and qualifications for performing appraisals in federally related financial transactions.

therm – The basic unit for measuring natural gas use.

thermal boundary – The border between conditioned and unconditioned space where insulation should be placed.

thermal break – A material that does not transmit heat well, such as plastic, sandwiched inside the metal parts of the frame. This reduces the heat being transferred through the frame. Thermal breaks can be used in the spacer between panes of glass in multi-pane windows as well as in the main body of the frame.

thermal energy – The vibration and movement of the atoms and molecules within substances.

thermal resistance (R) – An index of a material's resistance to heat flow. *See* R and RSI.

thermal window – An insulating window or two panes of glass with air between.

thermo-solar energy – Electricity generated from the heat of the sun, and not, as photovoltaic panels do, from sunlight.

thermostat – Temperature sensitive control device that signals a heating or cooling system to operate if the temperature in the building reaches a preset limit.

third party – A person who may be affected by the terms of an agreement, but who is not a party to the agreement.

three-day notice to pay or quit – The initial notice given to a tenant to begin the eviction process, in the event of non-payment of rent. The tenant must pay the amount owed, or vacate the property.

threshold – A strip of beveled wood or metal used above the finished floor under outside doors.

tidal power – The power available from the rise and fall of ocean tides.

tidelands – Lands that are covered and uncovered by the ebb and flow of the tide.

tier – A row of townships running east and west parallel to and north or south of a designated base line.

tight buildings – Buildings that are designed to let in minimal infiltration air in order to reduce heating and cooling energy costs. In actuality, buildings typically exhibit leakage that is on the same order as required ventilation; however, this leakage is not well distributed and cannot serve as a substitute for proper ventilation.

tight money – An economic situation in which the supply of money is limited, and the demand for money is high, as evidenced by high interest rates.

time – The duration of a loan.

time adjustment – A term usually applied to adjustments made because of changing market conditions (not merely the passage of time).

time is of the essence clause – A clause in a contract that emphasizes punctual performance as an essential requirement of the contract.

time management plan – The written plan scheduling all of the required activities necessary to reach goals.

time value of money – The financial principle that a dollar in the present is worth more than a promised dollar in the future because of the present dollar's interest earning capability.

timely manner – *See* time is of the essence clause.

time-price differential – The difference between the purchase price of a property and the higher total price the same property would cost if purchased on an installment basis. Under the Truth-in-Lending laws, lenders must disclose the time-price differential in any kind of installment contract.

timeshare – A specialized type of resort property, in which a buyer can purchase the exclusive right to occupy a unit for a specified period each year.

TIMMUR – The mnemonic for fixed and variable operating expenses of real property: Taxes, Insurance, Management, Maintenance, Utilities, and Reserves. Fixed expenses include property taxes, insurance, and utilities. Variable expenses include management and maintenance.

tinted glazing – Tinted glass and tinted window films reduce the amount of the sun's heat entering the building.

T-intersection lot – A lot that is fronted head-on by a street. The noise and glare from headlights may be detractors from this type of lot.

title – Evidence that the owner of land is in lawful possession of land, publicly recorded in the county where the property is located.

title company – Company that performs a title search on the property and issues a title policy for the lender and the purchaser, to ensure that there is a valid mortgage lien against the property and title is clear.

title exception – An item listed in a title insurance policy that is not covered by that policy.

title insurance – An insurance policy that is an assurance of indemnification for loss occasioned by defects in the title to real property or to an interest therein which is insured.

title plant – The storage facility of a title company, in which it has accumulated complete title records of properties in its area.

title policy – A contract indemnifying against loss resulting from a defect in the title to the interest or lien in real property insured.

title report – A report which discloses condition of the title, made by a title company preliminary to issuance of title insurance policy.

title search – The review of all the recorded transactions in the public record to discover any defects or clouds on a particular title, which may interfere with the transfer of the property.

title theory – The practice in some states of keeping the title to a mortgaged property with the lender until the loan is fully repaid. The borrower holds equitable title, or the right to use and possess the property.

to let, to demise – These phrases mean the same as to rent.

topography – Nature of the surface of land. Topography may be level, rolling, or mountainous.

topsoil – The uppermost soil horizon (layer), containing the highest amounts of organic material; depth varies greatly from region to region.

tort – Legal wrong (other than breach of contract) for which civil remedies for injuries or damages are provided.

townhouse – A type of row house, usually of the same or similar design with common side walls or with a very narrow space between adjacent side walls. Also known as a row house.

township – An area of land, as described by the Public Land Survey System. One township measures six miles-by-six miles (36 square miles) and contains 360 sections, each one being one mile square.

township lines – Used in the Public Land Survey System, imaginary lines drawn every six miles north and south of the base line to form a horizontal row or tier of townships.

toxic chemical – Any chemical listed in EPA rules as "Toxic Chemicals Subject to Section 313 of the Emergency Planning and Community Right-to-Know Act of 1986."

toxic cloud – Airborne plume of gases, vapors, fumes, or aerosols containing toxic materials.

toxic pollutants – Materials that cause death, disease, or birth defects in organisms that ingest or absorb them. The quantities and exposures necessary to cause these effects can vary widely.

toxic substance – A chemical or mixture that may present an unreasonable risk of injury to health or the environment.

Toxic Substances Control Act (TSCA) – Law passed by Congress in 1976, which allows the EPA to determine which substances are hazardous to the health of human beings or to the environment.

toxic waste – A waste that can produce injury if inhaled, swallowed, or absorbed through the skin.

tract – A large specified area of land in an unimproved state.

tract house – A house built as part of a subdivision, using the same building plan as many other homes in the subdivision, as opposed to a custom house, which is built to the specifications of the owner.

trade association – A voluntary, non-profit organization of independent and competing business units engaged in the same industry or trade, formed to help solve industry problems, promote progress, and enhance service.

trade fixture – An item of personal property affixed to leased property by the tenant, as a necessary part of business. It may be removed by the tenant, upon termination of the lease. Depending on several factors, fixtures may become real property.

trade name – *See* fictitious business name.

trade references – Names of vendors or merchants from whom supplies, materials, and products are regularly purchased by the tenant for a business operation.

trading on equity – The practice of agreeing to purchase a property and then assigning the purchase agreement to another buyer before the sale closes. The original purchaser turns a profit by selling the paper.

transaction coordinator – People at a brokerage who keep the files of each transaction or listing current and active.

transaction sides – Each real estate transaction has two sides (buyer side and seller side).

transfer tax – A state tax imposed on the transfer of property.

transferability – The ability to transfer ownership of an item from one person or entity to another.

transition – Change in use, such as farm to residential to commercial.

transit-oriented development – A mixed-use community within an average 2,000-foot walking distance of a transit stop and core commercial area that mixes residential, retail, office, open space, and public uses in a way that makes it convenient for residents and employees to travel by transit, foot, bike, etc.

transmission line – An electrical conductor/cable that carries electricity from a generator to other locations for distribution.

transom window – A window that is hinged at the top and opens into the room.

traverse window – A window popular in modern construction, having sashes that open horizontally, sliding on separate grooves past each other.

treasury bill (T-bill) – Short-term debt incurred by the U.S. Government. A promissory note issued by the U.S. Treasury with a maturity date of less than one year after the issue date. Unlike a bond or note, a bill does not pay a semi-annual, fixed-rate coupon, or interest payment.

treasury bond – A bond issued by the U.S. Treasury with a maturity date from five to ten years after the issue date.

treasury note – A promissory note issued by the U.S. Treasury with a maturity date from one to five years after the issue date.

trend – A change in the market in a consistent direction that occur over a long-term period.

trend analysis – Analysis that uses an arrangement of statistical data in accordance with its time of occurrence, usually over a period of years.

trespass – Intentional and unauthorized entry upon another's real property.

trim – The finish materials in a building, such as moldings applied around openings (window and door trim) or at the floor and ceiling of rooms (baseboard, cornice, and other moldings).

triple net lease – A lease requiring the tenant to pay rent as well as part or all of the taxes, insurance, repairs, and other ownership expenses. Also known as an absolute net lease.

trust – A legal arrangement, in which property or money is transferred from the grantor (trustor) to a trustee, to be held and managed by that person for the benefit of a third party, or beneficiary.

trust deed – *See* deed of trust.

trustee – Under a deed of trust, a trustee holds naked legal title to property as a neutral third party.

trustee's deed – A deed given to a buyer of real property at a trustee's sale (foreclosure).

trustee's sale – The forced sale of real property, by a lender, to satisfy a debt. The sale is the final step in the foreclosure process.

trust fund account – A bank account set up, generally by the broker, into which all the money involved in a real estate transaction is deposited. Also called an earnest money or escrow account.

trust funds – Money or other things of value received from people by a broker to be used in real estate transactions.

trustor – The borrower, under a deed of trust.

Truth-in-Lending Act (TILA) – The Truth-in-Lending Act (TILA), Title I of the Consumer Credit Protection Act, is aimed at promoting the informed use of consumer credit by requiring disclosures about its terms and costs. The Truth-in-Lending Act requires disclosure of the finance charge, the annual percentage rate, and certain other costs and terms of credit. This allows a consumer to compare the prices of credit from different sources.

TSCA – *See* Toxic Substances Control Act.

T-shaped – A T-shaped center has two linear groups of stores forming the shape of the letter T. Anchor stores are located at each of the three ends, with parking on all sides.

T-TIP – The mnemonic for the four unities of joint tenancy: Time, Title, Interest, and Possession.

turnkey projects – Investors purchase projects that are ready for occupancy.

turnover rate – The rate at which personnel enter and leave a company.

two-step mortgage – A hybrid loan, between a fixed-rate and adjustable-rate loan, in which a lower interest rate applies in the first five to seven years, and is then automatically adjusted one time for the remainder of the loan period.

type of construction – Building classification, based on a structure's basic frame, wall, and floor construction.

U

UCC – *See* Uniform Commercial Code.

umbrella insurance policy – Supplemental insurance that covers the amount of loss above the limits of a basic liability policy.

unbalanced improvement – An improvement that is not the highest and best use of the land. It may be an over-improvement or an under-improvement.

underground storage tank (UST) – A tank located all or partially underground that is designed to hold gasoline or other petroleum products or chemical solutions.

underimprovement – An improvement which, because of a deficiency in size or cost, is not the highest and best use of the site.

underwriting – The process of determining a borrower's financial strength, so that the loan amount and terms can be established.

undivided interest – Co-ownership of property, in which an interest is held under the same title by two or more people or entities, whether their rights are equal or unequal in value or quantity.

undue influence – Using unfair advantage to get agreement in acceptance of a contract.

unearned increment – An increase in value to real estate that comes about from forces outside the control of the owner(s), such as a favorable shift in population.

unemployment rate – The percentage of people classified as unemployed, as compared to the total labor force.

unenforceable contract – A contract that was valid when made, but either cannot be proved or will not be enforced by a court.

unfair and deceptive practices – Sales practices that do not necessarily involve deception, but are still considered illegal by the Federal Trade Commission (FTC). A sales practice is unfair if it offends public policy, is immoral, unethical, oppressive, unscrupulous, or causes injury to consumers. An example of an unfair and deceptive practice is pressuring buyers, using intimidation and scare tactics.

unfinished areas – The areas of a home that do not have flooring, insulation, etc., similar to the rest of the house.

Uniform Commercial Code (UCC) – A comprehensive code of laws that governs commercial transactions. These laws help promote interstate commerce by making it easier to transact business in various jurisdictions. The UCC is accepted by every state except Louisiana.

Uniform Residential Appraisal Report (URAR) – In appraisal, an example of a summary report, probably the most widely used appraisal form.

Uniform Standards of Professional Appraisal Practice (USPAP) – A set of Standards and ethics, originally developed by nine appraisal associations to guide members in the development and reporting of appraisals. It is currently developed, published, interpreted, and amended by the Appraisal Standards Board of the Appraisal Foundation.

unilateral contract – A contract where a party promises to perform, without expectation of performance by the other party.

unilateral instructions – The buyer signs one set of instructions and the seller signs another.

unilateral rescission – Legal action taken to repeal a contract by one party, when the other party has breached a contract.

unimproved – Not improved, as not used, tilled, cultivated, or built upon.

unit – (1) A single object. (2) A standard of measure by which other quantities are evaluated.

unit cost – The cost in money of a standard quantity (e.g., a square foot or a cubic yard) of a particular item.

unities – The essential elements of a common law joint tenancy. i.e., unities of time, title, interest, and possession.

unit in-place cost method – A method of calculating the reproduction cost of a building. The construction cost per square foot of each component part of the building (including material, labor, overhead, and builder's profit) is multiplied by the square footage of the component part. This is the most detailed method of estimating value. Also known as the segregated cost method.

． **unit of comparison adjustment** – A sales analysis tool, wherein the sales prices of the comparables are converted to price per physical or economic unit, that is found to be closely related to selling price or value. The value of the subject property is suggested by multiplying its number of units by the price per unit of comparison properties found to be typical or appropriate.

unit of measurement – The particular measurement being used. The two most commonly used are square foot (area) and cubic foot (volume).

unjust enrichment – The situation where a person has received and keeps money or goods that belongs to another. A lawsuit may be necessary to get back the property.

unlawful detainer action – The legal remedy for recovery of possession of real property.

unrecorded contract – A written document that creates a legal relationship between parties, but does not encumber any property. It is not publicly recorded.

up desk – Handling calls from prospects, while at the front desk or reception area. A passive lead-generation technique used to answer calls about ads or questions about the purchase or sale of property.

UPTEE – The mnemonic for the five ownership rights in the Bundle of Rights: **U**se, **P**ossess, **T**ransfer, **E**ncumber, and **E**njoy.

URAR – *See* Uniform Residential Appraisal Report.

uranium – A radioactive, silvery-white metallic element with the atomic number 92.

urban growth boundary – A boundary which identifies urban and urbanizable lands needed during a specified planning period to be planned and serviced to support urban development densities, and which separates these lands from rural lands.

urban mall – Multi-level shopping center covering one or more city blocks.

urban property – Property within a town or city.

urban renewal – A process in which older or substandard housing areas are improved and modernized, or demolished and replaced.

urban runoff – Storm water from city streets and adjacent domestic or commercial properties that may carry pollutants of various kinds into the sewer systems and/or receiving waters.

urban sprawl – The unplanned and often haphazard growth of an urban area into adjoining areas.

urbanization – The clustering of people around big city areas for work and living.

usable area – (1) That portion of the gross area of a site that can be built on or developed. Also known as useful area. (2) The area of the building is the actual occupied space by the tenant.

use clause – A clause in a lease designating which parties are authorized to use the property and for what purpose.

useful life – The time frame when an asset (e.g., a building) is expected to remain profitable to the owner. *See* economic life.

use value – The value of a property under a given use. Also known as value in use.

U-shaped – The U-shaped center has a group of linear stores forming the shape of the letter U. Anchors are found in the center or on the two ends, with parking inside the U.

USonian style – This housing style cost much less to build, because there are no basements or attics and very little ornamentation. These houses were built from the Depression until the mid 1950s, becoming the model for early tract housing.

USPAP – *See* Uniform Standards of Professional Appraisal Practice.

usufructuary right – Right that allows the reasonable use of property that belongs to another.

usury – The act of charging a rate of interest in excess of that permitted by law.

utility – The ability of a property to satisfy a need or desire, such as shelter, income, or amenities.

utility value – The usefulness of the property to its owner.

U-value – A measurement of heat flow through a square foot of window in an hour for every degree Fahrenheit difference in temperature across the window. The lower the U-value the more slowly the material transfers heat in and out of a structure.

V

vacancy factor – Ratio of the number of vacant units to the total number of units in a specific property or area. Also called vacancy rate.

vacancy loss – Loss of potential income, due to vacancies.

vacancy report – List of units that are unoccupied and available for lease. Units being remodeled or repaired (due to extensive damage) are not counted as vacant.

vacant land – Land or site that is unimproved and does not have any structures.

valid – Sufficient in law; effective.

valid contract – A contract with all required elements and is therefore binding and enforceable.

VA loan – A government-guaranteed home loan offered to veterans.

valuable consideration – Something of value such as money, property, or personal services. Each party to a contract must give up something of value to make the agreement binding.

valuation – The process of estimating market value.

valuation date – The date on which the opinion of value applies. The date of appraisal is not necessarily the same as the date the report is written. Also called the date of value or date of appraisal.

value – The present and future anticipated enjoyment or profit from the ownership of property. Also known as worth.

value conclusion – *See* final value estimate.

value in exchange – The value of property in the marketplace. *See* market value.

value in use – The subjective value of an item or object to a particular user. *See* use value.

value-oriented mall – Large shopping center characterized by low-end, discount, and outlet stores.

vanilla box – A leased space having only walls, concrete floor, lighting, HVAC, standard plumbing, bathrooms, and electrical outlets.

variable expenses – Operating expenses that change, depending on level of occupancy.

variable interest – Interest rates fluctuating up or down according to current cost of money.

variable rate mortgage (VRM) – A mortgage in which the interest rate varies, according to an agreed-upon index, resulting in a change in the borrower's monthly payments.

variance – An exception granted to existing zoning regulations to allow the building of a structure or a use that is not otherwise acceptable under current zoning law.

variance analysis – An analysis of reports, provided by software programs, which offers an explanation for variances from the budget.

variate – In statistics, a single random variable with a numerical value within a particular sample.

vendee – The buyer under a contract of sale (land contract).

vendor – The seller under a contract of sale (land contract).

Venn diagram – Relationship between numbers in a set or groups of objects that share something in common (although the commonality might be that they have nothing in common).

ventilation – The controlled movement of air into or out of a building, by circulation through a series of vents or an air conditioning system.

venture capital – Unsecured money used for investing. Due to the risks involved, venture capital usually commands the highest rate of return for its investment.

verification – (1) Sworn statement before a duly qualified officer to the correctness of an instrument's contents. (2) In appraisal, an inquiry into the circumstances surrounding and affecting a sale.

verification of deposit (VOD) – A form completed by the borrower's bank to confirm the status and balance of the borrower's bank accounts.

verification of employment (VOE) – A form completed by the borrower's employer to confirm the borrower's employment and employment history.

verify – Make sure information presented in the appraisal is correct.

vernacular style – vernacular buildings are seen as the opposite of whatever is academic, or high style. The traditional architecture of a region. Often times, traditional architecture is a result of response to the regional climate and land conditions.

vest – To give an immediate fixed right to property.

vested interest – (1) Having an absolute right or title, without contingency. (2) Having the right to use a portion of an investment fund, such as the right to withdraw from an individual retirement fund.

vestee – Present record owner.

vestibule – A small entrance hall to a room or building.

vesting – The way title will be taken.

vicarious liability – Liability that does not result from an individual's personal actions, but from his or her relationship to the party creating the liable situation. For example, brokers are vicariously liable for the actions of associate licensees working for them, even if the broker has done nothing wrong personally.

victorian style – A style of housing popular in the late 1800s, characterized by ornate embellishments.

vigas – Roof beams that protrude through the walls and help support the roof.

villa – A one-story residence, usually built as a condominium. Villas are typically built in units of two or four and include parking and a small yard.

virtual office – A company with no physical office.

virtual tour – An online open house for a property, offering sweeping views of the interior and exterior of the property.

visible light transmittance (VLT) – The measure of the amount of light that comes through the window.

vision statement – A mental image of what you want to happen in the future.

void – An agreement which is totally absent of legal effect.

voidable – Subject to being declared void.

voidable contract – An agreement that is valid and enforceable on its face, but may be rejected by one or more of the parties.

void contract – A contract that has no legal effect, due to lack of capacity of one of the parties to the contract or an illegal subject matter.

volatile organic compounds (VOCs) – Chemical compounds that have a high vapor pressure and low water solubility. VOCs are often components of petroleum fuels, hydraulic fluids, paint thinners, and dry cleaning agents.

volume – Measurement of the amount of space that a three-dimensional object occupies. In real estate, volume is normally measured in cubic feet or cubic yards.

voluntary conveyance – A deed that conveys mortgaged property that is in default to the lender. An alternative to a foreclosure action. It is also called a deed in lieu of foreclosure.

voluntary lien – A lien intentionally created or entered into by a debtor.

W

wainscoting – Wood paneling or tiles that cover an interior wall from the floor halfway to the ceiling. The remaining portion is painted or wallpapered.

waive – To abandon or to relinquish a right to enforce or require anything.

waiver – The relinquishment or refusal to accept a right.

walk-in – Prospects who have sought out a brokerage, due to advertising, such as newspaper ads or a brokerage sign on the building.

walk-through – The buyer's final viewing of the property, prior to closing, to verify that the property is in substantially the same condition as it was when the purchase offer was made.

walk-up – An apartment building of more than one story that does not have an elevator.

wall – A vertical divider of framing, sheathing, and plaster or wallboard, which is used to partition a building into rooms by surrounding certain areas.

warehouse – Type of industrial property primarily used for storing products and maintaining inventory.

warehousing – The process of assembling a number of mortgage loans into one package and holding them for a period of time, prior to selling them to an investor. They are held while waiting for a lower discount.

warm calling – The practice of making unsolicited calls to people you know, in order to get new business.

warranty – A guarantee that certain facts are true.

warranty deed – A deed used, in some states, to transfer title to property, guaranteeing that the title is clear and the grantor has the right to transfer it.

waste – Destruction or injury to real property.

wastewater – Water that carries wastes from homes, businesses, and industries; a mixture of water and dissolved or suspended solids.

wastewater treatment plant – A facility containing a series of tanks, screens, filters, and other processes by which pollutants are removed from water.

WASTO – The acronym for five ways to acquire or convey property: Will, Accession, Succession, Transfer, or Occupancy.

water – Water on the surface flowing in a stream or underground (percolating) is real property. If it is taken and bottled, then it becomes personal property.

water budget – The estimated water use within a facility. Flow rates of fixtures and appliances, occupancy, and landscape needs are calculated.

water contamination – Impairment of water quality to a degree that reduces the usability of the water for ordinary purposes or creates a hazard to public health through poisoning or the spread of diseases.

water harvesting – Collection of both runoff and rainwater for various purposes, such as irrigation or fountains.

water pollution – Presence of harmful material, such as industrial waste or sewage, in water in sufficient concentrations to make the water unusable.

water pressure test – Water pressure can be tested by turning on all faucets and flushing all toilets at the same time.

water quality – Chemical, physical, and biological characteristics of water with respect to its suitability for a particular use.

water reclamation – Reuse of effluent from wastewater treatment facilities through irrigation, land application, or other recycling methods.

water rights – The right of an owner of land to use water adjacent to or below the surface of the land.

watershed – Area of land that, as a result of topography, drains to a single point or area.

water supply system – The collection of pipes and valves that deliver potable (drinkable) water to a building.

water table – The natural level at which water is found, either above or below the surface of the ground.

water treatment – Removing undesirable chemical substances from a water supply through aeration and conditioning.

watt – The measurement of the actual amount of electrical force available to do work.

wave power – Creating power from the energy by ocean surface waves.

wear and tear – Depreciation of an asset, due to ordinary usage.

weatherstripping – Material used around windows and doors to prevent drafts.

web page – A single page of data as a part of a website.

website – A grouping of web pages, images, or other digital information that is hosted by a web server.

web traffic – The amount of data sent and received by visitors to a website.

weep holes – Openings that allow trapped water to escape and for ventilation of brick.

weighted average technique – A method of averaging, used in appraisal.

weighted rate – A method of determining overall capitalization.

wetlands – Areas where water covers the soil or is present, either at or near the surface of the soil, all year or for varying periods of time during the year, including the growing season.

white noise – Sound that has constant energy per frequency.

whole-house fan – A fan typically centrally located in the ceiling of a house that draws fresh outside air into the living space, flushes hot air up to the attic and exhausts it to the outside.

will – A written instrument, whereby a person makes a disposition of his or her property to take effect after their death.

willingness to pay – Relates to a person's character and is associated with a person's credit history.

wind energy – Conversion of wind energy into a useful form of energy, such as electricity, using wind turbines.

wind farm – A cluster of wind turbines (up to several hundred) set up in areas where there is a nearly steady prevalent wind, either on land or offshore.

wind turbine – Wind energy rotary device that converts the wind's kinetic energy into electricity.

window-to-floor ratio – The ratio of total, unobstructed window glass area to total floor area served by the windows, expressed as a percentage. This value can also be further subdivided by solar orientation (such as south-facing window-to-floor ratio).

witnessed will – Will usually prepared by an attorney and signed by the maker and two witnesses.

wood rot – Damage to wood, caused by fungi.

workers' compensation insurance – Injury compensation insurance that employers are required to provide to the employees of the company.

workfile – Appraiser's records that contain all the documentation necessary to support the appraiser's analyses, opinions, and conclusions conveyed in the appraisal report.

working capital – Amount of money available to carry out daily activities. It is the amount available after deducting current liabilities from current assets.

working capital fund – Amount of money needed to meet immediate obligations and is generally equal to one month's expenses.

workouts – Methods of resolving borrower financial problems and avoiding foreclosure, such as lengthening loan terms and reducing payments.

wraparound mortgage – *See* all-inclusive-trust-deed.

writ of attachment – The document recorded in the public record, by which the court holds the real or personal property of a defendant as security for a possible judgment, pending the outcome of a lawsuit.

writ of execution – A legal document issued by a court, forcing the sale of a property to satisfy a judgment.

writ of possession – A document that is executed at an eviction hearing that authorizes the sheriff's office to evict the tenant.

wrought iron – An easily-molded form of iron, used for decorative railings, gates, furniture, etc. The term is loosely used to describe steel or aluminum used in the same manner.

X

"X" – A person, who cannot write, may execute a document by placing an "X" (his or her mark) where the signature is normally placed. Beneath the mark, a witness then writes the person's name and signs his or her own name as a witness.

xeriscape™ – A patented name for landscaping that conserves water, by using a wide variety of plants appropriate to the natural environment.

Y

yard – A unit of measurement three feet long.

year-to-year tenancy – A tenancy that continues from one period to the next automatically, unless either party terminates it at the end of a period. Also known as periodic tenancy.

yield – The interest earned by an investor on an investment (or by a bank on the money it has loaned). Also called return or profit. *See* return on investment.

yield capitalization – A capitalization method that discounts future benefits at appropriate yield rates, producing a value that reflects the income pattern, value change, and yield-rate characteristics of the investment.

yield rate – The yield expressed as a percentage of the total investment. Also called rate of return.

Z

zenith – The point on the skydome directly overhead, the 90-degree solar altitude angle.

zero energy building (ZEB) – Zero energy buildings produce as much energy as they consume. ZEBs are autonomous from the energy grid supply and produce energy on-site.

zero lot line – The construction of a building in which one side of the building lies directly on the lot's boundary line. This is prohibited in some areas.

zeroscaping – The use of rock and hardscape, with only a few sparse plants. This is a type of low water landscaping. Since it uses so much rock and hardscape, zeroscaping tends to be hot.

zone – An area subject to designated for specified use and purpose.

zoned system – A system of heating or air-conditioning that maintains different temperatures or conditions in different areas or zones in a house.

zoning – The regulation of structures and uses of property within selected districts. Zoning laws affect the use of land, lot sizes, types of permitted structures, building heights, setbacks, and density.

zoning law – A type of law that regulates land use, executes master plans, and controls the mix of properties in a particular area. Also known as a zoning ordinance.

zoning variance – An exemption from a zoning ordinance or regulation permitting a structure or use that would not otherwise be allowed.

List of "Green" Terms

A

acid rain
active solar
adobe
adobe bricks
aerator
afforestation
agricultural waste
air barrier
air changes per hour (ACH)
air cleaner
air collector
air conditioner
air conditioning
air flow volume
air pollution
air-pollution abatement
equipment
air quality standards
algae discoloration
amperage
ampere
annualized fuel utilization
efficiency (AFUE)
anthracite
appliance
aquastat
aquifer
arid
artesian well
asbestos
asbestos abatement
asbestos containing material
(ACM)

Asbestos Hazard Emergency
Response Act (AHERA)
ash
asphalt
atmosphere
automatic damper
avulsion

B

backup generator
bamboo
biodegradable
biodiversity
biofuel
biomass
biomass energy
biomass waste
bioremediation
bitumen
bituminous coal
black liquor
blacktop
blackwater
blower door
boiler
BPI Building Analyst
British Thermal Unit (BTU)
brownfield
BTU
building ecology
building envelope
Building Performance Institute
(BPI)
building-related illness (BRI)

C

carbon cycle
carbon dioxide (CO2)
carbon footprint
carbon monoxide (CO)
carbon sequestration
carbon sink
carrying capacity
caulk
cellulose insulation
central heating system
cesspool
chemical energy
chimney
chlorofluorocarbons (CFCs)
circuit
circuit breaker
Clean Air Act
clean air delivery rate (CADR)
Clean Water Act
clear cutting
climate
climate change
closed-loop recycling
coal
coefficient of performance
    (COP)
color rendition (CRI)
combustion
combustion efficiency
compact fluorescent lamps
    (CFCs)
compost
composting
composting toilet
Comprehensive Environmental
    Response, Compensation
    and Liability Act (CERCLA)
compressor

concrete
condensation
condenser
conduction
conductor
conduit
conservation
constructed wetland
contaminant
contamination
convection
cooling capacity
cork oak
cradle-to-grave analysis
crude oil
current (electric)

D

dam
damage
damper
daylight factor (DF)
daylighting
decibel (dB)
deciduous
deforestation
dehumidifier
demand
densitometer
Department of Energy
depleted uranium
depletion
depressurization
dew point
direct sunlight
directional growth
double-glazed window
drain field
drip irrigation
dry rot

dual-glazed window
duct blower
ductwork

E

earth-sheltered construction
earth-sheltered home
eco-efficiency
ecological economics
ecological footprint
ecology
ecosystem
edible landscaping
efficacy
effluent
electric baseboard
electrical energy
electricity
electricity distribution system
electric power
electric power grid
electric power plant
electromagnetic spectrum
embodied energy
emission standards
Endangered Species Act
energy
energy audit
energy conservation
energy crop
energy efficiency
energy efficient mortgage
energy efficient ratio (EER)
energy efficiency retrofit
energy factor (EF)
EnergyGuide label
Energy Information
    Administration
energy payback time
energy recovery

ENERGY STAR®
engineered lumber
environment
environment surroundings
environmental degradation
environmental impact
environmental impact report
    (EIR)
environmental impact
    statement (EIS)
Environmental Protection
    Agency (EPA)
erosion
estuary
ethanol
eucalyptus
eutrophication
evaporation
evaporative cooler
exfiltration
expansive soil
exposure

F

Fahrenheit
feedstocks
fenestration
fiberglass insulation
filter
fireplace
first-hour rating
flow hood
flue
fluorescent lighting
forced-air system
formaldehyde
fossil fuels
frost line
fuel cell

fuel efficiency
fuel oil
fungi
furnace
fuse

G

gas-filled windows
gasification
gasoline
gentrification
geotextiles
geothermal energy
geothermal heat pump
geothermal power
glazing
global cooling
global warming
grayfield
graywater
gravitational energy
green building
green energy
greenfield
green flooring
greenhouse effect
greenhouse gases (GHG)
greenhouse gas intensity
green properties
green roof system
green wash
grid
groundwater

H

habitat
hazardous household waste
hazardous waste
heat gain

heating capacity
heating seasonal performance
    factor (HSPF)
heat loss
heat-pump
heliodon
heliostat
HERS
HERS Index
HERS Rater
HERS rating
high-efficiency particulate air
    (HEPA) filter
high-mass construction
home energy rater
home energy rating
home performance contractor
hot dry rock
household hazardous waste
human comfort zone
humidifier
humidistat
humidity
humus
HVAC
hydrocarbon
hydrochlorofluorocarbons
    (HCFCs)
hydrogen
hydrogen sulfide (HS)
hydronic heating
hydroelectric power

I

ice dam
incandescent lamp
indirect lighting
Indoor AirPlus label
indoor air pollution
indoor air quality

induction
infill development
infiltration
infrared camera
infrastructure
insulation
integrated design
integrated pest management
  (IPM)
intelligent building
irrigation

J

joule

K

kerosene
kilowatt (kW)
kilowatt hour (kWh)
kinetic energy

L

lagoon
lamp
landfill gas
leaching field
lead (Pb)
LEED
leichtlehm
lethe
life cycle assessment (LCA)
life-cycle cost (LCC)
life cycle of a product
light
light and air easement
light construction
lighting fixture
light pipe
light shelf

lignite
linoleum
liquefied natural gas (LNG)
load
louvers
low-e window glazing
low- or no-VOC paint
lumen (lm)
lumen method
luminaire
luminous ceiling
lux

M

manometer
masonry
mass transit
mechanical energy
mechanical ventilation
mercury vapor lamp
methane (CH4)
microclimate
micro wind turbine
mildew
mold
multiple-glazed window
municipal solid waste (MSW)
municipal waste
municipal waste-to-energy
  plant

N

National Environmental Policy
  Act (NEPA)
native vegetation
natural cooling
natural gas
negative pressure
neotraditional planning

net energy production
new urbanism
nit (nt)
nitrogen
nitrogen oxides (NOx)
noise criteria (NC)
noise reduction (NR)
non-renewable fuels
non-renewable resources
nuclear energy
nuclear fuel
nuclear power
nuclear waste

O

ocean energy systems
off-gassing
ohm
oil
open loop recycling
open space
organic matter
orientation
ozone (O3)
ozone depletion
ozone layer

P

particulates
passive building design
passive cooling
passive solar design
passive solar system
peak-hour demand
pedestrian pocket
pedestrian scale
pellet stove
performance-based retrofit
perimeter heating

perlite
permeability
phenolic laminate
phenols
phosphorus
photocells
photometer
photovoltaic
pitch control
pollutants
pollution
polyvinyl phloride (PVC)
post-consumer recycled
content
potable water
potential energy
prescriptive building retrofit
pressure dose
programmable thermostat
propane

Q

R

radiant barrier
radiant energy
radiant heating
radiation
radioactive waste
radon
rain forest
rainscreen
rammed earth
recovery rate
recycled material
recycling
reflectance
reflected glare
reflection

reflective insulation
refrigerant
relative humidity
remediation
renewable
renewable energy
renewable resources
renovation
RESNET
resource recovery
resources
retrofit
return air
rigid board insulation
rockwool insulation
RSI
runoff
R-value

S

scenic easement
scrubber
seasonal energy efficiency ratio
  (SEER)
sealed combustion
septic system
septic tank
sewage system
sewer
shading coefficient (SC)
sick building syndrome (SBS)
single-glazed window
site assessment
skylight
sludge
sludge composting
small wind turbine
smart building
smart grid

smart growth
smart meter
smart sprinkler controller
smog
sodium silicate
softscape
soil
solar access
solar altitude
solar array
solar azimuth
solar collector
solar easement
solar energy
solar heat gain coefficient
  (SHGC)
solar power
solar radiation
solid waste
spectrophotometer
stack effect
standby losses
storage capacity
storm window
sulphur dioxide
superfund
superwindows
supply air
surface water
sustainable agriculture
sustainable development
sustainably-sourced materials
system capacity

T

tankless water heater
temperature
therm
thermal boundary

thermal break
thermal energy
thermal resistance (R)
thermal window
thermo-solar energy
thermostat
tidal power
tight buildings
tinted glazing
topography
topsoil
toxic chemical
toxic cloud
toxic pollutants
toxic substance
Toxic Substances Control Act
   (TSCA)
toxic waste
transit-oriented development
transmission line

U

underground storage tank
   (UST)
uranium
urban growth boundary
urban renewal
urban runoff urban sprawl
U-value

V

ventilation
visible light transmittance
   (VLT)
volatile organic compounds
   (VOCs)

W

wastewater
wastewater treatment plant
water
water budget
water contamination
water harvesting
water pollution
water pressure test
water quality
water reclamation
watershed
water supply system
water table
water treatment
watt
wave power
weatherstripping
wetlands
white noise
whole-house fan
wind energy
wind farm
wind turbine
window-to-floor ratio
wood rot

X

xeriscape™

Y

Z

zenith
zero energy building (ZEB)
zeroscaping
zoned system

List of Mnemonics

ADAM E. LEE – Eight ways to terminate an easement: Abandonment, Destruction, Adverse possession, Merger, Express agreement, Lawsuit, Estoppel, and Excessive use.

COALD – Duties an agent owes a principal: Care, Obedience, Accounting, Loyalty, and Disclosure.

DUST – Elements of value: Demand, Utility, Scarcity, and Transferability.

LAND – Elements of a valid lease: Length of time, Amount of rent, Names of parties, and Description of the property.

MARIA – Tests of a fixture: Method of attachment, Adaptation, Relationship of the parties, Intention, and Agreement of the parties.

PANCHO – Requirements for adverse possession: Possession, Adverse, Notorious, Continuous, Hostile, and Open.

PEPS – Forces influencing value: Physical and environmental characteristics, Economic influences, Political (Governmental) regulations, and Social ideals and standards.

PETE – Types of government controls: Police power, Eminent domain, Taxation, and Escheat.

TIMMUR – Fixed and variable operating expenses of real property: Taxes, Insurance, Management, Maintenance, Utilities, and Reserves.

T-TIP – Unities of joint tenancy: Time, Title, Interest, and Possession.

UPTEE – Ownership rights in the Bundle of Rights: Use, Possess, Transfer, Encumber, and Enjoy.

WASTO – Ways to acquire or convey property: Will, Accession, Succession, Transfer, or Occupancy.

Formulas to Compute Types of Interest

Simple Interest:

$$I = PRT$$

I = Interest
P = Principal
R = Rate
T = Time

Add-on Interest rate:

$$AIR = \frac{2IC}{P(n + 1)}$$

AIR = add-on interest rate
I = number of installment payments per year
C = total loan charge
P = principal
n = number of installments in the contract

Compound Interest:

$$Cs = Bd\ (1 + i)n$$

Cs = compound sum
Bd = beginning deposit
i = interest rate per period
n = number of periods

Percentage Formula

Percent × Paid = Made

Variations:
Interest rate × Principal = interest earned

(An interest rate is a percentage of principal)

Rate of return × amount invested = profit
(A rate of return on an investment is a percentage of the amount invested)

Tax rate × assessed value = annual tax

(A tax rate is a percentage of assessed value)

Commission rate × selling price = commission amount

(A commission rate is usually a percentage of selling price)

Percent of net profit × cost = profit amount

(A net profit is a percentage of cost)

Percent of gross profit × selling price = profit amount

(A gross profit is a percentage of selling price)

Area Formulas

Area = Length × Width
Length = Area ÷ Width
Width = Area ÷ Length

Area of a Square = Length × Width
Area of a Rectangle = Length × Width

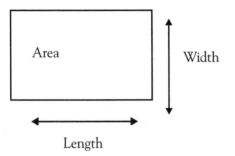

Area of a Triangle = Altitude × Base ÷ 2

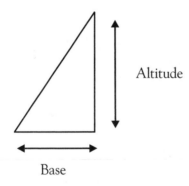

Percent, Decimal, and Fraction Equivalents

Equivalent Amounts

Percent	Decimal	Fraction
4 1/2%	0.0045	45/1000
6 2/3%	0.0667	1/15
10%	0.10	1/10
12 1/2%	0.125	1/8
16 2/3%	0.1667	1/6
25%	0.25	1/4
33 1/3%	0.333	1/3
50%	0.50	1/2
66 2/3%	0.6667	2/3
75%	0.75	3/4
100%	1.00	1/1

Measurement Equivalents

Unit	Equivalent
Mile	5,280 feet; 320 rods; 1,760 yards; 80 chains
Rod	5.50 yards; 16.5 feet
Square mile	640 acres; 102,400 rods
Acre	4,840 sq. yards; 160 sq. rods; 43,560 sq. feet
Acre foot	43,560 cubic feet
Square yard	9 sq. feet
Square foot	144 sq. inches
Chain	66 feet; 100 links; 4 rods
Kilometer	0.62 mile; 3,280 feet, 10 inches
Hectare	2.47 acres